I was Saved in a Living Room

The Definitive Guide to One-on-One Home Evangelism

Les Miller

TEACH Services, Inc.
PUBLISHING
www.TEACHServices.com • (800) 367-1844

World rights reserved. This book or any portion thereof may not be copied or reproduced in any form or manner whatever, except as provided by law, without the written permission of the publisher, except by a reviewer who may quote brief passages in a review.

This book was written to provide truthful information in regard to the subject matter covered. The author assumes full responsibility for the accuracy of all facts and quotations as cited in this book. The opinions expressed in this book are the author's personal views and interpretation of the Bible, Spirit of Prophecy, and/or contemporary authors and do not necessarily reflect those of TEACH Services, Inc.

This book is sold with the understanding that the publisher is not engaged in giving spiritual, legal, medical, or other professional advice. If authoritative advice is needed, the reader should seek the counsel of a competent professional.

Scripture quotations marked "NKJV" are taken from the New King James Version®. Copyright © 1982 by Thomas Nelson, Inc. Used by permission. All rights reserved.

Copyright © 2013 TEACH Services, Inc.
ISBN-13: 978-1-4796-0006-9 (Paperback)
ISBN-13: 978-1-4796-0007-6 (Hardback)
ISBN-13: 978-1-4796-0008-3 (ePub)
ISBN-13: 978-1-4796-0009-0 (Kindle/Mobi)
Library of Congress Control Number: 2012952449

Published by

www.TEACHServices.com • (800) 367-1844

Dedication

To my beautiful wife, Melissa, whom the Lord gave me when I needed her most, your consistent example of kindness was His love in action, which opened my heart to the truth.

Working for God

Working for God what a wonderful thing,
For He is our Father, Creator and King.
Wtinessing to others, a lifelong call,
And doing the work, is the purpose of all.

Using our talents to teach of His love,
Searching the scriptures to further know of.
Sharing the peace and joy that is real,
Giving and helping each person to feel.

Each is a teacher of morals and values,
Reason and sense is the path to the truths.
What a privilege to bring a soul back,
To the Father of love, who leaves none to lack.

We walk the path daily in humility,
Seeking to find those who want to be free.
Telling the story of God's only way,
Helping each know, to prepare for 'The Day'!

by Melissa Miller

Table of Contents

Dedication iii

Preface vii

Chapter 1   My Story 9

Chapter 2   How to be an On-Fire Christian 13

Chapter 3   How to Find Interests 22

Chapter 4   The Psychology of Giving Bible Studies 30

Chapter 5   The Long Program 42

Chapter 6   The Short Program 70

Chapter 7   Topics to Cover as the Need Arises 96

Chapter 8   Mentoring New Converts 129

Chapter 9   Understanding Evangelicals 139

Chapter 10   The Three Angels' Messages in One, Easy Five-Minute Lesson 153

Appendix A   Understanding Temptation 164

Appendix B   Dimensions of the Cross 167

Preface

Welcome to *I Was Saved in a Living Room*, a semi-autobiographical treatise on the subject of evangelism and soul-winning. This book specifically deals with home Bible study in a three-fold approach. The main body of the book shares the lessons I've learned while giving one-on-one Bible studies. But before I share what I have learned, I want to share with you how I learned these lessons through my own conversion story. I close the book with a summary of what these lessons mean for us today along with comments on how they can help us "finish the work" and preach the "gospel of the kingdom" in all the world through the final outpouring of the Holy Spirit known as the latter rain. The lessons themselves are Bible studies that present the truth as it is in Jesus, coupled with instruction on how to present those studies to change human lives.

A word of warning first! This book is primarily meant to teach born-again, on-fire-for-God Seventh-day Adventist Christians how to best share their faith and tell others what they need to know to be ready for Jesus' second coming. If you are not a born-again, on-fire-for-God Seventh-day Adventist, please turn immediately to the chapter titled "The Long Program." Go through every Bible study in order, looking up each verse in your own Bible and reading the descriptions with them. Then continue doing the same thing in the next chapter, the "Short Program." Please prayerfully consider how each truth presented there relates to every other and relates back to the fact that Jesus Christ died and rose again for your sins. Apart from the Bible study chapters, the rest of this book outlines presentation techniques and styles similar to a sales training manual, but with one important difference: offering people eternal life in God's kingdom is not the same as selling them a vacuum cleaner.

The Lord says in Hebrews 4:12 that His word is a "two-edged sword." Where there is guilt and burden in the life of a sinner, God's mercy takes it all away, lifting the sinner to new heights of peace, joy, and freedom. Where there is pride and self-reliance, particularly on the part of those who should know better, the ones inside the church, His truth cuts down to size anyone harbouring such a spirit. However, this is in mercy and only to grant a new Spirit from above. This sword is a tool to be held in the hands of His warriors. They are His chosen vessels for communicating the only true message of salvation to this dark world. With it they will tear down "principalities, ... powers, ... rulers of the darkness of this world, [and] ... spiritual wickedness in high places" (Eph. 6:12).

The Lord wants you to take up the sword. With a little practice, you will wield it well and see those around you take their stand for God as a result of His blessing on your efforts. Don't just read this book; use it to His glory.

It is awkward to always write politically correct using gender-neutral terms such as person or individual. I remember when my wife and I bought our first home. There was a clause in the contract that said, masculine singular includes feminine and plural where applicable. While most of the time I will use "him" to describe the friend you are trying to reach, "her" or "them" is included as well. Please note that what is written in this book applies to all of God's children.

Chapter 1

My Story

My name is Les Miller, and I've been a Seventh-day Adventist Christian since 1988. I live in Airdrie, Alberta, Canada. I came to know Jesus for the first time when I was ten years old. Having been raised in the United Church of Canada, a union of the Methodist, Congregationalist, and Presbyterian churches that formed in the 1920s, I had a basic knowledge of the Bible. However, to say the least, I was a nominal Christian.

At the age of ten I went to a nearby Bible camp run by the Baptists. It was there I learned for the first time that I was a sinner with no hope of salvation except for a born-again relationship with the Lord. I saw from the Bible that I had no power on my own to be good and that Jesus' death and resurrection were the only way to pay for my sins. My heavenly hopes were only possible by accepting Him into my heart, so I gave my heart to God. But I didn't fully understand what it was I had done by accepting Him. I certainly was not on fire for God, but something was different. I did have a basic desire to be good instead of bad. This, of course, caused me problems.

As I grew older the weight of the world with all its temptations, especially from peer pressure, made me give up trying over time. My Sunday School class gave me a Bible when I was fifteen, and I decided to read it for myself. Over the course of seven years, I read approximately one page per night. But I tried the way of the world as well. By age twenty-two, I came to realize I had become a bad person by my wrong choices. I was scarred and changed, and there was nothing I could do about it.

My darkest hour was when I moved out on my own at the age of nineteen. Living about five hours from my family, I experienced firsthand the life of the prodigal son. Still Jesus helped me. I went to some meetings with a Pentecostal coworker and stood again to give my heart to the Lord. However, in the follow-up literature they gave me, something didn't seem right. By this time I had almost finished reading the entire Bible. I couldn't quite put into words exactly what I was thinking, but somehow I could poke holes in their doctrinal beliefs.

Then I found what I was looking for. God brought a Seventh-day Adventist woman into my life. What I saw in Melissa Ryane, the woman whom I later married, was a peace and a strength I had never seen in anyone else. No Christian from any faith I'd encountered had the peace she had. They all spoke words. With Melissa, I saw the gospel in action. She was living proof there is power in the blood of Jesus.

I Was Saved in a Living Room

I set out to win her heart, and on May 17, 1987, we were married. The marriage preparation class with her pastor, Richard Warman, turned into a Bible study for me. Although I learned anew that Jesus died on the cross for my sins, I learned it in a deeper and much more meaningful way than I had as a child. I saw it as more than a covering of the individual wrong things I had done. I saw it as a total and complete restoration to innocence, which is what it really is.

Along with the hope of being made new by the Holy Spirit, I also learned pure doctrine for the first time. The doctrines he shared with me formed a complete circle of truth so pure it was obvious. Each individual truth was clearly related to all the others. I could not poke any holes in the logic of what was presented to me as I had been able to three years earlier. It wasn't just 'doctrine,' it was truth. The Holy Spirit weighed down on me my need of Jesus, and for the first time in my life, I knew what being a born-again Christian really was. I had found a truth as big as all of world history, which at the same time applied to my own life. In this new relationship with the Savior, I knew what it meant to say, "He died for me," and I knew the day would come when He would return to claim me as His own.

"All who are pursuing the onward Christian course should have, and will have, an experience that is living, that is new and interesting" (*Testimonies for the Church*, vol. 2, p. 579). As a child, I had considered ministry in the United Church as a career, and I brought these aspirations with me into my newfound faith. Three times in four years the Lord made it obvious He wanted me in the ministry. By saying I didn't have enough money to afford college, what I was really saying was that I didn't have enough faith to go.

So instead, in His mercy the Lord led me to a trade. I became a painter and later a painting contractor. Now I am an industrial painter. This was something I fought the whole time because, despite my lack of faith, I still wanted to serve God through ministry. Actually, I wanted to be an evangelist. In 1995, after turning down the Lord's calling three times, I tried to make it happen *my* way. First, I took a three-week training seminar for lay evangelists in South Dakota from Pastor Louis and Carol Torres, who were at the time with Amazing Facts. The seminar was titled "Send Forth Reapers." That course later evolved into the course they now teach at Mission College of Evangelism in Gaston, Oregon. Around that time the Alberta Conference of Seventh-day Adventists was instituting a new part-time lay pastor program.

Beginning in April 1996, Pastor Kelly Schultz and I spoke at a crusade in the town of Canmore, Alberta. Along with my wife's help, we planted the Mountain Sanctuary Seventh-day Adventist Church that resulted from those meetings. I hoped this would lead directly into a full-time call to the ministry. I was bitterly disappointed when, fourteen months later, the conference secretary said, "Thank you, but we're going to go in another direction." So it was back to painting full time.

In the next chapter I'll be defining what I call "the sleeping church mentality." Though I was very enthusiastic in my approach to the work in Canmore, you could say I was still a sleeping Christian in some sense because I thought that if I couldn't have the actual job of pastor I couldn't do very much in the way of outreach. All the work I did as a paid missionary was driven by public sermons and crusades.

My Story

I wanted to reach as many people as possible and didn't see the value in working with one person at a time. Upon pondering the situation in the next few years, I saw for the first time that despite fighting Him the Lord was still working out His plan for my life. Painting is a very transient profession. When the season is over and work slows down, layoffs come. In moving between various painting employers, I learned many different tricks of the trade they don't teach in the apprenticeship classes. Although I tried to get out of painting so that I could be in the ministry, I became a skilled painter.

I also saw that the Lord had done the same for me in ministry as well. I never went to school to learn hermeneutics, but after giving more than 160 sermons at Mountain Sanctuary and elsewhere, I knew how to preach. I never studied eschatology, but after interacting with people from many faiths at these various painting companies, I was led to study my Bible quite a lot to find answers to all the doctrinal challenges they gave me, especially on questions about end-time events.

In Canmore, Pastor Schultz allowed Melissa and I to prayerfully make a lot of the decisions ourselves. Serving on the board in what later became our home church taught me how to interact within the church leadership structure. I never studied European history, Seventh-day Adventist church history, or any of the other required courses for a theology degree. However, now I know what it takes to see a soul come to Christ, which is the real work of a pastor. Pastor Schultz and I did one crusade together, and a year later I did another as sole speaker. I never got a permanent job out of it, but I am an evangelist. I am a one-on-one evangelist.

The most gratifying experience the Lord gave me came in 1999 when Adrian, an employee of mine who was searching for the truth, began studying the Bible with me. I had previously had little interest in one-on-one outreach methods, but it was evidence that the Lord was working on my heart and was still willing to use me. Over the course of almost two years, off and on, Adrian and I studied together. I drew from the studies Pastor Warman gave me, and by watching his reactions, adapted them to meet his needs. In July 2001 he took a stand for Jesus, got baptized, and is now on fire for God. What I learned from the experience of winning him to Christ is what this book is about.

I was reading an Amazing Facts pamphlet by Joe Crews called *The High Cost of the Cross* where I learned the value of one person: "Christ's love for people is repeatedly dramatized in the Bible. We see it in His time-consuming, one-person interviews. Some of His most significant discourses were delivered to single individuals. We see it also in the dangerous voyage He made across the sea to deliver the Gadarene demoniac. It occupied fully two days of His precious time to cross that stormy water and return. Only one man was directly contacted during that unpleasant excursion, but that man, later turned the whole countryside toward the Savior.... Is one soul worth such an infinite price? In the light of eternity the answer is yes. Consider the amazing fact that one redeemed soul will outlive all the combined years of earth's total population: Eventually, in eternity, the life of that one person will outstrip by a million times all the life spans of all the inhabitants of this world put together" (pp. 27–29).

This book was written by a layperson for laypeople. My experience as a publicly oriented, paid worker does not in any way compare to the joy I felt in successfully reaching one friend. You can have that experience too. And you can experience this before you become perfect. God forgives us of our sins every day, so why do we think we need to be free of sin before He can use us? Too many times we hear of stories with the underlying message that the church members aren't good enough and that's why we don't see more success reaching others.

"In the last solemn work few great men will be engaged.... God will work a work in our day that but few anticipate. He will raise up and exalt among us those who are taught rather by the unction of His Spirit than by the outward training of scientific institutions. These facilities are not to be despised or condemned; they are ordained of God, but they can furnish *only the exterior qualifications*. God will manifest that He is not dependent on learned, self-important mortals" (*Testimonies for the Church*, vol. 5, pp. 80, 82, emphasis mine).

"The laborers will be qualified rather by the unction of His Spirit than by the training of literary institutions" (*The Great Controversy*, p. 606). Think about that. A college degree will not give you the fire of the Holy Spirit; it will only help to properly direct the fire you already have.

By God's grace we are doing many wonderful things in our public work. However, as we so often hear, we could do better. Church leaders tell us that when a church works to prepare a territory first by sending out people to give Bible studies in the community they get more results from the Revelation seminar. That is exactly what we need—more church members giving Bible studies in their own homes. Would you like to learn what it takes to be used by God to do that? Do you have a hope in your heart that He will give you success from your outreach efforts on this side of heaven?

This book is the result of the initial studies given to me in 1987 and 1988. This book also provides information about how I applied them over the years. As the Lord has brought me into situations with believers and non-believers, I have observed the process of change the Holy Spirit makes in someone's life using the truth. I have also learned why some don't accept the truth no matter how hard we try. These observations are contained here for your benefit. They are intended to help you as you "fight the good fight of faith." I have also included suggestions as to how we as Adventists can improve our outreach efforts.

Throughout this book are "Words of Advice" sidebars. They contain tidbits of useful information, most of which I have received from interacting with various church leaders over time. These lessons I consider to be essential for anyone wanting to learn to win souls. I have already mentioned the impact that Richard Warman, Kelly Schultz, and the Torres family had on me. Now I would like to introduce a few others who have influenced me. These include Randy Barber, current senior pastor of Calgary Central Seventh-day Adventist Church; Ken Eirich, a previous pastor of what is now my home church in Airdrie, Alberta, Canada, and his wife Nancy; and Lester and Bernice Carney who came to Mountain Sanctuary soon after it was established upon their retirement from conference leadership. A few others round out the list, some of whom I met only once. I hope their words will impact you as they have me.

Chapter 2
How to be an On-Fire Christian

What do we mean when we say "the church is asleep"? In order to be awake, we must first understand what it means to be asleep. But I hope we can study this matter in a way that focuses on what we need to be on fire for God.

Why hasn't the latter rain outpouring of the Holy Spirit come yet? Have you ever heard a sermon, read a book, or watched a video that tries to give an answer? Most of the time when you hear about getting ready for the last days, the emphasis is on your own personal need of the Lord as if all you have to do is sit at home, become perfect, and the Holy Spirit will do your work for you. There's usually a very heavy hand of guilt involved as if to say "since we're still here, we're not good enough."

Quotes such as this one from *Christ's Object Lessons*—"When the character of Christ shall be perfectly reproduced in His people, then He will come to claim them as His own" (p. 69)—are given to support this. Or there is an emphasis on how close we were to the second coming in 1888 but that we weren't ready. Another popular theme is to focus on the parable of the wise and foolish virgins in Matthew 25 and end the sermon with a warning not to miss out. However, there's usually little to no advice on how to make sure you have the Holy Spirit in you.

Not only have I heard sermons like this, but I have preached sermons like this. Never again though! They don't help. People in the church who get upset at the complacency their brothers and sisters seem to have concerning outreach have to remember three things. It isn't that they don't want to do outreach; it is that they don't believe they can, don't believe they should since they are not pastors, or have tried and the people around them have said no.

Let's be realistic about things. We are waking up as a church, and we are getting closer than ever to the final outpouring of the Holy Spirit. With the rise of institutions such as Mission College of Evangelism and others that teach a more compacted yet comprehensive course than that of our four year colleges and universities, I'm sure you'll agree we are seeing the fulfillment of what is written in *The Great Controversy* on page 606: "Thus the message of the third angel will be proclaimed. As the time comes for it to be given with greatest power, the Lord will work through humble instruments, leading the minds of those who consecrate themselves to His service. The laborers will be qualified rather by the unction of His Spirit than by the training of literary institutions."

Although the day is close, we aren't there yet. So what else do we need? *The Great Controversy* paints a picture of what revival in the last days will be like: "Servants of God, with their faces lighted up and shining with holy consecration, will hasten from place to place to proclaim the message from heaven. By thousands of voices, all over the earth, the warning will be given. Miracles will be wrought, the sick will be healed, and signs and wonders will follow the believers" (p. 612).

Now let me ask you, what is there in this quote that proves this day has not yet come? You will likely answer, "I know, we're not seeing miracles, right?" That's not the answer. Key in on the phrase "by thousands of voices." What we have right now in the Seventh-day Adventist Church is *one voice* again and again via satellite.

Let's say the same thing a different way. To be a sleeping Christian is not to be against the faith but to be living on a very basic level of faith alone. Sleeping Christians are focused on living a happy, comfortable life in this world and on getting themselves to heaven with a minimal regard for the salvation of others. A sleeping church is a church where the members come to the worship service to watch the leaders, treating them as movie stars and thinking the only contribution they can make is to put money into the offering plate so the bills can be paid. To be a sleeping church or a sleeping Christian is to spiritually overweight. We feed on the Word continually but do not get enough spiritual exercise through outreach endeavors. Still another way to make the point is to say that when a church is sleeping, it does not really believe in the fundamental Protestant doctrine of the priesthood of every believer.

> **Words of Advice**
>
> Ken Eirich once remarked to me in a discussion about Ellen White's various statements on the fact that the delay in the second coming is our responsibility as God's gospel workers. "I'm glad that generation failed, because it gave time for me to be born and have my chance to make a decision."

Certainly the sleeping church mentality is nothing new, nor are we as Adventists the only ones suffering from it today. Although churches and church members fall asleep, that doesn't mean the Lord has or will cast them off. Jesus said we're to come to Him as a child with that naiveté, trust, and innocence of heart that so many of us have who don't seem to have the confidence to be successful as outreach workers. It was Martha who complained to Jesus that she had to do all the work while Mary sat and listened to Him. Jesus' acceptance of Mary and His words to Peter in John 21:17, "feed my sheep," show how He feels about sleeping church members. However, as Luke 10:40 points out, Martha was "cumbered about much serving." She'd likely be the one to preach a guilt sermon on getting ready for the last days.

"For who will hearken unto you in this matter? but as his part *is* that goeth down to the battle, so *shall* his part *be* that tarrieth by the stuff: they shall part alike" (1 Sam. 30:24). David's command teaches us that anyone involved in the cause of the Lord will be rewarded. To be led to a position supporting the existing organization is what is meant by "guarding the stuff." I like to call it "inreach." So teaching Sabbath School or being an elder is equal to the frontline work of bringing people to the Lord and His truth for our time.

As of 2012 Ken Wiebe is president of the Alberta Conference. In 1995 he was senior pastor of Calgary Central Church. That year he ran an *It Is Written* lay training course in preparation for an upcoming citywide crusade with evangelist Leo Schreven. Quoting from witnessing statistics, he told us that 98 percent of Jehovah's Witnesses and 60 percent of the membership of the Alliance Church were actively involved in some form of regular, weekly faith sharing effort. On the other hand, the number for Adventists was only 2 percent. So instead of a 50/50 ratio as the verse above points out, we had a 2/98 ratio of outreach versus inreach in North America in the mid 1990s. No wonder pastors were preaching so many guilt sermons.

In *The Ministry of Healing* Ellen White said, "Everywhere there is a tendency to substitute the work of organizations for individual effort. Human wisdom tends to consolidation, to centralization, to the building up of great churches and institutions" (p. 147). The church is asleep when we trust more in the system than in the Savior. Church members need to stop hiding behind the organized effort of paid workers and take responsibility for outreach themselves. You and I are the ones God has called to "go into all the world." Don't expect 3ABN or *It Is Written* to do your job for you. Don't believe only a chosen few, well-educated, professional pastors or evangelists can have the privilege of reaping souls for Christ. God can use you to bring people to Him. Believe, receive, and you will achieve.

"The Lord will work in this last work in a way very much out of the common order of things ... contrary to any human planning ... God will ... [take] the reins in His own hands ... The Spirit is poured forth upon all who will yield ... and, casting off all man's ... binding ways and cautious methods they will declare the truth with the might of the Spirit's power" (Robert Olsen, *The Crisis Ahead: A Compilation from the Writings of Ellen G. White*, pp. 73, 74).

> **Words of Advice**
>
> Once in conversation, Ken Eirich shared with me how he feels compassion for the laity, and how it makes so much sense to him that the Lord would raise up a system of ministers to do His work on earth. "To have to work all day, come home at night, do your housework, and then to have to work on a sermon, it's hard."

That's a good way to look at it. Church members show they are in this mentality by some of the common catch phrases they say. For instance, have you heard people say:

"It's all up to the Holy Spirit. It's not my job to convert anyone."

"I don't believe in using big meetings; I practise friendship evangelism."

"I want to be a missionary in my own hometown."

"I just want to set a good example. It's about developing a Christ-like character."

"Crusades are all about numbers."

"If I could just reach one person."

All these statements are simply ways of saying, "It's not that I'm against doing outreach, I am simply too afraid to go beyond my comfort zone. I only want to do outreach among people around me that I personally know, for example my friends and family." This is the epitome of the sleeping church mentality.

Although it is true that the Holy Spirit does the converting, He uses us as His ambassadors (2 Cor. 5:20–6:1). Friendship evangelism does not mean just trying to reach your friends; it means being a friend to everyone you meet. In Mark 5:18, 19 the demon-possessed man was told to tell his "friends" about what God had done, but Luke 8:39 records that he shared the message with the entire city. The whole point of being a missionary is to get away from the trappings of normal life by going somewhere unfamiliar so you can totally focus on sharing God.

Jesus came from His heavenly home to be a missionary to us (2 Cor. 8:9). Abraham was not a missionary in Ur; God called him to come out from his family (Gen. 12:1–3). The Ethiopian eunuch in Acts 8:29–31 needed Philip to guide him even though Philip was still a sinner. You can't become perfect before you engage in outreach; in fact, the purpose of outreach is also to help you grow (1 Tim. 4:16).

Evangelistic meetings are about getting hearts to surrender to the Lord, but obviously they focus on getting as many people as possible. Why else did Peter and the other disciples count the fish in John 21:11? And what's wrong with going after a few big fish? If I could just reach one person implies that I'm only trying to reach one person. Cross reference the ten lepers Jesus healed (one out of ten thanked Him) with the parable of the sower (one in four of the seeds grew), and you will see that to actually reach one person, you have to try to reach forty.

I think the sleeping mentality in our church came about for three reasons. Firstly, as the Millerite movement was in full swing and the date for the expected second coming came closer, more and more believers quit their jobs, sold their possessions, and became full-time preachers. After the Great Disappointment they had to go back to work. As life resumed the fire of the movement died down.

Words of Advice

While leading out in starting the Canmore Church, I was privileged to attend the ministers meetings that year. Dale Kongorski, the conference president who had hired me to be a lay pastor said in prayer, "Lord, we're sorry, get the lay people to help us." This typifies how the leadership of the church feel. They want to see revival come and don't want the average church members depending on them to finish the work.

God knew it would happen. Did you ever notice that the first and third angel's messages are given with a loud voice, but the second one isn't? The key to getting over this aspect of the sleeping church mentality is to admit that while most of us can't go into ministry full-time we can spend our spare time participating in whatever ministry work we are led to do. Instead of a vacation, take a short-term mission trip. While there's nothing wrong with hobbies such as stamp collecting, scuba diving, or watching sports on TV, aren't there things you could do to help advance God's cause instead? I encourage you to take the part of your life where you devote it to personal interests and devote your extra time to God.

Secondly, when you become a believer, it takes time to really get to know the Bible. After attending one prophecy seminar and reading a few books, I could tell my friends what was going to happen. However, I could not prove it from the Bible myself yet. Ken Eirich had this to say in *Amazing Journey Amazing Grace: The Incredible Story of How God Led Two Pentecostal Pastors Into The Seventh-day Adventist Church*, a book he co-wrote with his wife: "Nancy and I had all too often witnessed people in the church simply parroting the teachings of pastors or televangelists, what they heard from others, or read in a book—without fully understanding the doctrine or the teaching themselves. We also knew that the vast majority of Christians did not know how to explain what they believed to someone else, and even fewer knew how to use the Bible to support their beliefs" (p. 169).

This was in reference to their days as Pentecostal pastors. Obviously we aren't the only ones who are asleep. If you feel this quote applies to you, the best advice I can give is to stop treating your favorite ministers as if they are movie stars. Let's rephrase 1 Corinthians 1:13, 14 and give it a modern twist: "Now I say this, that each of you says, 'I am of Doug Batchelor,' or 'I am of Mark Finley' … Is Christ divided? Was Shawn Boonstra crucified for you? Or were you baptized in the name of Dwight Nelson?"

Frank Tochterman, former Alberta Conference president, once said at an Airdrie Church business meeting, "It's the people who read that stay in the church." It takes effort on your part to be informed as to what you believe. You have to stretch yourself by actually studying the Bible for yourself to learn how to share its message. That is how to be strong in your faith.

Words of Advice

The friend who took me to the first crusade I ever attended, a man named Rey (pronounced Ray) McKibben, informed me he had invited fifty-six people, seven of whom showed up. And they weren't the seven he expected would come. Rey picked myself and two others up on a Sabbath evening, brought us to the meeting, took us all out for ice cream after sundown, and said, "This is courtesy of your friends, the Seventh-day Adventists." This was an example to me of an Adventist who was going well beyond his comfort zone.

The third reason is really the main reason. What is holding people back when they are in the sleeping church mentality? Fear. People are afraid to stretch themselves and reach out to strangers. It is hard to take when people turn down your offer of the truth. But let me remind you. Did Noah fail? His job was to get the whole world to accept or reject the present truth for his day. He did his job, and yet his family were the only ones to be saved.

Another fear is that of being overwhelmed. If you live in a large city with hundreds of thousands of doors, you'll never have time to knock on all of them. You just have to do your best and leave the rest up to God. "But ye shall receive power, after that the Holy Ghost is come upon you: and ye shall be witnesses unto me both in Jerusalem, and in all Judaea, and in Samaria, and unto the uttermost part of the earth" (Acts 1:8). Notice the order mentioned by the Lord. They were called to fill a small circle, which grew in three stages. It was more important to get something done in Jerusalem first, and then after they had gained experience in preaching and had the time to get the church structure well established, the message then went beyond there. When you get overwhelmed by this kind of fear, work together with friends in the church. That will help you to feel as if you are getting something done.

In addition to this, once you do find someone who is interested in Bible studies, the task of reaching that person can also be overwhelming. Paul spent a year and a half in Corinth planting the church there (Acts 18:11). Expect people to take that long to make a decision for Christ, and expect to spend equally as much time afterward mentoring them in the church. That means that from the first time the two of you open your Bibles together, you need to be ready to make a three-year commitment if you have to. I have no advice for you on how to overcome this fear other than to say once you have experienced the joy of successful outreach you will be hooked!

Words of Advice

In regard to how much leaders are trying to advance the cause of God, Carol Torres said, "Sometimes the paid workers feel overwhelmed with the size of task of reaching the world and work themselves to an early death. It is better to practice temperance. Work enough so that you're still healthy, and you can be used longer."

Randy Barber agreed when he said, "Don't feel guilty about relaxing."

Ellen White wrote in *Mind Character, and Personality*, volume 2. "I was shown that Sabbathkeepers as a people labor too hard without allowing themselves change or periods of rest. Recreation is needful to those who are engaged in physical labor and is still more essential for those whose labor is principally mental. It is not essential to our salvation or for the glory of God to keep the mind laboring constantly and excessively, even upon religious themes" (pp. 735, 736).

But these together do not constitute the greatest fear in our hearts. I know this fear firsthand as I have felt it and later found victory over it. The greatest fear we have is the knowledge that a human being cannot convert anyone. You only find that out when you try to.

Just as a parent stands in the place of God for a child who cannot comprehend Him, so a Bible study giver stands in the place of God for someone searching. When you agree to give a Bible study, *you are in essence holding that person's eternal destiny in your hands* until she is enlightened by the Holy Spirit and makes a decision. It is the most overwhelming feeling of all. It is the real reason so many of us are content to let the pastor do the work of outreach.

So how do we conquer this fear? By following and believing what I said to Adrian the very first time we opened our Bibles together. "I am only here to help you; this whole thing is between you and the Lord. I am only a rubber glove in His hand." This takes the pressure off you to bring a candidate all the way to church membership because God might use someone else for that. And it takes the pressure off him or her to make a decision because of your desires. The person can be free to come to Christ in his or her own time.

The "rubber glove" description is the very best way to illustrate what you are to be in order to achieve success. You admit you can do nothing, yet you go forward in total faith and resignation to His will for the study. You keep sharing, believing each time you do that the Holy Spirit drives the truth home in glorious power beyond your comprehension. With this in mind, and a drive for souls, you will see marvelous results.

You can be a successful outreach worker. You can see the Lord using you to change lives through your efforts. If you don't know enough yet, you will learn as you go, and you will become a stronger Christian for it. Plan and act as if it all depends on you. Think, talk, and pray as if it all depends on Him. "Joshua had received the promise that God would surely overthrow these enemies of Israel, yet he put forth as earnest effort as though success depended upon the armies of Israel alone. He did all that human energy could do, and then he cried in faith for divine aid. The secret of success is the union of divine power with human effort. Those who achieve the greatest results are those who rely most implicitly upon the Almighty Arm" (*Colporteur Ministry*, p. 110).

The parable of the sower gives us great insights on how to rise up out of slumber and be on fire for God. To save space we will just go through Jesus' explanation in Mark 4. "The sower soweth the word" (verse 14). You are the sower, and the rest of the parable lists the reactions that occur from the sowing of the Word. Also, you once had the Word sown in you. This parable has a double meaning. Instead of four kinds of people and four kinds of experiences, these are also the pitfalls you yourself must get past in order to get to the good ground.

"And these are they by the way side, where the word is sown; but when they have heard, Satan cometh immediately, and taketh away the word that was sown in their hearts" (verse 15). How many people are there today who, in the final judgment, will be shown that their last chance came in the form of a Christian knocking on their door, to which they said, "Not now, the game is on TV," or something like that. First, you must accept the Word. If you are in the faith now, then you have passed this test. The next two pitfalls are for those who have been given study, conversion, and baptism.

"And these are they likewise which are sown on stony ground; who, when they have heard the word, immediately receive it with gladness" (verse 16). Beware of emotional religion; it doesn't last.

"And have no root in themselves, and so endure but for a time: afterward, when affliction or persecution ariseth for the word's sake, immediately they are offended" (verse 17). The weakness here is faith in people, rather than in the Lord. This experience lasts only as long as the good feelings do, and when it comes time to pass any tests of faith, there is not enough stamina. The Beatitudes of Matthew 5:3–12 are similar to this parable in that they describe the growth process we all have to go through. New converts go through the whole thing in miniature at the onset of their Christian walk. So there will be an initial round of persecution that will weed out this stony ground group.

> **Words of Advice**
>
> Andrew Chin, former Calgary Parkdale Church pastor, now retired, said this in a sermon he gave on how the Lord used a series of tests to whittle down Gideon's army from about 10,000 to just over 300. "The last test shows that in order for God to use you in His work, the cause has got to be more important to you than your own needs."

"And these are they which are sown among thorns; such as hear the word, and the cares of this world, and the deceitfulness of riches, and the lusts of other things entering in, choke the word, and it becometh unfruitful" (verses 18, 19). After some time in the faith a person comes to a crossroads where he realizes that there are more sin issues to face, even though his walk has been a real one. Or as the person ages, the nostalgia of remembering earlier times in life sets in, and this person seems to forget the pain these old sin struggles caused. Then the question becomes whether to continue in Christian growth or let the struggles take over. For these people, although they have changed, more changes are still needed.

"And these are they which are sown on good ground; such as hear the word, and receive *it*, and bring forth fruit, some thirtyfold, some sixty, and some an hundred" (verse 20). There is fruit on the good ground. The parable started with a seed, and the harvest of a crop is always more seeds. So the thirty, sixty, or 100 means you have become thirty, sixty, or 100 times better as a person by continuing down the path God has laid out for you in life. At the same time, it also means 30, 60, or 100 people have been reached as a result of the seeds you have sown. *If you want to be in the good ground, helping others get to heaven has got to be above getting there yourself because that is what the good ground is about!* That is how to overcome the sleeping church mentality. That is how to be an on-fire Christian.

Let's end this chapter on a positive note. In December 1995, Evangelist Leo Schreven spoke at a citywide crusade in Calgary, Alberta. Leo was gracious enough, since I wanted to learn about evangelism, to let me sit in with him during some of the behind-the-scenes activities. I was allowed to observe the visitation sessions where he sought to get people to make the decision to accept all that they'd heard. A gentleman named Rob came. After hearing about the signs and manner of the second coming of Christ; who the beast really is; the truth about the Sabbath, Sunday, death, heaven, hell, healthy living, and much more; Rob leaned over to his sister whom he'd brought to the session and said, "Sis, you've gotta know Jesus." That's what it's all about.

Words of Advice

Another thing sleeping Christians like to say is "crusades don't work." Here's a thought on that: "The purpose of a public meeting is to provide a forum whereby those ready to make the decision are brought to this point. The real work of evangelism, where you get the most decisions, is in the home visitation that comes along with a crusade," said Lester Carney.

Chapter 3

How to Find Interests

There's a great quote you can lift slightly out of context from *The Acts of the Apostles* that gives insight on how to be on fire for God. The passage refers to the fact that the sleeping church mentality had its beginnings in the time of the apostles. "The persecution that came upon the church in Jerusalem resulted in giving a great impetus to the work of the gospel. Success had attended the ministry of the word in that place, and there was danger that the disciples would linger there too long, unmindful of the Saviour's commission to go to all the world. Forgetting that strength to resist evil is best gained by aggressive service, they began to think that they had no work so important as that of shielding the church in Jerusalem from the attacks of the enemy. Instead of educating the new converts to carry the gospel to those who had not heard it, they were in danger of taking a course that would lead all to be satisfied with what had been accomplished. To scatter His representatives abroad, where they could work for others, God permitted persecution to come upon them. Driven from Jerusalem, the believers 'went everywhere preaching the word'" (p. 105).

Did you catch the tip on how to be on fire? "Strength to resist evil is best gained by aggressive service." This idea ties in perfectly with what we saw in the last chapter from the parable of the sower. Now what does aggressive mean? Certainly it does not mean rude or annoying service, does it? No, it means a proactive approach, looking for people who are interested rather than waiting and hoping they will come to you someday.

So how do you find someone who is interested in the gospel? Before I share some thoughts with you, I must stop here and give this warning from *Christian Service*. "There will come times when the church will be stirred by divine power, and earnest activity will be the result; for the life-giving power of the Holy Spirit will inspire its members to go forth and bring souls to Christ. But when this activity is manifested, the most earnest workers will be safe only as they depend upon God through constant, earnest prayer. They will need to make earnest supplication that through the grace of Christ they may be saved from taking pride in their work, or of making a savior of their activity. They must constantly look to Jesus, that they may realize that it is His power which does the work, and thus be able to ascribe all the glory to God" (p. 98).

If you take the advice in the instructional portions of this book too far, you will be tempted to make a savior out of doing the work. When you get to the Bible study chapters, be sure to go through them so you can understand every single study to the fullest extent possible. You have to know the truth for yourself first before you can share the truth and win others to Christ.

> ## Words of Advice
>
> Within the last few years there has been a worldwide cultural revolution through what is now called "user generated content" on Web sites such as Youtube and Facebook. Bulletin boards, blogs, and videos are everywhere. Instead of waiting for someone else to tell us what to think, being fed in a top down sort of system, we all get to have our say. What this amounts to is the highest fulfillment of the principles of democracy and the doctrine of the priesthood of every believer ever seen in world history. If Adventists will embrace it, this new attitude will prepare us to receive the latter rain like never before.
>
> The symbolism of rain for the Holy Spirit is something very significant. Rain falls from above, and it falls everywhere, one drop at a time. It falls just where it is needed, on parched soil, to cause growth. The focus here is on the individual membership being empowered and going out everywhere to shine for God, drawing in souls who are also receiving the same rain. This is highly compatible with the idea that we don't need a priest to be a go-between for us in order to be saved. Don't look for it to happen around you. Don't look for it to happen at the conference office first. Surrender yourself to God; pray for His power in your life. *The greatest evidence the latter rain of Hosea 6:3 is finally coming down to the Seventh-day Adventist Church will be when there is an incredible upswing in interest on the part of the membership toward outreach.* It's a revival among the people, not the leaders who are there to serve us until we are ready. I do believe that upswing has begun. By reading this book I know you also want to be a part of that upswing.

The first rule is the most important of all. In order to reach people around you, you need to be nice to them! They have to see a power and a peace working in you that they don't have. One of the greatest evidences that evangelism is a miracle of the Holy Spirit is in the fact that you can't actually make them want this peace. They have to want it for themselves, or there's nothing you can do. That desire for God's peace comes from God working in their lives already. Prayer is also a key component. Pray in faith that the Lord will use you to draw people to Him.

I have experienced this firsthand. As I moved around in the earlier days of my painting career, I often worked for companies for a short time, but many times I made a special connection with just one person, and I knew the Lord had called me to that place just to work with that person and touch their life before He moved me.

Why does God deserve all the glory? His strength is made perfect in weakness because we need to constantly recognize that His power flowing through us is what really does the work of changing lives around us. It is His word, and as we share it, He blesses those who receive it. As Creator of the entire universe, everything is dependent on Him. The atoms in our own bodies would fly apart without His command to hold them together. He keeps the earth in its precise orbit. As redeemer of humanity all three members of the Trinity have played their part in the plan of salvation and its application to us.

He also deserves the glory because He knows you, your style and approach to witnessing, and what you think about His truth—what you've learned and what you still need to learn. He will guide you to the place where the kind of witness you have to offer is the right kind for those who will hear it, even if you don't think it's very good. Even when we think our efforts are feeble, His power will multiply them, just as Jesus multiplied the loaves and fishes when feeding the five thousand. What you have to offer is what someone can handle and needs to hear. If not, the Lord will keep that person from you. Remember Esther. She was placed in the right place at the right time to serve as a witness. The last part of Esther 4:14 says, "Who knoweth whether thou art come to the kingdom for *such* a time as this?"

Here are some ideas to keep in mind as you look for interests. The most logical choice before one ventures beyond their comfort zone is to work within that comfort zone as much as possible. Therefore, start with people you already know well, such as your friends and relatives. Coworkers may be next. Try to think of people you barely know but see often such as bank tellers or cashiers at the grocery store.

We discussed the fears that many Adventists have in the last chapter. I would liken facing your fears to when you go camping and you wake up each morning in a nice cozy warm sleeping bag but don't want to leave it. You stay in there a while because it seems as if the air around you is colder. You finally decide to brave the elements, and once you're up, it's not so bad. Then you can get on with your day. Being in the warm environment of your comfort zone is pretty much the same.

Look for what God is doing in the lives of people around you. The Lord will give you opportunities to share with people what they need to hear. "It is the very essence of all right faith to do the right thing at the right time. God is the great Master Worker, and by His providence He prepares the way for His work to be accomplished. He provides opportunities, opens up lines of influence and channels for working. If His people are watching the indications of His providence, and stand ready to co-operate with Him, they will see a great work accomplished. Their efforts, rightly directed, will produce a hundredfold greater results than can be accomplished with the same means and facilities in another channel where God is not so manifestly working" (*Testimonies for the Church,* vol. 6, p. 24).

One of the best ways to turn casual conversations into witnessing opportunities is to keep this thought constantly in the back of your mind "Have I got a book (or video) for you!" In other words, as you begin to get to know someone, ask yourself, "What are this person's likes, dislikes, hobbies, interests, or felt needs?" Then seek to provide them with something that relates what you've discovered about them to the Advent message. Of course, be sure to back this up with friendship as well. Be genuine in your approach.

Here are some examples. Is your friend a smoker? Give him or her stop-smoking materials. Do you know an expectant mother? There's a study later on called "Bible Words of Hope and Encouragement for Expectant Mothers." Daniel 7:9 describes the Father as sitting on his throne with "wheels as burning fire." That may encourage a handicapped friend to feel that God identifies with his plight. I found a statement once that said God gives extra angels to the blind. Tell your blind friend she has two guardian angels instead of one. Is your potential interest a deep thinker? Give him *The Great Controversy*. Or are you dealing with someone more touchy feely or someone who knows little about the basics of knowing Jesus? Then maybe start with *The Desire of Ages* or *Steps to Christ* instead. Whenever people come to me sincerely asking about the creation/evolution debate, I've seen them seriously ponder the thought, based on Ellen White, that Adam and Eve were twelve feet tall and a tyrannosaurus would have been to them as an elephant is to us.

Maybe this person is a science fiction fan? Tell him or her that the Bible does actually say there's life on other planets. There's a study here in this book on that topic. A good way to catch the interest of people who grew up watching Star Trek is to run through the basic plotlines of the first six Star Trek movies with them. Star Trek 1 has a character looking for its creator. The theme of creation is dealt with in Star Trek 2, which ends with Mr. Spock dying to save the rest. He rises from the dead in the third installment in the franchise and then returns to earth in the fourth movie. Star Trek 5 sends the characters off on a journey to heaven while Star Trek 6 ends with a new era of peace. Does that sound familiar? That's the exact same storyline and in the exact order as the Bible.

Hearing talk of Star Trek, Star Wars, Harry Potter, Lord of the Rings, etc., may at first make you think your friend has no interest in spiritual things. But remember, Jesus told us to be "sheep among wolves" and "wise as serpents but harmless as doves." If this person in front of you is watching something you know to be wrong, instead of telling them what they believe in is of the devil, offer a book, pamphlet, or video that ties into the gospel message. For instance, you could offer a science fiction fan the Amazing Facts "Cosmic Conflict" DVD and say, "It's the story of Adam and Eve done up like Star Wars." Someone who's into astrology or Nostradamus might enjoy reading something about Ellen White if you tell them God has a true prophet for our time.

The point is, agree with them where you can and save whatever you don't agree with for later. That's the essence of being nonjudgmental. There is some truth in every one of the devil's counterfeits. *Whatever that truth is, capitalize on it.* Paul concurs in 1 Corinthians 9:19-22: "For though I am free from all *men*, I have made myself a servant to all, that I might win the more; and to the Jews I became as a Jew, that I might win Jews; to those *who are* under the law, as under the law, that I might win those *who are* under the law; to those *who are* without law, as without law (not being without law toward God, but under law toward Christ), that I might win those *who are* without law; to the weak I became as weak, that I might win the weak. I have become all things to all *men*, that I might by all means save some" (NKJV).

> **Words of Advice**
>
> Sleeping members may also expect that, unless they have validation from the organized church, they cannot do anything. Remember Randy Barber's words, "You don't need permission from a church board or a conference committee to give a Bible study."

The important thing when looking for interests is to see everyone as a potential interest and act accordingly. Prayerfully look for every possible opportunity you can find. Persistence is the key. You need the heart of a salesperson. In order to find one serious interest, you must try to reach forty.

It will help to examine the analogy so often used to describe evangelistic outreach of sowing, cultivating, and reaping. Just what is each phase of growth? Public meetings are often referred to as "reaping" events where a harvest is gathered of souls who make their decision to join the church. But those decisions can also be made in a living room, as was the case with me.

So what needs to be done ahead of time to bring that about? The "sowing" is the planting of a "seed" represented by a small amount of truth, such as a tract or the example of a dedicated believer. Whoever the interest is, they are heading in a direction away from heaven. Even the smallest amount of truth that goes against the trend of this person's entire life will be noticeable to that person. The seed must germinate, and as Jesus said, "he knoweth not how" (Mark 4:27; read also verses 26–29).

One very important thing has to be mentioned here. As you go out with gospel seed and share, you must wait for the Holy Spirit to cause the germination to take place, which is simply when the person in question shows some level of interest for more. You cannot generate any interest by your own power. If you try too hard at this stage, you may push the person away.

From here on let's personalize this discussion by using a name to describe a Bible study candidate rather than continually referring to them as "the interest," "the candidate," or "him or her." This will help you get a picture in your mind of a person God can use you to reach. Let's call this person IAIN, which stands for "Interested and in Need."

> **Words of Advice**
>
> Ken Wiebe once related to me what he was taught in seminary. "My Professor said clearly to us, 'Don't think you're the ministers, they [the laity] are the real ministers. You get to do Bible things all day, which shields you. You don't have to work with people who smoke, drink, and swear. You're not fighting the battle like they are.'"

After the planting comes the cultivating. That is where unselfish love emerges in a very large way. My wife was used in several ways she did not realize until I told her later how they influenced me to desire study with her and the pastor. One event took place when we were engaged. It was Easter weekend and we were watching a movie about Jesus' life and death. She cried as she watched the crucifixion scene. It was so real for her, and it made me think that I needed something more too. Another time we were late for something, and her not swearing under stress impressed me as to the amount of peace in her heart. On two separate occasions while I ate meat and she didn't, she expressed concern over my enjoyment of my meal. Because her love for me was greater than a difference between us humbled and moved me.

Cultivation also takes the form of feeding the interest with more truth. A Revelation seminar, which focuses on sharing deeper truths and encouraging individuals to make a commitment to those truths, will be much more effective in getting results if there are church members out in the community giving Bible studies first. "But this *I say*, He which soweth sparingly shall reap also sparingly; and he which soweth bountifully shall reap also bountifully" (2 Cor. 9:6). It is the time spent ahead of the meeting looking for IAINs and sharing the basic truths with them, step by step, that really makes the series successful. People who come off the street and hear that the seventh day is the true Sabbath can't possibly stand for it in their own strength. They need a true conversion to Christ in order for the rest of the message to make sense.

So as you are out sowing seed like crazy, looking for those opportunities, and someone finally comes back to you for more, share with that person again. When IAIN comes back the third time, that's the indicator you have a serious interest on your hands and a God-given opportunity. Take the plunge and ask if the two of you can get together to explore IAIN's felt need a little further with a Bible study.

As far as any further advice on finding people for God, let's consider organized church efforts. There are of course many seminars and community outreach activities your church may already be running or may want to run. Support them and prayerfully look for opportunities to make friends with those non-Adventists who attend. Outreach opportunities may include cooking courses, Breathe Free plans, stress seminars, soup kitchens, thrift stores, and ADRA work.

Does your church have a Web site? Can they put sermons or Bible studies of some sort on there? Can they have a feedback section? Each of our Adventist media ministries such as *It Is Written* sends information to local churches when people in their communities order materials from the offers at the end of the show. Has anyone been designated to follow-up on those contacts?

At my church we have a "Vegetarian Club" that has been operating for more than twelve years now. Once a month we have a potluck meal and a speaker or video presentation on a certain health topic. At each meeting a newsletter is handed out with health articles and some spiritual thoughts sprinkled here and there. There is also a literature table with more Christian materials. The club always does a Christmas dinner with a Christian singing group to take advantage of the more spiritual mood people are in that time of year.

Maybe your church could run programs such as this and designate a few of the more evangelistically minded members to be the ones who give Bible studies to any new interests that come out of them. As you likely already know, when churches run these types of programs they have to be done unselfishly with no baited hook. Jesus set the example in healing all ten lepers though only one came back to thank Him. Now the idea of no baited hook does not mean hiding who we are and what we believe in. If we help people for this

> **Words of Advice**
>
> Randy Barber provided advice to a spouse regarding outreach and it's stretch on the couple's finances and time. "If he can score six Bible studies in one night, God will put the gas in the car. Also, negotiate one or two nights per week and commit to working then. On the other nights leave it alone and do your duty in the home."

life only and don't at least give them a chance for heaven, what good is that? You let them know who you are and those who want to know more about what you believe in and Whom you believe in will come to you.

On top of all these ideas don't forget about good old-fashioned knocking on doors. Revelation 3:20 depicts Jesus knocking at the door of our hearts. Why can't it also be understood as a prophetic reference to the need for house to house work in the last days? Here's how *Gospel Workers* puts it: "As soon as a new field is entered, educational work should begin, and instruction should be given line upon line, precept upon precept, here a little and there a little. It is not preaching that is the most important; it is house-to-house work, reasoning from the Word, explaining the Word. It is those workers who follow the methods that Christ followed who will win souls for their hire. Over and over again the same truths must be repeated, and the worker must place his entire dependence on God. And what rich experiences the teacher obtains when instructing those in darkness! He too is a learner, and as he explains the Scriptures to others, the Holy Spirit is working in his mind and heart, giving him the bread of life for hungry souls" (p. 468).

Whatever ways you look for interests, keep this important rule in mind *the farther away IAIN is from the truth, the smaller the pamphlets you give out, the shorter the answers to his questions!* And as soon as you can, get him Bible verses to prove your points. Human beings are constantly reasoning from their own opinions, and they need to be in the mindset of submitting to God in order to understand truth in a way that will change their lives for the better. If your witnessing ends up being your opinion against theirs, you're not really helping them to change.

Rahab's life story went through seven distinct phases that shows IAIN's spiritual growth:

She was a prostitute – Thus she was living a life of sin.

She hid the spies – Here we have recognition of God and His truth in the form of those He sent.

She lies to hide them – In doing the wrong thing for the right reason, she shows what's in her heart.

She's rescued when the walls of Jericho fall – This is the beginning of salvation, being born again.

She stays outside the camp at first – This indicates progress in spiritual growth, which takes time.

She joins Israel – This of course relates to church membership, such as from a reaping event.

Finally, she's listed as an ancestor to the Messiah – In other words, she's given a part to play in saving others.

When we do outreach, God can use us to help people at any step in this process. If it is your heart's desire to see people start their journey to heaven as a result of the Bible studies the Lord guides you to give, the advice in the next chapter will give you what you need to be the best outreach worker you possibly can be.

Words of Advice

Say you're using a prepackaged video or pamphlet Bible study program that incorporates everything we believe into twenty sessions. Night sixteen is the one that asks for a decision. You share with three friends. Friend one is ready at night six. What do you do? How do you compress the rest of the program to make sure she doesn't get bored? How do you know she is ready? Friend two won't be ready in twenty, but would be in twenty-four, what do you do? Which topics do you need to expand on? Friend three will never take a stand, and he's only trying to convince you your church is a cult. What do you do? When do you realize your time could be better spent finding someone else and let him go?

There are many advantages to prepackaged outreach materials. They can wait for IAIN to be ready to read on his own time; they can wear a resistant IAIN down each time he reads them by their consistency; and through duplication they can go farther and wider than a person can. But you have one advantage as a trained outreach worker they don't have. Adaptability!

Chapter 4
The Psychology of Giving Studies

"Natural means, used in accordance with God's will, bring about supernatural results" (*Selected Messages*, book 2, p. 346). We love to use this quote when we give health talks to the public to show the value of eating right in relation to true spirituality. God has the real power and does the real work. But when we do our best within the realm He has given us to work in, how much better can the results be. It's the same with giving Bible studies to someone who is interested and in need. There are certain rules, which if you follow, will be more conducive to enlightening a searching soul. These rules constitute the focus of our discussion here.

The most important thing is of course love. The truth must always be presented in love. IAIN must see that you care about him. *Evangelism* says, "Do not make prominent those features of our message which are a condemnation of the customs and practises of the people, until they have opportunity to know that we are believers in Christ" (p. 231). What you have to offer has got to be something IAIN will see as a benefit to his own life. "If we wish to do good to souls, our success with these souls will be in proportion to their belief in our belief in, and appreciation of, them" (*Mind, Character, and Personality*, vol. 1, p. 255).

The next rule is also equally important. You need to keep up your own devotional life. George Vandeman in *Helping for the Heart* put it this way, "I have discovered that if anything will unsettle the skeptic, it likely will not be argument, however sane or sound. Rather, it will be the degree of personal conviction. And that conviction depends upon the reality of one's own commitment to a risen Lord" (p. 113). Prayer is another key component to success. The Lord can use your efforts only as you draw on Him for strength and give Him the proper recognition, which is what "glory" really is. Through prayer, His power is added to your words. And His Spirit guides you to give what words and Bible texts are needed to reach IAIN.

I once watched a TV documentary about lasers showing how a 3D hologram is made. At one point in the show there was a chemically treated photographic glass plate that clearly showed an image of a boat. Then the narrator said, "Now watch what happens when we break the glass." At first I thought I would see a single boat shattered to pieces, which could be re-assembled like a jigsaw puzzle. But no! There was a full and complete boat in each piece, simply shown from a different angle. It is the same with doctrine if it is presented correctly. Each truth relates to every other and is only a different version of the one great truth.

This one great truth must always be kept in mind when sharing any Bible lesson. It's the theme of the great controversy between Christ and Satan, good and evil. In every generation this conflict has existed. All of world history shows the unfolding of one great plan on the part of God. It is called the plan of salvation. IAIN must come to realize his or her own place in this plan, because each life is a miniaturized version of the same conflict. The following are a series of questions each study should contain the answers to:

1. What is the main point of the lesson?
2. Can you think of any real world example from your own life that illustrates this point?
3. How does it relate to the first coming of Jesus? The second coming of Jesus? IAIN's own need of Jesus? The great controversy being played out in world history? And the previous studies?
4. How can this study be used to plant seeds for further studies?
5. Are there any sins to avoid?
6. Briefly discuss what counterfeits exist in the world. And when the study transitions into the differences in Christian faith that exist, discuss also what counterfeits there are in other churches.
7. What small decision can IAIN make now that will be a step forward toward your goal for him of making the great decision to take a stand for all the truth? Each study must end with a mini-decision to accept what was presented. That will lead to the great decision.
8. What should you say in your closing prayer?

When you first begin studying together, ask him about his spiritual knowledge and experience with God to this point. What does he already know of truth and salvation? Are there any topics in your study plan you can cover more quickly? How can you best find answers to these questions that will speak to his background, culture, and life experience?

The real art to giving Bible studies is not just getting the message across but watching for a reaction and being there with appropriate words to help your interest move along on her journey to heaven. Learning to share truth is like learning to play the piano. You practice until you "know it." For the first while you are concentrating to remember which key is Middle C or F Sharp. Then once the structure of the keys and the notations is in your head, you can just look at a page, and the melody naturally flows out of you. It's the same with Bible verses and points of truth. When you "know" what it is you are sharing, you can keep one eye on your

> **Words of Advice**
>
> Louis Torres said, "When you meet someone new, size that person up. Do they need to be sown, cultivated, or reaped?"

study notes and the other eye on IAIN. This gives you adaptability since each conversion is different. Your trust is not as much in the structure of the program as in the Holy Spirit applying the program to each person's need. The answers to these questions can naturally flow out of you. This will free you from having to follow your notes to the letter and help you to be more open to the Spirit's promptings as you see them in IAIN's reaction.

In every study, somehow, someway, work in the fact that Christ died for this person. IAIN is searching. He doesn't know what he is searching for; you do. It's a true relationship with Jesus. In order to help IAIN find what you have found, there are three questions on his heart that need answers. They are the three great questions of life itself. The studies you give to IAIN need to be grouped to answer these questions:

1. Who is God?
2. What has He done for me?
3. What does He want me to do for Him in return?

As you seek to answer these questions, the answers will be applied by the Holy Spirit into IAIN's life, and you will see changes in him as the Holy Spirit keeps working on his heart, drawing him in to make that decision to accept all he has heard. These questions and their answers also indicate the order in which IAIN needs to be won to the truth. Now again, keep watching for those reactions. You can cover more quickly what he already believes. But IAIN has to make certain decisions in a certain order.

First, IAIN needs to accept the authority of the Bible, that the God of the Bible is God, that Jesus is a real person from history, and that the stories of the Bible are true. As the study begins and IAIN is not very well acquainted with Jesus personally, he will likely only give intellectual assent. At this point openness is all that is needed. For example, on the topic of Creation, Hebrews 11:6 is clear, "For he that cometh to God must believe that he is, and that he is a rewarder of them that diligently seek him." IAIN may not be overly enthusiastic about believing in Adam and Eve yet. As long as he does not strongly disagree, keep going forward.

The next step is conviction of his sinfulness. IAIN must give himself over to Jesus. In some way the Holy Spirit will break him, and he will need to make the decision to accept Christ and stand for the truth to be made new. "For every one that doeth evil hateth the light, neither cometh to the light, lest his deeds should be reproved. But he that doeth truth cometh to the light, that his deeds may be made manifest, that they are wrought in God" (John 3:20, 21). The first thing to happen when IAIN comes to the light is that his own dark spots will be revealed to him. That he is even willing to admit this to himself is a sign of the Holy Spirit working on his heart. Someone who loves evil will turn away at this point.

The next item for consideration is that the Lord has a right to dictate to humanity the duties He has placed upon us all. However, the only time IAIN will be willing to make changes in his life will be when he is in love with Jesus. There is much value in the phrase, "I am leading this person to

> **Words of Advice**
>
> Bernice Carney said, "The pastors who give Bible studies see their churches grow."

Christ." That is just what you are doing. Keeping in mind the three great questions of life, how much emphasis do you need to place on God and His love, and how close is IAIN to responding to that love with a decision and commitment? Pay attention to the kind of questions and comments he poses when you study. Let him guide you, in essence, to meet his needs. He will respond to what the Holy Spirit weighs upon him.

IAIN is on a path you have already covered. You know where it leads, and he is looking to you for guidance. You face him and stay in front of him just far enough to put down a gem of truth, which he picks up. You then step back, thus leading him forward. If he picks up the gem, you lay down another, and he steps ahead to take it as well. Continue to feed and he will continue to grow.

Words of Advice

The very first session should be some sort of overview study that briefly encapsulates many of the truths to come without giving away too much either. As a fisher of men, this is your hook. Several studies are included in this book as suggestions. You could go with one of the two studies on Daniel 2, "Bible Proof There's Life On Other Planets" or "The Search For Truth."

Before IAIN is convicted of his sinfulness, he may have some obvious bad habits (such as drinking alcohol) that he honestly doesn't see as being wrong. Pointing it out now will alienate him. You have to overlook it for the moment. Let it slide off you, so to speak, until the Holy Spirit does His work. IAIN may spend a long time simply considering all you have to show him. When he is considering what you have to offer, you may go through much frustration. It is a hard balance between enough encouragement to keep up his interest and avoiding overload so as not to push him away. You will have to accept some inconvenience in your schedule to accomplish the end result of leading him to Christ. Try in every way you possibly can to make it a regular habit to study together. A weekly schedule is the ideal, but in today's multi-media world with people who are so busy, biweekly meetings will more likely be the case.

As long as the mini-decisions continue to be "yes" each week, even if there appears to be very little change, do not worry. Trust that the Lord will work with the effort you are making. If IAIN shows no interest in, or some animosity, to a particular topic but is willing to continue studying others, keep things going and put that one issue on the shelf for now. Always be ready and watching, because at some point he will change for better or worse. Suddenly, and sometimes very quickly, things will fall into place. They will make sense, and he will be ready to make that great decision. Which way he goes depends on whether or not he loves the truth more than his sins.

The process of conviction can be illustrated in the story of the prodigal son found in Luke 15:11–20: "And he said, A certain man had two sons: And the younger of them said to his father, Father, give me the portion of goods that falleth to me. And he divided unto them his living" (verses 11, 12). Many of us come to points in our lives where we decide to leave the protection of the Lord. In the parable the father gives the son his inheritance. Cross-reference this with Mathew 5:45 and you will realize the inheritance here is one of earthly blessings.

"And not many days after the younger son gathered all together, and took his journey into a far country, and there wasted his substance with riotous living" (verse 13). The son leaves his father for the world. Our heavenly Father in His infinite mercy gives us blessings in this life. To live only to consume those blessings is the main concern of worldly-hearted people. In the story the son's heart is only filled with thoughts of pleasure and self-indulgence, but these do not last, nor can they.

Words of Advice

Since IAIN's knowledge and interest may be lower at first, adapt the study to fit him. Keep it about forty-five minutes with a dozen texts. Questions asked should have short answers. Do your best to keep all the socializing at the start and pray before and at the end of each study. As soon as IAIN is ready, get him to pray as well. Leave each week as soon after the closing prayer as you can so his last thought will be about the study.

"And when he had spent all, there arose a mighty famine in that land; and he began to be in want. And he went and joined himself to a citizen of that country; and he sent him into his fields to feed swine" (verses 14, 15). The famine here is the famine of the bread of life. Benefits have now been wasted, and the son realizes there was no real fulfillment in them alone. However, he still believes in the world and its ways, though now it is costing him.

"And he would fain have filled his belly with the husks that the swine did eat: and no man gave unto him" (verse 16). After trying to recover what he lost by his own power, he sees finally that sin only disappoints. He has sunk to a new low. Once he realizes the error of his ways, he desires peace again.

These first points are where the Lord can use you to plant seeds. People on this earth are either enjoying their evil deeds or are beginning to recognize that they are suffering for them. God will introduce them to you and call you to witness to them. The Lord's purpose is to use you to offer them mercy. The significance of turning the other cheek to sinners around you, especially the ones still enjoying their sins, is that you are offering love to the undeserving. Deep down they know what they are doing is wrong, and deep down they expect nothing but retribution for it. When you love them, it allows the Holy Spirit to work on their hearts, showing them how undeserving they really are. If there is any hope for them to change their wicked ways, it is as they feel this weight the Spirit puts upon them, because with that weight there always comes an offer of a way out. Even in the presence of a Christian, they will see their need of something better. They will be convicted of their own sinfulness.

"And when he came to himself, he said, How many hired servants of my father's have bread enough and to spare, and I perish with hunger!" (verse 17). He "comes to himself"; the son is sane once more after so much self-abuse. Now he feels the need of home. He remembers what it was like to live in comfort. We all need to go through experiences that generate this desire in us. We all need to hunger for real bread—the bread only Christ can offer.

"I will arise and go to my father, and will say unto him, Father, I have sinned against heaven, and before thee, And am no more worthy to be called thy son: make me as one of thy hired servants" (verses 18, 19). The son "rises," showing he now wants to walk upright as a man of dignity. He is humbled by his wrongs. He not only admits he sinned against his fellow man but also against the Lord Himself. He doesn't expect special treatment, for he knows he committed those wrongs. Now his heart is ready for the Father to receive him again.

> **Words of Advice**
>
> As IAIN's conviction deepens, you may see a change in his countenance as if to say, "Even though I am so bad, do you (and therefore does God) still love me?" The answer has to be yes.

This is most likely the point IAIN is at when he expresses an interest for study. This would correspond to the seed beginning to emerge from the soil in several of Jesus' parables. You are to cultivate that soil with mercy and truth that his iniquity can be purged. "And he arose, and came to his father. But when he was yet a great way off, his father saw him, and had compassion, and ran, and fell on his neck, and kissed him" (verse 20). The father never left the border of his own land until he saw the son. The Lord will not compromise Himself. Though as soon as there is evidence of repentance, then God comes rushing into IAIN's life like the father. The son is "a long way off." Let's say he is a smoker. He is on his way back to God not when he quits, but when he wants to quit with all his heart.

"It is true that men sometimes become ashamed of their sinful ways, and give up some of their evil habits, before they are conscious that they are being drawn to Christ. But whenever they make an effort to reform, from a sincere desire to do right, it is the power of Christ that is drawing them. An influence of which they are unconscious works upon the soul, and the conscience is quickened, and the outward life is amended. And as Christ draws them to look upon His cross, to behold Him whom their sins have pierced, the commandment comes home to the conscience. The wickedness of their life, the deep-seated sin of the soul, is revealed to them. They begin to comprehend something of the righteousness of Christ, and exclaim, 'What is sin, that it should require such a sacrifice for the redemption of its victim? Was all this love, all this suffering, all this humiliation, demanded, that we might not perish, but have everlasting

> **Words of Advice**
>
> Richard Warman said, "When studying with someone, always leave the person wanting a little bit more."

life?'" (*Steps to Christ*, p. 27).

The father kisses the son, which is the son's first realization of his father's presence. Now IAIN is not just talking about his problems, but he is expressing his overall need of God. Now he begins to see God working in his life. As the rest of the parable describes, the father restores his son to the household. *Steps to Christ*, page 27, continues with, "The sinner may resist this love, may refuse to be drawn to Christ; but if he does not resist he will be drawn to Jesus."

> ## Words of Advice
>
> Bible study and the giving of one's heart to the Lord is an intensely personal experience. IAIN must be allowed to control his own witnessing. Louis Torres said, "Don't talk about joining the church in front of his friends. You will only embarrass him."

The process of conversion is simply one where IAIN is broken before God, who makes him anew. It will happen at different times and in different ways for each IAIN you meet. To help IAIN along, share your own testimony of what the Lord has done for you. Tell of your own joy at receiving Him. Don't glorify your sins with a detailed account, but do let IAIN know Jesus has worked in your life. Remember, there is great significance to the illustration in Revelation 3:20 of Jesus standing at the door and knocking. The Lord is standing at the door of IAIN's heart. IAIN must be the one to open the door and let Him in. He has to be led through a prayer where he with his own words says that he would like to accept Jesus as his Savior. And accepting Him into his heart means that IAIN now gives Jesus complete control of his life.

> ## Words of Advice
>
> Louis Torres, in referring to John 3:8 using Jesus' illustration of wind for the Holy Spirit, said, "You can't see wind, but you can see its effects in blowing branches and rustling leaves." Here is his list of various signs of conviction. Positive signs: tears of joy, verbalizing, contemplation, facial expressions of peace, questions, agreement, relief, surprise, and acceptance. Negative signs: anger, excuses, tears of sorrow, verbalizing, facial expressions of guilt or fear, rejection, changing the subject, joking, silence, tone of voice, objections, avoidance, and squirming in the chair.

Go as fast as he is willing to follow. As his interest level grows, you will see in IAIN an increasing openness to all spiritual things. As an Adventist, you know there is such a thing as false and true Christianity. In making the transition into the commitment studies (the ones that answer the third great question), begin introducing this difference. This is the background theme to the entire Short Program, which includes a specific study on the topic. This is also explored further in the last two chapters.

"We must in our work not only strike the iron when it is hot but make the iron hot by striking" (*Evangelism*, p. 647). I have heard more than one story of someone who needed to hear the message many times in order to stand for it. Daniel 8:27 says, "And I Daniel fainted, and was sick certain days; afterward I rose up, and did the king's business; and I was astonished at the vision, but none understood it." Daniel couldn't handle what had been given to him in vision for many years. During that time his life went back to normal. "No," may mean "not yet." If IAIN ceases to continue studying with you, do not feel one bit of guilt. If you have seen no sign of change by the time you get to a study on baptism, make that your first opportunity to strike and ask him about getting baptized.

> ## Words of Advice
>
> Kelly Shultz spoke about a situation where one woman was considering the Advent message while at the same time attending another new church in Canmore. "Whoever offends her first will lose her. Just keep showing her Christian love. If someone over there says, 'What are you keeping that old Sabbath for?' we'll have her." At this time we'd shared all the truth with her, and she was taking time to absorb it. Later, when she did stand with us, she said what made the difference for her was our sincerity.

As mentioned previously, knowing the truth gives you adaptability. An example of this came from my experience in giving the studies Pastor Warman gave me to my friend Adrian. (The studies constitute the majority of what's in the Long Program.) When I went to pass them on, things went differently. I could see the basics weren't catching Adrian's interest, so I rearranged them to fit into a break down of the three angels' messages of Revelation 14:6–12 (which fills most of the Short Program). I also quickened the pace, which kept his interest, but didn't convert him. He went through a first round almost completely. When I made a call for him to take a stand for what he'd been shown, he said he was not ready, and we didn't see each other for about five months. During that time I kept up my faith and prayed for him continuously.

Later on the Lord brought us back together by sheer coincidence. This time the Lord was obviously weighing him down, and we studied together again, focusing more on his receiving Jesus as his Savior. The first time he learned doctrine that made sense in his head. The second time he learned truth that came alive in his heart by a miracle of the Holy Spirit.

Under the Lord's guidance, you are controlling the study and IAIN in it. Don't let that control go beyond the study. For instance, don't try to sway IAIN to your point of view on political issues. Speak softly, calmly, and lovingly. Phrase all comments in a way that is positive. Louis Torres said, "Never get angry, because then that which is holy will have been brought down to a common level." Give Bible answers to all his questions. Don't belittle the study time with jokes or humorous anecdotes. Don't sensationalize it with conspiracy stories that go beyond what the Bible says or put down other churches.

Also, there must be nothing noticeable from you to distract the study in any way. Your dress, hygiene, and personal habits must be proper. Don't do anything to draw attention to your own sin struggles or faults. Never flirt. Billy Graham has a policy of never being alone with a woman who is not his wife. This can also be an advantage if IAIN is a lady with small children who will distract her. The third person can help occupy them.

> **Words of Advice**
>
> Carol Torres on flirting: "Satan has a woman for you in every city."

There is a time to point out error and sin, both in the church and in the world. However, the main point of every single study has got to be what is right with the truth and not what is wrong with everyone and everything else. Too much refuting is a form of validation. It says that what is being refuted is worthy of refutation. Be proactive; win souls rather than arguments.

Studying with members of other churches can be a unique challenge. If IAIN was an evangelical Christian previous to studying with you, she most likely has already gone through the process of conviction and prayed a prayer of general surrender to Jesus. If so, just as Catholicism ultimately trusts in a ceremonial religion (they think salvation comes from participating in certain ceremonies rather than by experiencing a change of heart), so Protestantism can do the same thing. A word-for-word reading of an invitational prayer printed on the back of a tract can become ceremonial, or a failure to move on to higher truths as referred to in Hebrews 6 can mean a stunting of her spiritual growth. If so, IAIN needs to understand that present truth is a continuation of her Christian experience. She will be reconvicted on issues of growth, such as the Sabbath and the truth about death.

Romans 7:9 can be modified to help you understand what life is like for an evangelical who discovers that Sunday is not the true holy day, "I was alive [in my born-again faith] without the law once [before being brought into contact with this new truth]: but when the [fourth] commandment came, sin revived, and I [and all that I thought I knew of what being born-again really meant] died."

> **Words of Advice**
>
> Louis Torres had a story of two different ladies coming to him after he covered jewelry in the evening meeting of a crusade. One came up expressing gladness at being freed from jewelry, while the other said, "How could you be so rude! You knew I was the only one here wearing any jewelry, and you singled me out." This is an example of positive and negative conviction.

Respect that the Lord has led her that far. Your hope is that He will use you to help her go farther. Leo Schreven told the story of a Lutheran lady who came to one of his crusades. She had been a matriarch in her home church for decades, always holding positions of major responsibility. One year she didn't take a post and no one knew why. At the end of the crusade she said, "Now I know why the Lord did not want me to take a place on the church board this year, because now He wants me to join this church."

When you see any evidence of conviction manifesting itself, pour on the prayer. Pray for IAIN, and pray for the tact, wisdom, and strength to make the call for a decision at the appropriate time. Pray also for love and tenderness. As you make that call for decision, do it without fear, and leave the results to the Holy Spirit. Treat any issue that comes up with scripture. "Then Philip opened his mouth, and began at the same scripture, and preached unto him Jesus. And as they went on their way, they came unto a certain water: and the eunuch said, See, here is water; what doth hinder me to be baptized? And Philip said, If thou believest with all thine heart, thou mayest. And he answered and said, I believe that Jesus Christ is the Son of God" (Acts 8:35–37). That Phillip "preached" to the eunuch implies he covered doctrine as well as the cross. That the eunuch wanted to get baptized supports this. The decision came when the eunuch realized there was nothing holding him back. Most of us won't realize this ourselves; we need to be asked.

Claim Bible promises for the Lord's help. You will see results. "So shall my word be that goeth forth out of my mouth: it shall not return unto me void, but it shall accomplish that which I please, and it shall prosper in the thing whereto I sent it" (Isa. 55:11). If there are no tears of joy at being forgiven or no anger because of cherished sins being revealed, there is one other sign of conviction to look for. IAIN really believes what you've shared with her, when she *shares it with someone else*!

Most likely after IAIN has come to know the Lord, he will make some sort of "great confession" to you. Keep that in confidence for life. Assure him that victory is possible through Jesus. Pray with and for IAIN. However, do not check up on his progress later. This will only serve to remind him of sins that are now buried at the bottom of the sea. IAIN may also give you some sort of gift. Accept it as a gift of the heart to God. Since He used you to reach IAIN, that's what it is. Also mark the occasion of IAIN's baptism with a gift appropriate to the amount of time and effort you put in to reaching him.

When IAIN is newly converted and on-fire for the Lord, his family and friends will either accept or reject him and his new message. If these people are still willing to associate with him, there is hope for them no matter how much animosity they currently show to the truth. If they cut him off completely as soon as he shares, then they are not rejecting him, but the message the Lord gave him. Advise him to let those individuals go.

In John 21:3 Peter says, "I go a fishing." This was sort of a "once more for old times sake" situation. Just before IAIN gets baptized, he may say he has done or wants to do one more thing from his old life. What's happening here is he is testing how he feels about what choice he has made and he needs to see that his old ways really do cause pain to his new heart. He needs to say goodbye to his old life on his own terms. Continue the plan for baptism and don't worry about it.

> ## Words of Advice
>
> *Gospel Workers* documents the story of a dream given to Ellen White that relates evangelistic work to fruit picking. Here is an overview: "It does not hang on the outside of the bushes; you must search for it. True, you cannot pick it by handfuls; but by looking carefully among the green berries, you will find very choice fruit" (p. 136). "You see that the fruit which I have gathered is large and ripe. In a little while other berries will ripen, and we can go over the bushes again.... You must hereafter work with more zeal and earnestness ... or your labors will never be successful.... You should be diligent, first to pick the berries nearest you, and then to search for those farther away; after that you can return and work near by again, and thus you will be successful" (p. 139).

In conclusion, giving Bible studies does have its fair share of heartaches, but the joys far outweigh them. "Let him know, that he which converteth the sinner from the error of his way shall save a soul from death, and shall hide a multitude of sins" (James 5:20). The history of the entire world will be altered for good every time someone takes a stand for Jesus, as there are now so many bad things that will never happen because he or she has chosen a better way. The effect a new soul who is on fire for the Lord has will ripple through hundreds of people previously untouched by the church's outreach efforts. It will serve to be a great encouragement to those in the faith who may be on the way to losing their first love. Seeing success is also the best way to build up your own faith. "The truth is soon to triumph gloriously, and all who now choose to be labourers together with God, will triumph with it" (*Testimonies for the Church*, vol. 9, p. 135).

> ## Words of Advice
>
> Balance two seemingly opposite concepts together when deciding if a person is ready for baptism. First, IAIN is ready for baptism when he is in love enough with God to be able to say yes to all the baptismal vows. You may see the conversion early and have to cover some things in a summarized way, but only consent to baptism if you have shared all things that IAIN needs to know. The section "Binding Off Thoroughly" in *Evangelism* reiterates this well (pp. 321–326).
>
> However, if IAIN indicates a desire for baptism but you're still wondering whether he has completely grasped the truth or not, it's just as much an act of faith for the pastor to give the baptism as it is for IAIN to receive it. You won't be going into his house to check and see if she really has removed all the pork, liquor, and coffee from her pantry. *Testimonies for the Church*, volume 4, says, "There will ever be some who do not live out their profession, whose daily lives show them to be anything but Christians; but should this be a sufficient reason for any to refuse to put on Christ by baptism into the faith of His death and resurrection?" (p. 41).
>
> Lester Carney adds to the berry picking analogy: "You have to pick the fruit when it is ripe. You test to see if you can pick it by tugging on it. If it comes off the vine, it is time for it to be picked. If you tug and one comes off that is not fully ripened, it can ripen in with the others you have picked. If you tug on one that is bruised or blemished and it comes off, you have to pick it anyway."

Chapter 5

The Long Program

The following is a set of studies to be used to take an IAIN with little or no knowledge of God and bring that person step by step into a conversion experience. Each one is linked to the other and is designed to be presented in order. Before you go into a Bible study with IAIN, be sure to have gone over what you want to share ahead of time, keeping the questions listed in the last chapter in the back of your mind. Each text is listed with a brief explanation designed to capture the essence of the thought it expresses. Put these explanations into your own words as you share. The Bible verses are listed rather than typed out so you can use any translation.

Open the study with prayer and read the first text, making comments as you feel led. Then get IAIN to read the next text. Help him find it in his Bible if he doesn't know the books of the Bible yet. Make further comments as you both go through each text, being sure to watch him. What is he reacting to and how is he reacting? As soon as IAIN shows he is ready have him pray as well. One week you open and he closes, and then it's reversed the next time. It's very important for IAIN to use his own Bible when studying with you, so he can see the truth for himself, and not just because you told it to him.

As you consider the questions listed in the previous chapter, you'll be better able to tie each verse to every other and each study to every other as well. The "Extra Thoughts" section is there to help you with questions that might naturally come up as a result of the study, to stimulate discussion, and to provide promptings for what to say to bring conviction as the Lord may lead you.

The eight questions to keep in the back of your mind from the last chapter are repeated here.
1. What is the main point of the lesson?
2. Can you think of any real world example from your own life that illustrates this point?

> **Words of Advice**
>
> A gentleman whom I met only once at Mountain Sanctuary worked in the Treasury Department of the North American Division and had been a paid worker in the church for many years. He told me, "I never think so much of my own experience that I don't think I can learn from others, or don't think I need the basics myself anymore. I recently signed up for and re-took the Discover Bible study course by mail. I hadn't done that in years, and I still learned new things."

3. How does it relate to: the first coming of Jesus? The second coming of Jesus? IAIN's own need of Jesus? The great controversy being played out in world history? And the previous studies?
4. How can this study be used to plant seeds for further ones?
5. Are there any sins to avoid?
6. Briefly discuss what counterfeits to the main point there are in the world. And when the study transitions into the differences in Christian faith that exist, discuss also what counterfeits there are in other churches.
7. What small decision can IAIN make now that will be a step forward toward your goal for him or her of making the great decision to take a stand for all the truth? Each study must end with a mini decision to accept what was presented. That will lead to the great decision.
8. What should you say in your closing prayer?

Words of Advice

What differentiates the leadership from the laity in their approach to outreach is that while the layperson starts with friendship and hopes to share truth the pastor approaches things the other way around. In order for us to completely fulfill our calling as church members, we'll have to think like the leaders do.

Many people need to be shown by example how to do things. I do have demonstration Bible studies and several lectures based on the instructional portions of this book on several different Web sites for you to watch if you'd like. There are elements in them that are slightly different than what's in this book and vice versa, so you need both. On 3angelstube.com click on "Presenters" then "M" and "Les Miller"; on Youtube look for "lesmillman", on Vimeo.com look for "Bible truth for everyday life"; or visit airdriesda.org and click on "Video Bible Study."

Here are the topics and the order of presentation recommended. They are set up to answer the three great questions IAIN has in his or her heart as noted:

Preliminaries
1. Fulfilled Prophecy Proves the Bible (Daniel 2)
2. How to Study the Bible

Who Is God?
3. Getting to Know the Father
4. Getting to Know the Son
5. Getting to Know the Holy Spirit

What Has He Done for Us?

6. Heaven's War/Satan's Fall
7. The Story and Meaning of Suffering
8. Creation
9. Christ and Redemption
10. The Second Coming of Jesus
11. Confession
12. Forgiveness
13. Justification
14. Sanctification

What Does He Want Us to do for Him in Return?

15. The Ten Commandments
16. True Grace Is Power to Live Right
17. The Ceremonial Laws
18. The Sabbath
19. Now Sunday
20. What Happens After Death?
21. Judgment and Final Death
22. Baptism
23. Communion and Foot Washing
24. The Importance of Health
25. Christian Standards, General
26. Christian Standards, Tithe
27. Christian Standards, the Place for Jewelery
28. The Ten Tests of a True Prophet
29. The Remnant Church
30. The Unforgivable Sin

Study #1 – Fulfilled Prophecy Proves the Bible (Daniel 2)

- Amos 3:7   The Lord gives evidence by speaking ahead of time what will happen.
- Jeremiah 51:36, 37, 57, 58   The first great world empire of Babylon was overthrown by the Lord. As He said, it has never been inhabited to this day.
- Isaiah 45:1–5, 13   This message to Cyrus was spoken 150 years before he was born. The reference to the "two leafed gates" describes how he came to conquer the city of Babylon. He diverted the river so his troops could walk in under the first gate on the outer wall. The inner gates had been left open during a drunken party spoken of in Daniel 5.

The Long Program

The time of the Babylonians marks an important point for us today. Before this time, dates don't exactly line up. Those who don't believe the Bible see this as justification for their doubts. If people want to hear it, there is more than enough evidence to support the Bible in the archaeological record previous to this time period. However, from this point forward, we have a very accurate record of history.

- Daniel 2:1–3   The opening verses set the stage. The king's dream troubled him.
- Daniel 2:4–12   This shows the futility of all who claim spiritual power outside Christianity. New Age psychics, witches, clairvoyants, and astrologers are all frauds. The ones who seem to have power get it from Satan (see Deut. 18:9–14, 22).
- Daniel 2:13–24   The vast superiority of the God of heaven and earth is clear. Daniel received the dream and the interpretation in answer to prayer.
- Daniel 2:25–30   Daniel glorifies God and shows his own humanness. There is a lesson in religious freedom here since he did not take advantage of an opportunity to rid the kingdom of false prophets. The Lord wants free choice for all, even those who reject Him.
- Daniel 2:31–43   The dream and the interpretation are now given. A statue with four sections, each a different metal in descending order, is what the king saw. The metals themselves were central to the economies of the various kingdoms. Babylon, the head of gold, under Nebuchadnezzar ruled from 605 to 539 BC. Then shown as silver, the Medes and the Persians under Cyrus, listed above, took over and lasted until 331 BC. After which came Alexander the Great and the Greek, or Macedonian, empire represented by brass. The iron legs were the crushing power of Rome, ruling from 168 BC to AD 476. Rome transitioned into modern Europe, represented by the feet, which are part iron and part clay. Today's attempt at reunification through the European Common Market and the European Economic Union is actually the seventh time this has been tried. From Charlemagne to Hitler, conquerors have come and gone. Each has failed to break God's prophecy.
- Daniel 2:44–47   The happy ending to all world history. Jesus Christ Himself will come to this earth and fulfill this prophecy. We will see Him ourselves. The point of this Bible study program is to help you get ready to meet Him.

Daniel 2 gives us an advance look at the history of western society. Since it came true, we can therefore trust in God who caused this to happen. We can also trust the accuracy of the record in the rest of the book previous to Daniel's time. Adam and Eve, the flood, Abraham, etc. Are all true events.

Study # 2 – How to Study the Bible

- 1 Corinthians 2:14   You must have the Holy Spirit to understand scripture.
- 2 Timothy 3:15–17   Study the whole Bible. The point of study is to obtain salvation and perfection.
- Hebrews 11:6   It takes faith and diligence to understand.
- 2 Peter 1:20, 21   The Bible is not merely a human book; it is inspired by God. God gave men

the thoughts, and they put the thoughts in their own words.
- Isaiah 28:9, 10   The key to understanding Scripture is in cross-referencing.
- Amos 3:7   God gives evidence of Himself in Bible prophecies.
- Deuteronomy 29:29   Some things, however, we will never know.
- 2 Chronicles 20:20   All prosperity (physical, mental, financial, spiritual) is linked to following God.
- John 5:39   Once again, the whole point of study is focusing on salvation, which is only through Jesus. Christ is the central theme throughout the Bible.
- Luke 24:25–27, 44–47   Jesus had perfect knowledge of the Scriptures, and He taught men while on earth.
- Acts 8:30–35   We follow His example in sharing truth with others.
- Jeremiah 29:13   This is God's promise to us. He will be there if we look for Him. We can find salvation, peace, and spiritual prosperity in Him.

Study #3 – Getting to Know the Father
- Hebrews 11:6   To get to know God, we need FAITH!
- James 1:17   The Father is the highest authority in the universe.
- Isaiah 59:1, 2   We have cut ourselves off from Him by sinning.
- Hebrews 12:29   As sinners, we cannot look upon Him. His perfection is enough to completely destroy us.
- Isaiah 6:1–8   Here is a story of one man seeing God. His natural reaction was to see his own unworthiness. Notice God's reaction. All He wanted to do was forgive him and give him a new life.
- John 4:23, 24   Jesus tells us that God wants to have a relationship with us.
- Matthew 6:9   Pray to the Father.
- Micah 7:18, 19   Though we have cut ourselves off by sinning, God is merciful.
- 1 Corinthians 8:6   We start to see the mystery known as the Trinity. There is a oneness between the Father, Son, and Holy Spirit that we can never fully understand. The best way is to see the various roles that they play. The Father makes the decision, the Son gives the command, and the Spirit carries it out.
- John 17:1–6, 20–23   In coming to earth, Jesus connected us with the Father through Him.
- Romans 8:31–33   Because of Jesus, nothing stands in our path to God. We need to believe in and receive Him.
- Revelation 21:3   We will live with God forever in the earth made new.

Extra Thoughts:

Do you want God in your daily life? Pray for the desire to seek Him diligently.

Study #4 – Getting to Know the Son

- John 3:16, 17   Though sin cuts us off from God, He still loves us and wants us back.
- Colossians 1:13–18   Christ is part of God. He was there at Creation. Through His death and resurrection, we are forgiven.
- John 1:1–4, 14   Jesus was with the Father. Then He came to show us what the Father is like.
- Colossians 2:9   The best way to describe God is by using the word Godhead. The Trinity means the Father, Son, and Holy Spirit are one, yet separate. It is a mystery.
- Exodus 3:2–6, 14   Throughout the Old Testament, the "God" who dealt with man was the Son (Jesus). In the Old Testament, Jesus is also called the "Angel of the Lord" and "I AM."
- John 8:58   Jesus repeats His name "I AM."
- John 14:6, 9–14   We can access God through Jesus.
- Romans 6:23   Though sinners, Jesus came to give us life.
- 1 Timothy 2:3–6   God wants us all to be saved.
- Philippians 2:5–11   We are to be like Jesus.
- 2 Corinthians 5:18   God reconnects with us through Jesus.
- 1 Corinthians 15:20–28   The history of the world is outlined here. The fall, the cross, the resurrection, and the second coming.

Extra Thoughts:

Pray that God will help you understand the plan of salvation and will give you a personal relationship with Jesus.

Study #5 – Getting to Know the Holy Spirit

- Hebrews 1:1–3   God showed us His love with the gift of His Son (Jesus) and His Word.
- 2 Peter 1:21   The messages came from the Father through the Holy Spirit to the people.
- Ephesians 3:8, 9   The depth of God's love is a mystery to people.
- 1 Peter 1:18–21   From the beginning, Christ was our Creator and Redeemer.
- Genesis 1:1, 2, 26   All three of the Trinity were involved in Creation, and all three are involved in redemption.
- Deuteronomy 6:4   Here is the oneness of God.
- 2 Corinthians 13:14   All three work together for our salvation.
- Matthew 28:18–20   Jesus tells us to witness for Him and baptize others. This baptism is in the name of all three members of the Trinity.
- John 16:7–16   These are the roles of the Holy Spirit.
- John 14:16–18, 26   Jesus left the Holy Spirit to be with us until He comes again.
- Ephesians 3:14–19   The Holy Spirit brings Jesus into our hearts.

- Romans 8:11   The Father and the Holy Spirit give us our earthly life and the choice for a "new life" through our Christian walk.

Extra Thoughts:

Do you want the Spirit to work in your life and bring you to Jesus?

> ## Words of Advice
>
> Sometimes fanaticism can be a problem. Louis Torres was once asked why he didn't kneel every time he prayed. He took the person in question to Acts 2 and showed how they were sitting when the Holy Spirit was poured out. He then said, "Shun being another's conscience."

Study #6 – Heaven's War/Satan's Fall

- John 8:44   There is no truth in the devil.
- 1 John 3:8   Jesus came to destroy the devil's works.
- Revelation 12:4, 7, 9   The devil was once in heaven, but he rebelled and was cast to the earth.
- Ezekiel 28:11–19   The king of Tyre is used to describe the devil.
- Isaiah 14:12–20   Lucifer (the devil) was originally the highest angel in heaven, but he wanted to be God. At the final judgment, he will be destroyed forever.
- Zechariah 3:1–7   The high priest Joshua represents all who are sorry for their sins. The devil is trying to get in the way of our salvation.
- Revelation 12:12   The devil has a short time to tempt us.
- 2 Corinthians 11:12–15   Many of Satan's followers and he himself can appear to have the truth, but they do not.
- 1 Timothy 4:1   Many false ideas will exist in the last days that will draw people away from their faith.
- Malachi 4:1–3   The wicked (the branch), including the devil (the root), will be destroyed. Those who follow Jesus will be healed.
- Revelation 21:4, 5   The world will be restored.
- Job 1:6, 7   Before Christ came to earth, Satan had access to both heaven and earth.
- Luke 10:18   Once Jesus came, Satan's downfall had already begun.
- Job 38:4–7   At creation, all was happiness.
- Isaiah 66:22, 23   In the new earth, all will be happiness again.

Extra Thoughts:

Do you want freedom from the enemy? Do you want Jesus to bring healing to your life? Ask God to help you see Satan's deceptions clearly.

Study #7 – The Story and Meaning of Suffering
- James 1:17   God is the source of all good.
- Genesis 3:1–7   The story of the beginning of sin was a literal event.
- Romans 5:12   Because of sin, all must die.
- Isaiah 59:1, 2   Our sin has separated us from God.
- Acts 5:40, 41   Free choice can result in people causing suffering. Notice the depth of spirituality in those who suffered.
- Job 2:3–7   The devil focuses on hurting God's people, but the Lord limits him.
- Lamentations 3:31–33   God works in compassion.
- Psalm 119:71, 75, 76   He allows us to suffer so that we may learn.
- Hebrews 12:5–11   Like a father, God lovingly disciplines us.
- Hebrews 11:24–26   Christ's discipline is worth much.
- Romans 5:17–19   Through Christ's death, forgiveness for all sins is available. Suffering will cease in the end.
- Isaiah 53:5, 6, 10, 11   Christ suffered for our sins. God took our pain upon Himself by dying on the cross.
- Romans 8:28   Every experience in our lives is designed for our own good.
- 2 Corinthians 4:17   Our suffering will seem small compared to eternity.

Extra Thoughts:

Remember, God put His own Son through this same process of suffering. Because Jesus achieved the victory, He has what we need to achieve victory here too. When you suffer, remember how Jesus suffered for you.

Study #8 – Creation
- Genesis 1:1   In the beginning God created all. It was not an accident. This is the first Bible fact.
- Jeremiah 10:11–16   All other "gods" were created by humans and are figments of their imagination. He is the true God who is spoken of in the Bible. Notice the waters here correspond to the waters of the previous text.
- John 1:1–4, 14   Jesus is God along with the Father and the Spirit.
- Romans 5:8, 9   The same God who created the world came into it to show us His love.
- Isaiah 43:1   The same One who created all takes a personal interest in each one of us.

- Colossian 1:16–18   Christ was destined from the beginning to be the Creator and Redeemer.
- 1 Corinthians 8:6   This shows the oneness of God and that Christ is with God. Our very existence is by His power.
- Matthew 3:16, 17   The Father and the Spirit showed their approval of Jesus as He started His mission on earth. This was His planet, and He wanted to save it.
- Matthew 28:19, 20   The Savior told us to teach all nations. This includes teaching about Creation and redemption. He promises to be with us.
- Exodus 31:16, 17   The Sabbath of the Ten Commandments is a memorial of Creation.
- Ezekiel 20:10–12   Again this is mentioned. The Sabbath is a gift to aid in our spiritual growth.

Words of Advice

The "here a little there a little" method of teaching Bible truth through chain reference studies works well with those who are already familiar with the stories of the Bible. If you read the magazine put out by Adventist Frontier Missions, available at http://www.afmonline.org, you will note how the cultures those missionaries work in are almost completely unfamiliar with the stories we all take for granted. The people there are not of the Western mindset and need to be taught in a different way. If that is the situation you are in and you are dealing with a person who does not know the Bible at all, then much of the advice in this book is still applicable in the sense of the order of the various topics and the answers to the questions, but chain reference studies won't work to give those answers.

What you need to do in a situation like this is change the method of presenting the Bible studies. These studies normally have about twelve proof texts for a topic, and at least one of those texts comes as the summary of a story. An example might be Nehemiah 8:10: "The joy of the Lord is your strength." Maybe you have that verse in a study encouraging people's faith in tough times. So instead of using it with eleven other verses, tell the story surrounding it. After telling the story you then make the proof text in verse 10 the main point of that story. You then relate that point back to the felt needs of whomever you are sharing the study with. If you teach young children in Sabbath School, this can be a useful way of planting seeds in their hearts that will lead to baptism.

- Revelation 4:11   What gives Him the right to the worship He claims is that only He holds the power of creation. Keeping His Sabbath the way He wants you to will help you to accept Him as Creator.
- 2 Corinthians 4:6   His power is enough to create light. It is also enough to enlighten our hearts with His truth and the gift of His Son.

- Psalm 51:10   We cannot prove Creation by attempting to disprove evolution. Rocks only prove evolution if you already want them to. The real proof of Creation is not in geology but in the new life God can create in you. Only God can do this. He uses the same creative power to forgive you that He used to create you in the first place.

Extra Thoughts:

Do you want this awesome and powerful God on your side? Do you want Him to show you His truth and change your life? He can; all you have to do is ask Him.

Study #9 – Christ and Redemption

(Note: For this study, repeat the first five texts from the previous one, and then branch off in another direction by reviewing these texts.)

- Ephesians 2:8–10, 13   It is His efforts and power that save me and not anything I have done.
- Isaiah 41:10, 13   He who is powerful enough to hold this earth in orbit will hold you steady in your life.
- Isaiah 40:25–31   He never tires. His might is always available to help. When we depend on Him, we have all the strength we need.
- Jude 24, 25   God's power is so great that He can make us perfect. He has a plan for our lives, and it fits with His plan for the whole world.

Extra Thoughts:

Do you see and feel the Lord reaching out to you personally? Would you like to give your heart to Him?

Study #10 – The Second Coming of Jesus

- John 14:1–3   Jesus Himself promised He would return.
- Acts 1:9–11   A repeated promise is given by the angels at His ascension. Notice they comment on how He will come again.
- Revelation 1:7   This will be a universal experience. Everyone will see Him.
- 1 Thessalonians 4:16, 17   Jesus is coming back for all His people. This includes those who lived and died in any age throughout history and the ones alive at the time of His return.
- Matthew 24:3–7   All these signs have been fulfilled in the last 100 years. There were more wars, earthquakes, and famines in the twentieth century than ever before.
- Luke 21:25–27   Notice the power and great glory.
- Daniel 12:4   Modern technology is a fulfillment of prophecy.
- 2 Timothy 3:1–5   This is definitely a description of today.
- Revelation 6:12–17   The three great signs: the Great Lisbon Earthquake occurred in 1755; the dark day and blood red moon took place in May 1780; and the most fantastic meteor

shower in history fell on November 3, 1833. The rest is yet to come.
- Matthew 24:14–27, 44   Now is the time to get ready.

> ## Words of Advice
>
> Randy Barber said, "Friendship is the mortar that holds the bricks of truth together." That thought provides its own description of what the relationship should be between you and your Bible study student. Without friendship, the wall of truth will fall apart. Friendship surrounds the truth, and there is friendship between each individual truth, but bricks take up more space on a wall than the mortar that surrounds them. Let the truth be the main reason for the study.
>
> In dealing with a couple who did not want to give up a cherished sin and no longer continued studying with us, Kelly Schultz said that compromising our message to keep their friendship was not worth it.
>
> Louis Torres also noted that in a situation where a pastor is studying for a long while with someone, never gets the decision, and then an evangelist gets it, it is because the friendship has taken first place in the Bible study.

Extra Thoughts:

Just what do you need to do to be ready? Seek the Lord and all His truth.

Study #11 – Confession

- Proverbs 28:13   It is impossible to hide from the Lord. To be fully repentant, we must admit our sinfulness.
- James 5:16   When we sin against others, we must confess to them. Prayer gives God the opportunity to heal our hearts.
- 1 John 1:9   Cleansing is promised, and He is faithful. Notice as well, He's just. His cleansing is a life-changing experience.
- Psalm 34:18   'Contrite' means to be completely sorry. He is nearest when we sense our own sinfulness.
- Romans 10:9, 10   You can't just feel repentance inside and not do anything about it. You must verbally admit it. Confess your sin, but also confess His goodness.
- Isaiah 53:12   We admit our guilt so Jesus can take it away. Christ's completed work on the cross gives Him the right to forgive us.
- Psalm 32:5   All sin is really between God and us. We are admitting it to Him.
- Psalm 86:5   He wants to forgive us. He longs to show mercy.
- Mark 1:5   Confession is a prerequisite to baptism.
- Psalm 32:1, 2   It's a blessing to receive forgiveness, which comes from confession.

Study #12 – Forgiveness

- 1 John 1:7–10   Admitting our sins is our job. Forgiving them is His.
- Isaiah 1:18   When He forgives, it's as if we've never sinned.
- Isaiah 55:7   Two kinds of people are spoken of in this text. The "wicked man" is someone outside the faith who sins in obvious ways. The "unrighteous man" is inside the faith but has not attained to the full truth. He looks good on the outside, but he still sins in his heart.
- Isaiah 44:22   "Blotting out" implies a total erasing of sin and a complete restoration to God. He calls us back.
- Ephesians 1:7   Forgiveness is possible because Jesus died for each of us.
- Matthew 6:14, 15   His forgiveness is linked to how we pass it on.
- Psalm 86:5   Anyone who asks can be forgiven.
- Psalm 103:2, 3, 12   Here is a picture of His great mercy. What the Bible speaks of is a return to innocence He creates in us.
- Jeremiah 31:34   Once He forgives, it's final. It is a personal experience and it's also the best way to know Him.
- Psalm 32:1, 2, 5   Forgiveness automatically comes from the Lord after we confess our sins. It is a blessing.

Extra Thoughts:

Have you ever confessed your sins to the Lord? You may not have any one sin on your mind. Confession helps us to see our humanness and our need of Him. Pray a prayer similar to this, "Dear Lord, I know You are great and good. I understand now, like never before, that I need You to cleanse my heart. I offer it to You now. In the name of Jesus, I pray, Amen."

Study #13 – Justification

- Titus 3:7   We are justified by God's grace, not anyone else's.
- Romans 5:9   Jesus' death on the cross has justified us; therefore, we will be saved from punishment.
- Romans 3:23–26   We all deserve to die, but Christ is our substitute. Jesus was punished for our sins, making a way for God to save us. He is patient with us.
- Galatians 2:16   Believe in Jesus and what He has done for you. Trying to obey on your own will not work.
- Genesis 15:5, 6   When the Lord speaks to us on any given issue and we believe Him, that is an act of faith and He honors it.
- Philippians 3:9   Righteousness, the ability to live right, is from Him and not something we can give ourselves.
- Romans 5:15–17   No matter what we've done, God's gift is big enough to erase it. The

obedience of Jesus and the sacrifice He gave reverses the trend in motion that Adam began by sinning.
- Romans 4:4, 5   When you try in your own strength, you feel as if you owe God, and obeying becomes a burden. The Lord would also, therefore, owe you salvation. It would not be a free gift then. When you believe, He makes it happen for you.
- Romans 11:6   If salvation could be earned, it wouldn't be a gift.
- Romans 3:29, 30   God is God to everyone.
- Romans 4:25   Jesus took on Himself all the blame for our sins.
- 2 Corinthians 5:21   Again this is repeated with more emphasis on the goodness He gives us in return for believing.

Extra Thoughts:

When I come to Jesus just as I am, God looks at me through Him and says "perfect." It is as if I had never sinned.

Study #14 – Sanctification
- 1 John 4:7, 8   The first principle of Christianity is love.
- Romans 3:23, 24   Justification is a free gift. Jesus makes up for our guilt-ridden past.
- John 3:16   God's love is beyond compare; He gave us Jesus.
- Romans 6:23   Because of Jesus, we can live forever.
- Ephesians 2:8–10   We can't be good by ourselves, but when Jesus saves us, He can make us good.
- Romans 2:4   His goodness melts our hearts and changes our lives.
- Revelation 3:20   All He wants is to come into our hearts. We have to choose to let Him in.
- Titus 3:7   Because we are justified, we have a reason to hope.
- Romans 5:9   We have something wonderful ahead of us.
- Titus 2:13, 14   Jesus is coming back. He gave Himself to cover not only our past sins but to change us so we become truly good.
- Matthew 5:48   The Lord calls us to perfection.
- 1 Peter 1:15, 16   Followers of God are to be like Him. Holiness is complete perfection.
- 1 Thessalonians 4:3, 4; 5:23   Our part in doing God's will is to make sure nothing gets in the way. Every part of our life and our self is to be like Him, physical and mental.
- Acts 20:32   Just as God gives justification, so He gives sanctification through His word. He makes the changes. All we do is receive them.
- 1 Corinthians 1:30   It all comes through Jesus.
- Hebrews 10:10   The cross is enough to both justify and sanctify.
- John 17:17   The truth changes us, and as we receive the truth, we grow in perfection. The

Bible is spoken of as truth in this verse.
- Philippians 1:6; 2:12, 13   God can be relied on. He won't give up on us. Our part is to continue seeking Him and trusting He will work in our lives.

Extra Thoughts:

After receiving Jesus for the first time and being justified, one must go on to further growth in His grace. This is illustrated in the story of God saving Israel and bringing them out of Egypt, which is symbolic of rescuing us from sin. The trip through the Red Sea was like a baptism and then right afterward they were given the law, which instructed them on how to live as His people.

Words of Advice

Don't use a lot of college level, big words like "imparted" and "imputed" righteousness to explain these ideas. Morris Venden, in his book *Uncommon Ground*, repeatedly explains justification as "Christ working for us" and sanctification as "Christ working in us."

Study #15 – The Ten Commandments

- Exodus 20:1–17   These are not ten laws, but one. the Ten Commandments cover every conceivable kind of sin.
- Romans 3:23   Sin results in death. The only way to heaven is through Jesus.
- 1 John 3:4   Violating the law is a New Testament definition of sin. Sin is really the inability to obey.
- James 2:10–12   Even one sin is considered a sin. It is the "law of liberty" because it provides the means of freedom. If everyone obeyed the commandment to not steal, you would not need locks on your doors or burglar alarms.
- Romans 7:7   The law cannot save us. However, it can show us we need to be saved. It points out our sin.
- James 2:8, 9   Love is the foundation of obeying.
- Proverbs 28:9   Religion without obedience is just a big show.
- Isaiah 8:16, 20   True Christianity includes the law.
- Psalm 19:7   We are converted when we see our sin in the law and go to Jesus for healing.
- Ecclesiastes 12:13, 14   To obey Him is our purpose in life.
- Galatians 3:21–26   If obeying on our own could get us to heaven, then it would be the way. We need faith in Jesus, but this faith does not contradict the law.
- Ezekiel 36:26, 27   Faith includes the law in our hearts.
- Psalm 119:34, 174   This is the attitude Christians should have toward the law.

Study #16 – True Grace Is Power to Live Right

- Romans 6:14; 3:28; Galatians 2:16; Ephesians 2:8, 9   An examination of these verses on their own seems to suggest the law has no place in the Christian experience.
- Romans 6:1, 2; 3:31; Galatians 2:17; Ephesians 2:10   Here are some nearby verses that balance out the others. Christianity in no way negates the Ten Commandments.
- Isaiah 64:6   This verse provides a symbolic use of clothing to illustrate goodness. Our own goodness is not good enough.
- Zechariah 3:3–7   The illustration continues with the Lord taking our goodness away and giving us His.
- Revelation 19:8   Does it not make sense that if God gives you His goodness, you will actually be good?
- Ezekiel 36:26, 27   Many people today quote Bible verses as if to say New Testament faith excuses our sins. This is not true. God is offering us an empowerment to live above sin.
- James 2:17, 18   Faith is what being a Christian is all about. But real faith flows out from one's heart into actions that are tangible.
- Galatians 2:20   I have a new purpose when Jesus changes my life—I live for Him.
- Revelation 16:15   To be naked is to have experienced the knowledge of your sin and asked Him to take it away but never asked for the power to follow through. These people think they have faith, but when Jesus comes they are not saved.

Extra Thoughts:

Would you like to fully experience His love? Ask Him to give you victory over your own sin struggles.

Study #17 – The Ceremonials Laws

- Deuteronomy 4:12, 13   The Lord started Israel off with a great revealing of Himself. He spoke the Ten Commandments and wrote them Himself on stone. This implies permanence.
- James 2:8–12   One sin or all sin is enough to break the law. Notice the term "royal law" is used.
- Romans 7:7   The purpose of the law is to point out sin.
- Ecclesiastes 12:13, 14   Life is summed up as obeying God's law.
- Exodus 40:20   The "testimony" is the Ten Commandments. They were put inside the ark of the covenant.
- Psalm 19:7   The Ten Commandments play an important part in our salvation. Without them, we wouldn't feel any need of Jesus. That is something that cannot be changed.
- 2 Chronicles 35:12   The "law of Moses" deals with offerings and ceremonial regulations.
- Nehemiah 9:13, 14; see also Deuteronomy 4:14   There are two distinct laws mentioned here.
- Leviticus 7:37, 38   The Lord commanded this law to Moses while Moses waited on Mount

Sinai. In other words, God did not write this law, but dictated it to Moses.
- Leviticus 23:26–28, 32   This is an example of many of these ceremonial laws. This was for a special holiday and was to be "a sabbath." This religious Sabbath occurred on whatever day of the week the holiday fell each year.
- Exodus 31:16–18   This Sabbath is the regular weekly Sabbath of the Ten Commandments. It is a special sign of faith in God.
- Colossians 2:14, 16, 17   This passage on judging each other refers to the holiday Sabbaths as they were part of the handwriting. This was Moses' handwriting, not God's. The word "ordinance" refers to a religious regulation and not a moral law.
- Ephesians 2:11–16   There was previously a difference between Jew and Gentile. The difference was the ceremonial law. Now God has done away with it, and all people can have access to Him through Jesus.
- Hebrews 10:1–9   The sacrifices and holidays in themselves had no power to change anyone. They were symbolic of the great sacrifice Jesus was going to make.

Extra Thoughts:

This study is to help in understanding difficult passages in the New Testament. When the law is talked of, which law is it? Does the passage refer to ceremonial or moral issues? Nothing in the Bible says the Ten Commandments can be changed or done away with.

Study #18 – The Sabbath
- Genesis 2:1–3   The Sabbath is a memorial of Creation. The Lord Himself caused it to exist by "blessing" it. This was His decision. It existed before sin.
- Exodus 20:8–11   Here are clear definitions of what constitutes keeping it holy. The word "remember" signifies that they already knew of it and were being told not to forget. The Sabbath is a central part of God's holy law.
- Mark 2:27, 28   Jesus, as God, confirmed the Sabbath. This is His day. He kept it.
- Exodus 16:4, 5, 15–29   The test of the manna was given before the law was spoken. They were to develop into the habit of Sabbathkeeping before the Ten Commandments were written down.
- Nehemiah 9:13, 14   This is a summation of the whole Mount Sinai experience. The Sabbath is mentioned on its own. This was more than one thousand years after the Ten Commandments.
- Luke 4:16   Jesus Himself kept the Sabbath.
- Luke 23:54–56   Even under such traumatic circumstances as the disappointment of seeing their Master dead, the followers of Jesus still kept the Sabbath.
- Acts 13:14, 42–44; 17:2; 18:4   Years after the cross, Paul kept the Sabbath. He observed the

Sabbath not just with the Jews, but with Gentiles also. The seventh day of the week is the Christian Sabbath.
- Isaiah 66:22, 23   The Sabbath will be kept in all eternity. This is a complete history of the world from beginning to end, and the Sabbath is in every part of it.

Study #19 – Now Sunday
- John 20:19   They were assembled for "fear of the Jews" and not to worship. They had not even fully believed His resurrection yet.
- Luke 24:44–47   Jesus refers to the resurrection day not as the first day of the week here, but as the third day of His time paying our debt to God. (Five other references simply mention the first day of the week as the day of His resurrection and attach no significance to it: Matthew 28:1; Mark 16:2, 9; Luke 24:1; John 20:1.)
- Romans 6:4   Baptism honors the resurrection. If things were to be changed, then why are there no Friday worship sessions to honor the cross? We honor the cross in the Communion service as Jesus commanded.
- Acts 20:7   This is a Sabbath meeting that ran long. This was a Saturday night, as the next texts will show.
- Leviticus 23:32   Bible time is kept from sundown to sundown.
- Genesis 1:13   Bible time starts with the dark part of the day first.
- 1 Corinthians 16:2   The verse says "lay by him in store." They are at home and not in church.
- Romans 14:5, 6   See verse 1. The issues discussed are about "doubtful disputations." The Sabbath question is indisputable (see the previous study). This chapter deals with holidays under the old covenant. Some Jews wanted to keep them still.
- Revelation 1:10; see also Mark 2:28   Jesus is Lord of the Sabbath.

Extra Thoughts:

The theory that Sunday honors His return from the grave is a Catholic doctrine. Converts Catechism of Catholic Doctrine *says, "Q. Why did the Catholic Church substitute Sunday for Saturday? A. The church substituted Sunday for Saturday, because Christ rose from the dead on a Sunday, and the Holy Ghost descended upon the disciples on a Sunday" (p. 50). As this study has shown, just because these events happened, it doesn't mean that they changed the worship day.*

> ## Words of Advice
>
> Here's two thoughts on sharing the Sabbath truth from Lester Carney. "As soon as the interest accepts a point of truth, move on. For instance, if the study is about the Sabbath and it is accepted immediately, turn it into how to keep the Sabbath."
>
> Lester Carney also said, "When you cover the topic of the Sabbath in a study situation, you have to get the person to make a decision to give it a try and come to church. Otherwise, when he or she doesn't and feels no ill effects, there will almost be a subconscious decision against it."

Study #20 – What Happens After Death?
- Genesis 2:7   Man does not have a soul; man is a soul. The combination of a physical body and the "breath" makes a soul.
- Job 27:3   This "breath" is also called "spirit" or "ghost." It is the energy God gives to make life. This energy is not a conscious entity of its own.
- Job 34:13–15   It is God alone who has the power of life and death. All life comes from Him and is not something anyone else can control.
- Ecclesiastes 12:7   Death is a breaking of the union.
- Ecclesiastes 3:19–21   Animals and humans experience the same thing at death.
- Psalm 146:3, 4; 6:5; Ecclesiastes 9:5, 6, 10   Death is a state of complete unconsciousness. The Bible uses the concept of "sleep" to refer to death almost seventy times.
- Job 14:21   Here is a statement of just how completely unconscious death is. When people visit the grave of a loved one, that loved one has no knowledge of it.
- John 5:28, 29   The resurrection is the day when the Lord makes the dead come to life again.
- Job 19:25–27   The resurrection is at the second coming of Christ for those who love Him.
- 1 Thessalonians 4:16, 17   Jesus Himself calls His friends out of their graves to be with Him forever.
- Psalm 17:13–15   The point to life is to get ready for that day.

Extra Thoughts:

The truth about death completely destroys all of the devil's lies. What we see in dealing with dead spirits in seances, channelling, appearances of Mary, the saints, dead relatives and ghosts are all really evil angels in disguise.

Study #21 – Judgment and Final Death
- Revelation 20:4   The judgment is a 1,000-year time period.
- 1 Corinthians 6:1–3   God's people examine the record of human history during the 1,000

years. We will judge all those who failed to go to heaven and the angels who were originally cast out.
- John 5:28, 29   There are two resurrections.
- Revelation 20:6   The ones Jesus saves come up first and reign (judge) 1,000 years.
- John 14:1–3   Jesus promised we'd be with Him. This judgment and rule is in heaven, not on earth.
- Revelation 7:9   Here is the vision given to John of the saved.
- Luke 17:26–30   This day comes by surprise to the last generation.
- Jeremiah 4:23–27; Isaiah 24:21–23   This is the condition of the earth once the wicked are dead and the righteous are in heaven.
- Revelation 20:1–3   The symbol of an abyss or bottomless pit describes the earth in this condition. The devil is confined here.
- Jude 6, 7, 13   The eternal fire of Sodom, a real place in history, was a fire of eternal results. There is no fire continuing to burn in the Middle East. Cross-reference this with Lamentations 4:6 and you'll see that the punish*ment* is eternal, not the punish*ing*.
- Malachi 4:1–3   Another text showing that eternal fire destroys forever. The wicked are reduced to ashes.

Extra Thoughts:

The events of Revelation 20 happen on the surface of the earth. There is no eternally burning hell in the center of the earth right now. The wicked are asleep in their graves and will be annihilated at the final judgment.

Study #22 – Baptism
- Mark 16:15, 16   Jesus calls His followers to go everywhere and preach. People accept the gospel by getting baptized.
- Acts 2:37, 38   Baptism follows our repentance. The Holy Spirit will help you live for God and give you a place in His cause.
- Acts 22:16   Once you've experienced conversion, why wait? There is nothing holding you back from being a Christian.
- Matthew 28:19   Baptism accompanies teaching. You must know what you are standing for and be ready to change your life according to Bible truth. The proper way to baptize is in the name of all three members of the Trinity.
- Galatians 3:27   It is a public way to show you have given your heart to Jesus.
- Romans 6:3–6; Colossians 2:12   The ceremony is specific. You must be immersed in clean water once and raised up. This symbolizes that you've chosen to die to your old life and have accepted the new life God has for you. Sprinkling is not true baptism.
- Matthew 3:13–17   Jesus set the example for all. His baptism covers any who could not get baptized. For example, there was no time to baptize the thief on the cross.

- Acts 10:47, 48   Baptism is for all people. There is no minimum age, but it must be a person's own choice. Therefore, christening babies does not agree with the Bible.
- 1 Corinthians 12:12–14   Baptism initiates church membership.
- Acts 8:35–38   Have you accepted Jesus with all your heart? Then there is nothing holding you back. Getting baptized and living for Him is the next logical step for you.

Extra Thoughts:

Notice from Mark 16:15, 16 how if you believe and are baptized you're saved, but if you don't believe, you're not, whether you actually get baptized or not. Faith is what it's really all about, which starts in the heart but flows out to real life. The act of baptism without that faith accomplishes nothing.

Study #23 – Communion and Foot washing

- Ephesians 4:5   God calls us to oneness.
- Colossians 2:12   Baptism symbolizes the change of heart we received by giving ourselves to Jesus.
- John 3:23   Water symbolizes cleansing.
- Acts 8:35–39   An example of someone giving their heart to God and being baptized.
- Matthew 3:13–17   Jesus is our ultimate example. The Lord's approval comes after the cleansing.
- Romans 6:3–6   Don't go back to the old way. Stay with God and His truth.
- John 13:1–17   This happened just before the Communion service was instituted. Verse 14 has the Savior saying we should follow Him in foot washing. This is to be done just before Communion. Verse 10 is the key. The ceremony of foot washing is like a re-baptism in miniature form. It reminds us of our continued need of His cleansing. By humbling ourselves as Jesus did, we are prepared to receive the bread and wine.
- 1 Corinthians 11:24-26   The Communion symbols teach us that Jesus died for us.
- Matthew 26:14–30   The story of Judas tells us we must be humble and true to Him to participate in the Communion service.

Words of Advice

Randy Barber was with us the night my friend Adrian made his decision to get baptized. After hearing his testimony, Pastor Barber helped by saying, "From what you have told me, you have experienced conversion. The next step for you is clear from the Bible. You need to get baptized."

Study #24 – The Importance of Health

- 3 John 2   John's wish is God's wish for all His people.
- 1 Corinthians 6:19, 20   Jesus not only redeems us for the next life, but this one as well. We are to use and take care of our bodies appropriately.
- 1 Corinthians 3:16, 17   It is a sin to waste this body. Cross-reference this study with the studies that teach the truth about death, and you'll see in heaven we will have real, physical bodies. Therefore, taking care of this body is essentially practice for the future because the body we have in heaven will have to last forever.
- 1 Corinthians 10:31   All things are to be done for God's glory. This includes eating and drinking.
- Leviticus 11:1–20   This is the list of clean and unclean foods (essentially predators and scavengers). Since there is no ceremonial significance to it, it is still valid.
- Isaiah 66:16, 17   A prophecy of the second coming. Notice the place for eating swine's flesh.
- Proverbs 23:29–35; 20:1   Drinking alcoholic beverages is a weakness and a problem. The gourmet attitude associated with wine is of no value. It makes complete sense that these texts cover any kind of drug that will do strange things to the mind. Nicotine and caffeine would also be covered.
- 1 Corinthians 9:25   For love to be the opposite of selfishness it must include complete self-control.
- Psalm 103:3   All true healing comes from the Lord. Doctors are but servants in His hands. He also heals with truth, telling us what's good and bad, so we don't put harmful things in our path.

Extra Thoughts:

Would Jesus waste food? Compare John 6:5–13 with Mark 5:1–14, and you will see pigs are not food.

Words of Advice

Remember, you are a facilitator to bring IAIN to the truth. Do everything you can to be humble and concerned about her well-being. If she gets the impression you are just there to get her to join your church, you will lose the study. Don't say anything of your own opinion; let the Bible speak for itself. Don't let it in any way be brought to a level of you against her.

Study #25 – Christian Standards, General

- John 15:5   In Jesus you can exist in this world of sin.
- Jeremiah 9:23, 24   Your place here isn't as important as knowing God.
- 1 John 2:16   All sin fits into these three categories.

- Psalm 101:3-7   Seek perfection in all areas of life so you can serve God. Let this principle apply to all you set before your mind's eye. This includes art, TV, music, etc. Also take stock of the activities of your life and ask prayerfully, "Is it really Christian?" Some things are just wrong like gangster rap or heavy metal music. Playing violent video games or watching Ultimate Fighting Champion would be other examples. Some things like card playing are so associated with gambling that they cannot be justified. Some activities don't seem to be wrong in and of themselves yet attract a wrong crowd, i.e. skateboarding, billiards. We must be careful how we indulge in them. Some activities may have nothing inherently wrong with them, like stamp collecting, scuba diving, having a model train set in your basement or playing or watching sports. However, so often people end up living for their hobbies. God has to be first.
- Philippians 4:8   This is not to say that everything in your life has to be directly religious. If there is something truly good in the world of art, science, literature, etc., God is there even if He isn't there by name.
- 2 Corinthians 6:14, 15   As a Christian you are pledging brotherhood with all who believe the same. To do so with those who don't is not right. This bars you from labor unions, political parties, activist groups and secret societies such as criminal gangs, lodges or college fraternities.
- Colossians 3:16, 17   Spiritual music is better than worldly music.
- 1 Samuel 16:23   "Spiritual music" is not only music with Christian words, but a style of music that is uplifting, ennobling, and inspiring with a calm rhythm and melody. Worldly music normally inspires a spirit of rebellion and self-exaltation.
- 2 Samuel 6:14   This religious dancing is lost to history. It is not the same as the dancing of today, which is associated with bars and loose morals.
- Leviticus 19:28   Tattoos are banned completely. If you already have tattoos, this does not ban you from becoming a Christian; you just can't get another one. Repenting of sin means now you won't do wrong things any more.
- Job 31:1   Men are not to treat women as sex objects.
- Isaiah 3:16–26   Women are not to present themselves to men or the world in general as sex objects.
- John 17:15–17   Jesus wants to strengthen us from within, not shelter us. While it is important to guard ourselves, we must not make the mistake of being so focused on avoiding sin that we become fanatical or try to hide ourselves so much from the world that God can't use us to witness to it.
- Romans 12:1, 2, 21   By seeking the truth and denying ourselves evil, we will be doing our part.

Extra Thoughts:

We can draw a lesson from Mark 2:23 where the disciples were accused of violating the Sabbath simply by grabbing a handful of grain. Yes, in Exodus 16 harvesting and cooking on the Sabbath were banned. But if we look to the rules themselves, we'll end up becoming fanatics. If we look to Jesus, who was with the disciples that day, He will guide us through the do's and don't of serving Him.

Study #26 – Christian Standards, Tithe

- 1 Timothy 6:6–10   Greed is a great temptation. We need to live for more than money.
- 1 Peter 1:18–20   The value of the cross is far above all earthly things.
- Deuteronomy 8:17, 18   The Lord controls your opportunities in life. What you have is part of His plan. The point to giving you wealth is so you can use it to further His cause in the world.
- Leviticus 27:30, 32   God claims 10 percent of all we have as His own.
- Genesis 28:22   Jacob the patriarch made this promise.
- Matthew 23:23   It must be done in the right spirit. Tithing is still required in the New Testament.
- Malachi 3:8–12   The only way we are allowed to test God is on the issue of money. Put Him first and He promises more than we can handle.
- 2 Samuel 24:24   The point to a sacrifice was not to kill something but to give something precious up for God. True spirituality is in giving.
- 2 Corinthians 9:7   This is in reference to free-will offerings, which were on top of tithe. Again true giving is not a burden.

Study #27 – Christian Standards, the Place for Jewelery

- Matthew 6:28–30, 33   Spirituality is simplicity according to our Savior.
- Jeremiah 9:23, 24   The real issue is self-glorification. In human nature men (discussed in this text), usually glorify themselves based on their strength, power, or riches, while women usually glorify themselves based on their beauty.
- 1 Peter 3:3–6   Inner beauty is what our Father in heaven really wants us to have. This is an issue especially affecting women.
- 1 Timothy 6:16   Only He dwells in light. Jewels normally consist of expensive metals and rocks that reflect light. Humans wearing these things are trying to create a light of their own to dwell in.
- Isaiah 3:13–24   Wearing jewelry is shown to be a thing of pride. Every possible kind is mentioned from head to foot. Also, changes of clothes, in other words being a slave of fashion, is condemned.
- Job 40:6–14   The Lord invites Job to try to glorify himself. Part of this invitation is to do it

by trying to make himself more beautiful than he is. Jewelry wearing is an attempt to add to the beauty that God has created in the human form.

- Leviticus 19:28   The verse banning tattoos from the Christian standards, general study is repeated here to make a point. God made our bodies as beautiful as they can be in this sinful world. Marking or piercing ourselves does not improve us but is in fact degradation. Only those whose hearts are truly enlightened by the Holy Spirit can see this.
- Hosea 2:13   The nation of Israel is called unfaithful here. Notice jewelry wearing is listed among her sins.
- 1 Timothy 2:9, 10   This is confirmed as applying in the New Testament as well.
- Deuteronomy 7:25; Colossians 3:5   Gold and silver throughout the Bible are allowed only when used for God's glory and banned when used for self-glorification. Greed (covetousness in King James English) is idolatry.
- Genesis 35:2–4   Idols, banned by the second commandment, include jewelry.
- Genesis 38:18; Luke 15:22   Two apparent contradictory texts are dealt with easily. In Bible culture these were identification badges much like our driver's license today. There is a principle that can be drawn out here. If something serves a purpose, can be worn without pride, and is common in the culture, it is permissible. The most notable examples today are wedding rings, watches, and eyeglasses. To be in harmony with the texts listed above, they should be inexpensive.
- Exodus 33:1–6   Yes, there are Bible examples of people wearing jewelry. However, there are also examples like this one of God calling people to make a higher commitment to Him with the removal of their jewelry. The Lord was about to lead His people into the earthly Promised Land. As we are now so near the time when the Lord will open for us the true heavenly Promised Land, is it not logical we need to be ready in the same way?
- Isaiah 31:7   A prophecy of people at the second coming of Jesus.

Words of Advice

You don't have to be the one to get the decision as long as IAIN makes that decision. Make use of health seminars, evangelistic meetings, or any public event your church is sponsoring. Don't worry about whether or not IAIN is ready for a more advanced message if you just started studying together. If he is not, he won't go. If he does not go, continue the study at its regular pace. This is a more important contribution to the work of the gospel than for you to attend the meeting.

> ## Words of Advice
> Human nature greatly values gold and jewelry. As my wife, Melissa, once said, "People are in essence wearing their money."

Study #28 – The Ten Tests of a True Prophet
(This study is based on chapter one of Rene Noorbergen's book *Ellen White Prophet of Destiny*.)

- Jeremiah 28:9   A true prophet is never wrong and does not lie.
- 2 Peter 1:20, 21   This person will not speak on his or her own behalf or give a private interpretation.
- Isaiah 58:1   A prophet is called to point out the sins of God's people.
- Isaiah 24:20, 21; Revelation 14:6, 7   A prophet is also called to warn of judgment.
- 1 Corinthians 14:3, 4   God sends a prophet to help the church.
- Isaiah 8:20; 1 Corinthians 14:32   The Bible and the Ten Commandments are the test. The teachings of a true prophet will completely harmonize with them.
- 1 John 4:1–3   The fact that Jesus is God and came into this world will not be denied. You can test a prophet by this fact.
- Matthew 7:16–20   A true prophet will have a solid Christian character. There will be real results from the person's ministry.
- Deuteronomy 18:9–12   Absolutely none of the false ways of the psychics, astrologers, or anyone who claims to talk to the dead will be used for divine prophecies.
- Lamentations 2:9   The Ten Commandments are a necessary requirement for a church to receive a prophet. Therefore, all true prophets are Sabbathkeepers.

Extra Thoughts:

On supernatural manifestations, see Daniel 10:7, 8, 17, 18 and Numbers 24:4, 16. Since the Bible predicts prophets in the last days (Joel 2:28), and since there are so many false prophets running around, does it not make sense that there are true prophets here as well?

> ## Words of Advice
>
> You will notice I have not included anything on Ellen White and how she passes the ten tests. There are many books, videos, and Internet resources available, and I leave you to find something that will be suitable to your friend's needs. I do recommend if you see any animosity on IAIN's part that you emphasize the gift and not the person. Tell also of Hazen Foss and William Ellis Foy. If you know the story, tell also of Mannilaq, an Innuit man who was given prophetic visions about the same time period as the others, but in an area untouched by white men at the time.
>
> If IAIN is getting tripped up by any anti-Adventist or anti-Ellen White publications, tell IAIN they aren't accurately teaching what we believe, they are giving their opinion of what we believe. You are showing IAIN from the Bible what we believe. Also make note of the mean-spirited un-Christlike manner in which they present their case. Would your friend ask a disgruntled ex-employee about the company that person worked for before taking a job there? It's the same with the church. We have to not only say the right thing, but we have to say it in the right way. If they aren't doing that, what are the odds that what they're saying is accurate anyway?

Study #29 – The Identifying Marks of the Remnant Church

With so many groups claiming to be specially favored, a lot of people don't think the Lord could have any one church now. However, on earth our Savior founded *one* church. Over time it has become many churches. Doesn't it seem likely that He always wanted only one?

When Jesus came, He gave witness to the truth because He was the truth. It's interesting to note that He hardly ever said word-for-word, "I am the Messiah." Instead, He let the evidence speak for itself. His church today would follow His example and not be telling everyone "we are the truth." That church would instead give Bible evidence to base a sound decision on. Consider the following verses and decide for yourself.

- 2 Timothy 3:16; 2 Peter 3:16   God's church uses the whole Bible and does not misquote Paul.
- Deuteronomy 7:6, 7   It's not a very large church.
- 1 Corinthians 1:11–13   It's not centered in one person (i.e., Luther, Lutherans). It is not a sect that split off from others.
- John 4:23; Ephesians 4:4   True oneness exists. That is doctrinal and organizational oneness. The popular idea today that we only need a "spiritual" oneness is not a true oneness.
- Acts 1:23–26   It will have peaceful church politics; therefore, no major schisms will have taken place in its history.
- 2 Corinthians 1:24   The human leaders are not seen as above the people.
- Ephesians 4:5; Acts 8:35–38   It baptizes by immersion those who choose to accept Jesus.

- 1 Corinthians 14:32   It holds to all true Christian doctrine. New truth never contradicts old truth.
- Revelation 12:6; 12:17; 17:3   The church that went into the wilderness did not stay true but became Babylon. This "rest of her offspring" or "remnant" is, therefore, a new church that came up after the Dark Ages, which ended in 1798 as discussed in the "Short Program."
- Matthew 28:18–20; Titus 2:14; Revelation 14:6   It is a missionary-minded group, teaching and preaching in the entire world.
- 3 John 2   Jesus' many examples of healing are reflected in the church—a relationship between spiritual and physical health is a concern for those truly following God.
- Revelation 12:17; 14:12; 19:10   There are three special last-day features of the remnant church. They are born-again Christians who are keeping all ten commandments and following the Spirit of Prophecy.

Extra Thoughts:

There is one church on earth that is truly one and has stayed one. This church uses both the Old and New Testaments; teaches and heals with a vast array of schools, hospitals, and disaster relief systems; came together from many faiths in the mid-1800s; baptizes by immersion with born-again theology; keeps all ten of the Lord's commandments; has the understanding of prophecy; has been gifted with a prophet; and is now in the entire world. The name of this organization is the Seventh-day Adventist Church.

Our drive and focus is serving the God who called us together, the God of the Bible who gave His Son to die and rise again that all might have new life. He wants you to be part of His people not only in receiving but also in giving the last message of hope to this dying world. (See 1 Peter 2:9 and 2 Cor. 4:5–7.)

Study #30 – The Unforgivable Sin
- Matthew 12:31   Every other sin is forgivable except this one.
- John 16:8   The Holy Sprit's role is to show us where we don't live up to truth.
- Genesis 6:3   Though God has incredibly great mercy and tries so many times and in so many ways to reach us, He does have limits.
- Ephesians 4:30   Our final decision to follow the Lord comes from our willingness to cooperate with Him. He does the sealing, but we need to make sure nothing is in His way.
- Acts 7:51   These were people who claimed to be on God's side, yet they were "stiffnecked"—they always resisted this call to cooperate.
- 1 Thessalonians 5:19   You are the one who puts out the fire He put in you. As this verse is written in the negative, you have a choice and can avoid this.
- Hebrews 10:26   To have been given mercy from Jesus and choose to go back to sin, there's nothing more He can do for you.
- Ephesians 4:19   When this happens, people's hearts are cold. They become unreachable.

The Long Program

However, it is their choice to give themselves over to sin.
- John 6:35–37   God has more than enough power to help us stay with Him.
- Revelation 22:16   All who really want the Lord can come to Him.

Chapter 6

The Short Program

This program is called the Short Program, not because it is a much smaller set of Bible studies, but because it contains compressed versions of the various Long Program topics and is designed to answer the first two of the three great questions more quickly. It is based on a breakdown of the three angels' messages of Revelation 14:6–12. The third question, "What does He want me to do for Him in return?" is answered by focusing more on present truth/prophecy issues for these last days. As you compare the first seven here to the first seventeen of the previous series, you will note the comments are similar. Where Long Program studies are repeated, you are asked to refer to that study. Again, putting the comments into your own words is best.

Neither program completely goes over everything. The first contains more basics for someone with very little Bible knowledge. This one takes that knowledge for granted. It can still be useful for sharing with someone relatively new to the Word if his or her interest is aroused by the subject of prophecy. With the idea of adaptability under the Holy Spirit's guidance in mind, topics from this program can be woven into a Long Program study, or a transition from the Long Program to this one can be made as is noted in IAIN's feedback regarding the studies. Use each program creatively to make IAIN's overall study experience interesting and bring the truth of God's last-day message to him or her.

I suggest you consider this example on how to share Bible truths from the world of sports. In any sporting event covered on radio or TV, there are always two announcers. One gives play-by-play commentary, the actual events of the game, and the other gives color commentary, much needed filler statistics and information to make the broadcast interesting. The first announcer tells you what is happening while the second one tells you what it means. Therefore, in order to best enhance each Bible study, discuss not only what the event is, but also what it means for IAIN today. Fit the event into the theme of the great controversy. For example, the pope is the antichrist; just as Satan was a usurper in heaven, so his man on earth is a usurper as

> **Words of Advice**
>
> As an example of planting a seed for further study, mention as you go through Daniel 2 that we have an accurate record of time from then to today. Then when you get to the Sabbath/Sunday issue, you have support for your argument that the weekly cycle was never changed if you need it.

well. The seal of God is the Sabbath; the issue is not the day but whether humanity is willing to make a complete commitment to the Lord or not.

Here are the studies in order. Each heading is a key word taken from the three angels' messages:

The Everlasting Gospel
1. The Bible: Its Proof and How to Study It
2. Getting to Know the Trinity
3. The Second Coming of Christ
4. Satan's Story and Why We Suffer
5. Creation and Christ
6. The Ten Commandments and True Grace
7. The Ceremonial Laws

Judgment Is Come
8. What Is Jesus Doing Now? (the 2300 Days)

Worship Him
9. The Sabbath and Sunday

Babylon Is Fallen
10. The Differences in False and True Christianity
11. Babylon and the Way of the Many
12. Who is the Antichrist?

The Warnings Against Receiving the Mark of the Beast
13. What Happens After Death?
14. Judgment and Final Death

The Mark of the Beast
15. The Seal of God
16. The Mark of the Beast

Here Is the Patience of the Saints
17. Christian Standards (Three Studies Compressed Into One)
18. The Importance of Health
19. Ten Tests of a True Prophet
20. The Remnant Church

21. Baptism

Study #1 – The Bible: Its Proof and How to Study It

- Daniel 2:1–3   The opening verses set the stage.
- Daniel 2:4–12   This shows the futility of all who claim spiritual power but are outside Christianity.
- Daniel 2:13–24   The vast superiority of the God of heaven is clear. Daniel received the dream and its interpretation.
- Daniel 2:25–30   Daniel glorifies God and shows his own humanness. There is a lesson in religious freedom here also.
- Daniel 2:31–43   The dream and the interpretation are now given. The king saw a statue with four sections, each a different metal in descending order. Babylon, the head of gold, ruled from 605–539 BC. Represented with silver, the Medes and Persians took over and lasted until 331 BC, after which came the Greek, or Macedonian empire, of brass. The iron legs were the crushing power of Rome, ruling from 168 BC to AD 476. Rome transitioned into modern Europe, the feet that are part iron and part clay.
- Daniel 2:44-47   The happy ending to all world history is when Jesus Christ will come to this earth and fulfill this prophecy.
- Amos 3:7   God gives evidence of Himself in fulfilled prophecies.
- Isaiah 28:9, 10   The key to understanding is in cross-referencing.
- 2 Chronicles 20:20   All prosperity is linked to following God.
- John 5:39   Once again, the whole point of study is salvation, which is only through Jesus. Christ is the central theme throughout the Bible.

Study #2 – Getting to Know the Trinity

- Hebrews 11:6   To get to know God, we need FAITH!
- Isaiah 59:1, 2   We have cut ourselves off from Him by sinning.
- 1 Corinthians 8:6   This verse points to the existence of the trinity.
- John 4:23, 24   God wants to have a relationship with us.
- John 17:1–6, 20-23   Jesus connects us with the Father.
- John 3:16, 17   Though sin cuts us off, God wants us back.
- Romans 8:31-33   Because of Jesus, nothing stands in our way.

> **Words of Advice**
>
> I met Frances Chant when she was managing colporteurs for Pacific Press in western Canada. She had this advice for Bible workers: "When dealing with multiple appointments in one day, don't promise a set time like 3:00 p.m. Say instead, 'I'll be there between 3 and 3:30.' This leaves you room in case you need more time with a client. Now you're not technically late for the next one."

- Colossians 1:13–18   Christ is part of God.
- John 1:1–4, 14; 14:6, 9–14   He came to show us what the Father is like. We can access God through Jesus.
- 1 Timothy 2:3–6   God wants us all to be saved.
- 1 Corinthians 15:20–28   The history of the world is outlined here.
- Hebrews 1:1–3   God showed us His love through Jesus.
- 2 Peter 1:21   The messages came from the Father through the Holy Spirit to the people.
- 1 Peter 1:18–21   Christ is our Creator and Redeemer.
- Genesis 1:1, 2, 26   All three of the Trinity were involved in Creation.
- 2 Corinthians 13:14   All three work for our salvation.
- John 16:7–16   These are the roles of the Holy Spirit.
- John 14:16–18, 26   When Jesus went home to heaven, He left us the Holy Spirit to help us.
- Ephesians 3:14–19   The Holy Spirit brings Jesus into our hearts.

Words of Advice

Those over forty-five years of age in the year 2010 in North America grew up with the Protestant worldview. Those under forty-five grew up in a world shaped by the revolutions of the 1960s when secular humanism took over our culture. One doctrine that gives Adventists a distinct advantage over other Christian groups in dealing with secular-minded people is that of "present truth."

When you see animosity manifested toward Jesus as "the way, truth, and life" to the exclusion of all other belief systems, go immediately to Romans 2:13-15. This provides an excellent balance between exclusiveness and inclusiveness in Christian faith. "Jesus is the only way" becomes "they knew Him by His character, not by His name." "The remnant church is God's only true church" becomes "wouldn't you like to be part of the remnant too?"

Study #3 – The Second Coming of Christ
- John 14:1–3   Jesus Himself promised He would return.
- Acts 1:9–11   A repeated promise is given by the angels.
- Revelation 1:7   This will be a universal experience.
- 1 Thessalonians 4:16, 17   Jesus is coming back for His people.
- Matthew 24:3–7   These signs were fulfilled in the last century.
- Luke 21:25–27   Notice the power and great glory.
- Daniel 12:4   Modern technology is a fulfillment of prophecy.
- 2 Timothy 3:1–5   The immorality in society can be attributed to the powerless religion

predicted in verse 5.
- Revelation 6:12–17   The three great signs: the Great Lisbon Earthquake occurred in 1755; the dark day and blood red moon took place in May 1780; and the most fantastic meteor shower in history fell on November 3, 1833. The rest is yet to come.
- Matthew 24:14–27, 44   While the true gospel is being proclaimed in the entire world, many false followers and pretenders will abound, so beware. It is time to get ready.

Study #4 – Satan's Story and Why We Suffer
- Revelation 12:4, 7, 9, 12   The devil has a short time to tempt us.
- Ezekiel 28:11–19   The King of Tyre describes the devil.
- Isaiah 14:12–20   Lucifer was once the highest angel.
- John 8:44   There is no truth in the devil.
- Genesis 3:1–7   The beginning of sin was a literal event.
- Zechariah 3:1–7   The devil is trying to stop our salvation.
- Acts 5:40, 41   Free choice results in causing people to suffer.
- Job 2:3–7   The Lord limits Satan and his destructive actions.
- Psalm 119:71, 75, 76   God allows us to suffer so we may learn.
- Hebrews 12:5–11; 11:24–26   Like a father, God lovingly disciplines His children. Christ's discipline is worth more than the pleasure of this world.
- Romans 5:17–19   Through Christ's death, forgiveness is available.
- Romans 8:28   Every experience we're given is for our good.
- 2 Corinthians 4:17   Life's pain is small compared to eternity.
- Revelation 21:4, 5   The world will be restored.
- Isaiah 66:22, 23   In the new earth, all will be happiness again.

Words of Advice

When dealing with Christians from other churches, remember that arguing is a sign of conviction. You need to carefully avoid getting drawn into an argument based on human opinion, but still stand for what's right. If people show closed-heartedness and tell you that you are being legalistic or doctrinal, you need to (at least once) be courageous and blunt enough to hit them with the truth head on as Jesus did with Nicodemus. When they start to go on about being "free" by grace and not needing to keep the Sabbath because they are "saved," ask them word for word, "Does God's love give you an excuse to sin, yes or no?" If the answer is yes, no matter how many texts they may quote to support their position or how moving their stories and illustrations may be, they are not true Christians. Don't be afraid of them or intimidated by their overconfidence, but remember to still love them as Jesus would.

Extra Thoughts:

Do you want freedom from the enemy? Do you want Jesus to bring healing to your life? Ask to see clearly through Satan's deceptions. Ask to have Jesus in your life.

Study #5 – Creation and Christ
- Genesis 1:1   In the beginning God created everything.
- Jeremiah 10:11–16   All other gods were created by man.
- Romans 5:8, 9   The earth's Creator came to the earth to save us.
- Isaiah 43:1   God takes interest in each one of us.
- Psalm 51:10   The real proof of creation.
- Colossians 1:16–18   Christ is Creator and Redeemer.
- 2 Corinthians 4:6   His power enlightens our hearts.
- Ephesians 2:8–10, 13   We are saved through faith.
- Isaiah 41:10, 13; 40:25–31   With Him we have strength.
- 1 Corinthians 8:6   This shows the oneness of God.
- Matthew 3:16, 17   The Father and the Spirit showed their approval of Jesus as He started His mission.
- Matthew 28:19, 20   He promises to be with us.
- Revelation 4:11   Only He holds the power of creation.
- Exodus 31:16, 17   The Sabbath is a memorial of Creation.
- Ezekiel 20:10–12   Again this is mentioned.
- Jude 24, 25   The power of creation is so great that God can make us perfect.

Extra Thoughts:

Jesus came to save the world He created. Is He your Savior? Do you want this powerful of a God on your side?

Study #6 – The Ten Commandments and True Grace
- Exodus 20:1–18   They cover every conceivable kind of sin.
- Romans 3:23   Sin results in death.
- 1 John 3:4   Violating the law is a definition of sin.
- James 2:10–12   Even one sin is enough to condemn us.
- Romans 7:7   The law cannot save us. It points out our sin.
- James 2:8, 9   Love is the foundation of obeying.
- Psalm 19:7   We are converted when we see our sin in the law and go to Jesus for healing.
- Romans 6:14; 3:28; Galatians 2:16; Ephesians 2:8, 9   These verses seem to suggest Christians don't need the law.

- Romans 6:1, 2; 3:31; Galatians 2:17; Ephesians 2:10   Here are some nearby verses that balance out the others.
- Ezekiel 36:26, 27   God empowers us to live above sin.
- James 2:17, 18   Real faith flows out into life through one's actions.
- Galatians 2:20   Through Jesus changing my life, I live for Him. All that I do is in the strength He gives me.
- Psalm 119:34, 174   This is the attitude Christians should have.

Extra Thoughts:

Most churches in the world teach that you cannot get to heaven on your own and that you need Jesus. But most do not emphasize that Jesus can help you right here and now with your problems. Look for differences in Christian faith that exist, and be aware that not all churches are the same.

Study #7 – The Ceremonial Laws
Please see the identical study in the Long Program.

Words of Advice

While speaking at a crusade once, Randy Barber had an audience member stand up in vehement disagreement with what he'd heard. This man was obviously a great believer in the popular system of prophetic interpretation called futurism whereas we follow what's known as the historicist view. After the meeting he was almost completely surrounded by well-meaning Adventists who tried to convince him that what he'd heard that night was truth though he would have none of it and was ready to debate anyone who talked to him. I asked Pastor Barber if there was any point in the church members doing this since he had already shared so much from the front. He said, "No, just leave him be. He's had his whole world torn out from underneath him tonight and needs to be loved. He'll have no peace until he looks at this again. God will give him another chance."

Study #8 – What Is Jesus Doing Now? (the 2300 Days)
- Revelation 14:7   The "judgment is come" indicates a present event when this prophecy is applicable. This is a judgment before Jesus returns.
- Daniel 8:14   A time prophecy of 2300 years was given for the cleansing of the sanctuary. What this means will be explained by this study.
- Acts 3:19–21   Notice, forgiveness does not come instantly but at a later date, the "times of refreshing." King James English uses the phrase "when the times of refreshing shall come" while some modern English Bibles may not.

- Daniel 9:20–27 The angel comes and explains what he does not understand, which is the previous vision in chapter 8. The 70 weeks "cut off" are cut off from the 2300 days. Both time prophecies, therefore, begin with the same date, 457 BC. The 70 weeks ended in AD 34. The rest of the 2300 days ended in 1844.
- Hebrews 8:1, 2 By 1844 there was no longer a sanctuary on earth as it was destroyed in AD 70. However, Jesus went into the original in heaven. The earthly one was only a copy. So since 1844, the heavenly sanctuary is what is being cleansed.
- Hebrews 9:11, 12, 28 Jesus bears our sins in the sanctuary, but then returns without them. Why? Because they have been removed from the records of heaven. This is the cleansing, the time of refreshing, and the judgment before Jesus comes to claim His people. They are all descriptions of one event going on now.
- Hebrews 11:13, 39, 40 Jesus give Himself up to suffer for our sins on the cross. It was like paying our debt by check, because the payment still had to be applied. The judgment Jesus is participating in now is taking what He did on Calvary and using it to make us clean. We are clean by faith as soon as we accept Jesus. We are clean in reality as soon as our name comes up before Him and He pleads to the Father on our behalf. The Father gave us the Son so we might be cleansed.
- Leviticus 23:27–29 The Day of Atonement was the cleansing of the earthly sanctuary.
- Leviticus 16:7, 9, 10, 16, 20–22, 29–33 A description of the ceremony itself is given here. The daily sacrifices symbolized the cross, while the yearly festivals symbolized the development of God's plan throughout history. The sins went each day onto the lamb, which carried them into the sanctuary. Then symbolically, they stayed there. Once a year the high priest went from the holy place to the Most Holy Place carrying the sins with him. It was then that they were completely wiped out of existence. The sacrificial goat and the high priest each show different aspects of Christ's work to save the world. The scapegoat is a lesson of the devil's fate for leading God's people to commit those sins. This atonement was for the whole congregation. All of God's people from throughout history are being judged right now. If they were truly sorry for their sins and if they were true in faith, Jesus can apply His sacrifice to them and save them when He comes again.
- John 14:1-3 Jesus goes to prepare a place for us. It is a spiritual preparation by removing our sins. Then we can be with Him for real in heaven.

> **Words of Advice**
>
> My wife Melissa's thoughts on the meaning of our modern technological age where so many have rejected God, Christ, and Bible truths such as Creation and the second coming, are as follows: "The devil is tempting us. His message is, 'Don't you want to stay? Don't you want to believe you can create heaven on earth yourselves?'"

- Revelation 22:11, 12   This declaration He will give just before He returns. He can give the reward when He comes because He has finished preparing a place for His people. From that point on, the world's destiny is fixed forever.
- 2 Peter 3:10–14   Life is very serious. We are so close to the end of the world. We need to be on guard and focused on living right continually.
- Daniel 12:4   The timing of the end is proven by our advanced world today.

Extra Thoughts:

According to Hebrews 10:9–24, we need boldness and must go to Christ with all our hearts. Sincerely repent of your sins, believe He loves and accepts you, and claim His promise of salvation. He wants to give it to you.

Study #9 – The Sabbath and Sunday

- Revelation 14:7   A reform in the area of worship is called for in our time.
- Genesis 2:1–3   The Sabbath is a memorial of Creation. The Lord Himself caused it to exist by blessing it. This was His decision. It existed before sin.
- Exodus 20:8–11   Here are clear definitions of what constitutes keeping it holy. The word "remember" signifies they already knew of it and were being told not to forget. The Sabbath is a central part of God's holy law.
- Mark 2:27, 28   Jesus, as God, confirmed the Sabbath. This is His day. He kept it.
- Nehemiah 9:13, 14   This is a summation of the whole Mount Sinai experience given about a thousand years later. The Sabbath is mentioned on its own.
- Luke 4:16   Jesus kept the Sabbath.
- Acts 13:14, 42-44; 17:2; 18:4   Years after the cross, Paul kept the Sabbath, not just with the Jews, but with the Gentiles also. The seventh day of the week is the Christian Sabbath.
- Isaiah 66:22, 23   The Sabbath will be kept in eternity, thus the Sabbath has been a central piece of history from the beginning of time through eternity.
- John 20:19   They were assembled for "fear of the Jews" and not to worship. They had not even fully believed His resurrection yet.
- Luke 24:44–47   Jesus refers to the resurrection day not as the first day of the week here but as the third day of His time paying our debt to God.
- Acts 20:7   This is a Sabbath meeting that ran long.
- Leviticus 23:32; Genesis 1:13   Sundown to sundown is how Bible time is kept.
- 1 Corinthians 16:2   The verse says "lay by him in store." They are at home and not in church.

Extra Thoughts:

There can be only one holy day for a holy God who never changes. The call to return to true worship in this first angel's message is a call to restore the Sabbath to its proper place. This is prophesied in Isaiah 58:12–14.

> ## Words of Advice
>
> Eugene Thorarinson, while he was head elder of Calgary Southside Church, gave me his take on the differences in mental dynamic he'd observed in the men and women who accept the Lord, get baptized, and join the church: "The men come in with the question 'Is this true?' For the women the question is 'Does this work for you?'" Both are equally valid questions. See John 10:37, 38.

Study #10 – The Differences in False and True Christianity

- Matthew 7:21–29   Read the passage and the following verses, which cross-reference with the key words in Matthew 7 (in the King James Version) to help explain the text.
  - "Not everyone"—2 Corinthians 4:3   People who don't understand don't have true faith.
  - "Lord, Lord"—Proverbs 28:9   God will not honor those who reject the law.
  - "Will of my Father"—Psalm 40:8   His will is His law.
  - "Many"—Matthew 20:16; 2 Corinthians 2:17   The majority called by God will not last until heaven.
  - "Works"—Isaiah 64:6   Human works are insufficient.
  - "I never knew you"—John 9:31; Psalm 50:16–23; Hosea 4:6   Again, the attitude one has toward the law makes the difference.
  - "Depart from me"—Psalm 119:115   All sinners will be removed by the Lord Himself.
  - "Iniquity"—Romans 3:23; 2 Thessalonians 2:12   Iniquity is to fall short, which implies an attempt at righteousness that does not go far enough. Being pleased with this half-effort makes one worthy of judgment.
  - "Hear, do"—James 1:22–25   The truths of the Bible must be lived and not just heard.
  - "House"—Matthew 21:12, 13   This is His house, a church.
  - "Rock"—1 Corinthians 10:4   Jesus is the Rock on which to build a church.
  - "Rain"—Psalm 72:6; Deuteronomy 32:2; Hosea 10:12; Isaiah 55:10, 11   The Lord rains down truth, righteousness, doctrine (His Word), and His Spirit.
  - "Flood"—Revelation 17:15; Isaiah 59:19   Water symbolizes people as well. A flood comes from the side, while rain falls from above. The devil counterfeits the rain by flooding the church with false Christians.
  - "Wind"—James 1:6; Ephesians 4:14; "sand"—Genesis 32:12; Daniel 8:12   Winds of doctrine come in, and people are sand. The devil floods the church with popular ideas that are of human origin and contradict or counterfeit Bible truths.

I Was Saved in a Living Room

- ○ "Great fall"—Daniel 2:44, 45   God will destroy all that is not of Him when He comes.
- ○ "Authority"—Isaiah 55:8, 9; "not as the scribes"—Colossians 2:6-10   Again, beware of popular religion!

Extra Thoughts:

This passage is a summary of the Sermon on the Mount in Matthew 5–7. In it, Jesus talked of the depth of what it means to be a follower of God. He spoke of loving our enemies and turning the other cheek, but He also emphasized the relationship the Ten Commandments has to practical faith when He spoke of murder and adultery starting in the heart. Many are being led astray by a false gospel. The broad way of Matthew 7:13, 14 is not worldliness but popularly taught religious beliefs, which compromise the law. The narrow way is doing the will of God completely.

This study's main focus is on false and true in the sense of teachings. However, like the Sermon on the Mount, much of the Bible emphasizes practical love in action as truth. This cannot be ignored nor can it be separated from the true Christian experience. Here's a few other references to look up if you would like: 1 Thessalonians 2:4-7; Philippians 1:15-18; James 1:27; Micah 6:8; Luke 10:25-37; Ecclesiastes 12:13; Galatians 5:13; Hebrews 12:14; 1 John 3:7-10, 24; 4:7, 17, 20; 2:3, 4; Isaiah 58; Psalm 51; Ezekiel 18.

- Matthew 24:40-51   Read the passage and the following verses, which cross-reference with the key words in Matthew 24 to help explain this text.
  - ○ "Two, field"—Matthew 13:38; 1 Corinthians 3:9; John 4:35   The field is the world: the two in it are workers for God.
  - ○ "Taken, left"—Matthew 24:38, 39; Luke 17:27, 36, 37   The one taken is "taken out," which is still an expression today for being destroyed.
  - ○ "Women"—Jeremiah 6:2   A woman is a symbol of a church. Two kinds of churches are referred to here. Revelation 12 and 17 each speak prophetically of two churches in the end.
  - ○ "Grinding"—John 12:24; 2 Timothy 2:15   Jesus is the grain, and grinding Him is preaching the gospel.
  - ○ "Wise servant"—There is no reference here, simply this point: Only Christians claim to be serving the Christian God. These two servants are not Christians versus others, but two kinds of Christians.
  - ○ "Meat"—Isaiah 28:9, 10, 13; 1 Corinthians 3:1, 2; 2:13; Hebrews 5:12-14   Deep truth is meat. Therefore, the good servant, in giving meat, implies that the evil servant is not. He is then only giving milk, or basic truth.
  - ○ "Due season"—Hebrews 6:1-6   Milk is important, but you must build your faith from the basics to something higher.
  - ○ "Shall find so doing"—2 Corinthians 5:17; 6:1   These good servants are rewarded while the others are not.
  - ○ "Ruler of goods"—Psalm 50:5   The blessing pronounced at the second coming of Jesus.

- ○ "Evil servant"—Romans 2:21–24; Philippians 1:15–18; Psalm 50:16–21   This servant, though a Christian, is cursed by God.
- ○ "Delayeth his coming"—Matthew 24:26   By believing false interpretations of prophecy, today's Christians are looking for end-time events that will never happen.
- ○ "Begin to smite"—Revelation 13:15–17; 1 John 3:15; 4:20; Galatians 4:2   This will lead them to try to hurt the true followers of God with the mark of the beast.
- ○ "Eat and drink with drunken"—Revelation 3:20; 17:6–8; John 12:43; Isaiah 29:9–13; 1 Thessalonians 5:1–10   A spiritual union of popular churches with the antichrist will happen. In attempting to win the world through compromise, the faith they offer to the world will be so watered down it will be worthless. This will result in these churches being deceived by the great counterfeit Satan will put on the world in the last days.
- ○ "Hour not aware"—2 Peter 3:10, 11   Jesus will take them by surprise.
- ○ "Portion with hypocrites"—2 Thessalonians 1:8   Again, they will be cursed.

Extra Thoughts:

This text is a prophecy predicting that those who stay with just the basics will be led to persecute those who study in depth when the differences between them become plain and obvious. It is important to note that Jesus said "but and if." These prophecies do not have to come true if people will choose to stand fully for God.

Words of Advice

Louis Torres once prepared a Bible study about the Sabbath for an interest, and the interest chose that particular week to bring a brand new couple to the study. Pastor Torres did not know what to do, as the obvious thought was these new people would be offended at such a strong message right away. So in his opening prayer he prayed that each one would take from the study what he or she needed. Louis and Carol met the couple more than three years later and were told the Sabbath went right over their heads that day. They were non-practicing Catholics who were motivated by the study to go back to church on Sundays, and continued that way for a year until seeing ads for a Revelation seminar. Then something clicked as to what the study was really about.

The point being: don't be afraid to let the Holy Spirit do more than you intend, and trust that the Holy Spirit plays a part in uncertain happenings.

Study #11 – Babylon and the Way of the Many

- Revelation 14:8   The prophecy says "is fallen." This is a trend in motion, which is not completely fulfilled until the end. It will be fulfilled when every country gives itself over to the

control of this worldwide union called Babylon.
- Matthew 26:28   Jesus died for "many," in other words, Christians are the many.
- Matthew 24:5, 12   False Christ's will trick many Christians who will lose their love for God before the end.
- Matthew 20:16   Of all the great number calling themselves Christians, only a small number will actually go to heaven.
- Matthew 7:13–15, 21–23   The reason for people falling away is they believe popular ideas instead of the truth. This study is best understood in the light of the previous studies on the differences in false and true Christianity. It must be carefully but completely stated that the way of the many is not the way of the world but the way of popular religion! A wolf in sheep's clothes is someone who appears to be a Christian, but is not.
- Malachi 2:7–9   Popular religion always denies the obligation of the law. The ministers who want to be popular do it by compromising on the issue of obedience. They are especially responsible. That is why these preachers have a bad reputation with mainstream society. A religion with no real commitment that just emphasizes good feelings is no real help.
- Revelation 17:9, 18   Rome is the whore of Babylon. The seven heads are the seven mountains the city of Rome is built around. The woman is a symbol of a church. This is the church of Rome, the Catholic Church. Through all its history it worked by political compromise. It is still that way today.
- 2 Peter 3:15, 16   Twisting of Paul's writings leads to false religion. This is very common in Protestantism now as the majority of churches use them to tamper with the Ten Commandments.
- 2 Timothy 4:3, 4   Many churches and church leaders are saying the same things. The people who seek them are not seeking truth but someone who will tell them what they want to hear.
- Revelation 17:1–6, 18   Catholicism is the "Mother of Harlots"; therefore, Protestant churches are her daughters when they act the same way. Look at what is happening today with the great moral decline of the past two generations. The majority of believers in God are gradually filling with rage at the sins of the world. Jesus told us to love our enemies. Our job is to show them the better way. If we get mad, we'll be led to try a way that is built on revenge. That is not something the Lord can bless.
- The attempts at world peace based on religious unity appeal to modern Christians; because by conquering the world, they will think they are converting it. This is the same way the early church fell away from the Lord. Only the full truth has the power of God behind it to change human lives. Compromising the truth to get more of the world into the church only creates a worldly church.
- Revelation 15:2   God's true people will gain the victory over last-day deception.
- Revelation 20:4   Here is a promise that the martyrs of all time will be rewarded. Those who

stood for the truth and the Lord and died as a result, throughout history, will be rewarded in heaven.

> ## Words of Advice
>
> The second crusade we did while at Mountain Sanctuary was in Banff, Alberta, home of the world famous "Banff National Park." Melissa and I had to face the excruciating disappointment of seeing someone come so close to taking a stand but turning away. Lester Carney told us that he has had that happen at every crusade he's ever done. Then he said, "Even Jesus Himself could not convert Judas."

- Revelation 20:10   This punishment is for those who believe the lie.
- Revelation 19:20; 16:13   Miracles and supernatural events are used to trick people. As we have the dragon in Revelation 12 and the beast and its image in Revelation 13, so a corresponding set of symbols is used here. The dragon is anything outside Christianity, the beast is the Catholic Church, and the false prophet is apostate Protestantism.
- Revelation 18:1–4, 8   This is the most important verse! "My people" are God's people. Because of all the believers still in Babylon, He has allowed it to continue until the end. His word is to call them to come out and take a full stand for Him and His truth.

Extra Thoughts:

Even though the churches have gone astray along with the world, God still loves them. Like in Old Testament times, He is raising up those who are following Him by calling to the rest to take their stand. Sometimes the most loving thing a person can do is to sound this wake-up call. Will you stand for God? Will you also work to reach others who will?

Study #12 – Who Is the Antichrist?
- Revelation 1:1   To say the Revelation will shortly come to pass shows that the theory placing all its events at the end is false. Therefore, those theories and the speculations they give on the antichrist are not reliable.
- 1 John 4:3   The "spirit" of antichrist starts as an attitude. In the time that John wrote these words, that spirit was already there.
- 1 John 2:18, 22   The attitude of the antichrist can manifest itself anywhere and anytime. What is to be looked for is not one man. From John's time forward, it has been the end, in the sense that this issue has continually repeated itself in every generation.
- 2 John 7–11   The text starts commenting on someone outside the church as antichrist by

denying Jesus. Then it moves into someone denying Jesus in another way, by changing pure Bible doctrine. To deny Jesus can be done with actions or words (see Titus 1:16). It is possible to be in the church in name and still be antichrist. "Anti" not only means "against," it also means "in place of."

- 1 Timothy 3:6   The instruction here is part of the qualifications for a minister in the church. Notice how they are at risk from falling into the devil's control through pride.
- John 16:2   Jesus' prediction for His disciples literally came true in their day. In another sense, our Lord's prediction came true in other generations with those who followed the truth being cast out of the organized church as it departed from truth during the Dark Ages. After the Roman Empire fell, the church reigned supreme. When it did, Bibles were banned from the common people and many false doctrines were taught. People who stood up against this faced torture and being burned at the stake.
- 2 Thessalonians 2:3, 4, 7, 10–12   Paul knew that the New Testament church would fall from the truth and the Lord just as Israel fell in the Old Testament. The one to be taken out of the way was the Roman Emperor. The one who rose up, the "man of sin," is the antichrist. The reference to opposing God comes from Daniel 7, which lists a power called the "little horn" who does the same thing.
- Daniel 7   There are thirteen identifying features of the antichrist in this chapter. The one who fulfills all of them is the one to watch. Following are the verses to specifically look at: verses 7, 8, 19, 20, 23–25.

1. "Little horn"—Daniel 2 has the same history with a different emphasis. The fallen Roman Empire evolved into several countries when the ten invading tribes moved in to claim the land. Those tribes were the Anglo-Saxons, Franks, Suevi, Visigoths, Burgundians, Alemani, Lombards, Ostrogoths, Vandals, and Heruli. Being a little horn, it is a little country. The little horn that came up is today the smallest country in the world, Vatican City, occupying a total of 108 acres. See Luke 1:68, 69 for use of the word horn.
2. "Eyes of a man"—Always headed by a man. Compare this to Daniel 2:38, 39 where the king was the head of gold and another came up after. Another empire came up, not another king. So the king is synonymous with the country he rules. It's not just the one man; it's the whole country. The Pope and the entire Papal system fulfill each of these points.
3. "Different"—This is a unique system. Every other empire in history was political. This was and is a union of religious and political kingdoms.
4. "Three other horns plucked up"—Three tribes—the Vandals, Ostrogoths, and Heruli—were completely destroyed as it rose to power.
5. "Stout"—It controls by guilt.
6. "Makes war with the saints"—A power that persecutes the Lord's people is shown. Through the Dark Ages, Bibles were taken away from the people. It is estimated that 50 million were

killed for their faith by this power over the time period described.

7. "Stamps residue with feet"—This is another way to describe persecution, but it is listed separately because of the noticeable method of persecution. Compare the feet here to the feet of the statue in Daniel 2, which described the nations that rose up after the fall of the Roman Empire. The church did the same thing in the dark ages that the Jews did when they put Jesus on the cross. They held their own religious trial and then handed the one on trial over to the government for punishment.

8. "Prevailed"—It stayed in control and appeared to win.

9. "A time, times, and half a time"—This phrase refers to three and a half years. Since a day equals a year in prophecy and a prophetic year is 360 days, this power rules for 1260 prophetic years. The final tribe to be removed was the Ostrogoths in AD 538. This marks the date for the start of the time period. It ended right on time in AD 1798 when Napoleon's General Berthier invaded and cut off its power.

10. "Whole earth"—Worldwide influence. As European countries discovered and colonized the rest of the world, it went with them. Christopher Columbus, upon setting shore for the first time in the New World, planted a cross and a hangman's noose. This was a way of bringing the Spanish Inquisition overseas.

Words of Advice

The further the study goes on, the greater the commitment IAIN will need to make. If there is any cherished sin she is holding on to, she might respond by accusing you of 'judging' her. Jewelry wearing can be one of these sensitive issues. Evangelist Leo Schreven would respond to comments he got about being judgemental by taking the audience back to the Bible verse which offended the commentator and asking, "Now, did I say that?"

11. "Came up among the ten horns"—Arose in the area and after the fall of the Roman Empire. In AD 533 Justinian, Eastern Roman Emperor, declared the bishop of Rome head of the church and gave him Rome to control. The pope was not free to exercise this power until the routing of the Ostrogoths out of Rome in 538.

12. "Speaks great words"—There are two Bible definitions of blasphemy. Mark 2:7 lists the claim of power to forgive sins. John 10:33 says it is claiming you are God (or God's special one). Each are claimed in the Catholic hierarchy. Priestly forgiveness at confession is supposed to be equal to the Lord's. Also the pope's triple crown implies a claim of dominion over heaven, earth, and hell and a claim to be God's representative on earth.

13. "Thinks to change times and laws"—Tries to change the law, but it is unchangeable. The pride and height of power this system attained to makes it think it can do even this. The only "time" mentioned in the Ten Commandments is the fourth commandment, which speaks of God's holy day, the Sabbath.

- Daniel 8:9–12, 24, 25   The description is one horn for the Roman Empire and the papacy. The pope is really more Roman than Christian. The empire changed from pagan Rome to papal Rome when it exalted itself to heaven in verses 10 and 11. It humanized the truth and set its focus on this world rather than Jesus in heaven. It grew by compromise and worldly greatness.
- Revelation 13:1–10, 18   There are parallels here to Daniel 7 and 8. The beast rules during the same time period; is worldwide in its reach; persecutes the saints; blasphemes; and receives worship.

There is one special identifier from verse 18 that only the pope fulfills—the number of 666. It came from sun worship. In ancient languages like Latin, letters were used as numbers. Ancient kings claimed to be children of the sun god and chose names whose numbers worked out to 666 in their languages. The pope's name is no different. "VICARIVS FILLII DEI" is Latin for "Vicar (representative) of the Son of God." Add the Roman numerals and you get 666 as shown.

V	=	5	F	=	0	D =	500
I	=	1	I	=	1	E =	0
C	=	100	L	=	50	I =	1
A	=	0	I	=	1		
R	=	0	I	=	1		
I	=	1					
V	=	5					
S	=	0					
		112			53		501

The total is 666.

Study #13 – What Happens After Death?

Please see the identical study in the Long Program. If you would like to give a more in-depth conclusion to the study that fits with the prophecy theme, try these Extra Thoughts for your wrap up.

Extra Thoughts: Read Job 14:10–15, and cross-reference the key words as follows:
- "Heavens no more"   see 2 Peter 3:10
- "Wrath is past"   see Revelation 15:1

- "My change comes"   see 1 Corinthians 15:51–54

Also, look up Ezekiel 18:4 and 1 Timothy 6:15, 16 as well.

Study #14 – Judgment and Final Death

Please see the identical study in the Long Program.

> **Words of Advice**
>
> I remember when Pastor Warman shared information about the first and second deaths with me. The first thought that came to my mind was, "Pretend you're a sociologist and analyze the two belief systems—which one is the most realistic?"

Study #15 – The Seal of God

- Revelation 14:1   The word "name" here is used in a figurative sense to imply character. These people are living the character of God.
- Revelation 22:4   To see God, we must be perfect. To "see" implies to understand. To be ready for heaven, we need to commit to achieving perfection now in order to understand.
- Ephesians 1:13   This is a three-step process of character perfection: "trusted … believed … sealed." The Lord reaches out to us, we accept Him, and then we're given the seal of the Holy Spirit. This is a faith experience for us to receive it.
- 2 Corinthians 1:21, 22   The seal of God is something He gives. It has to do with being born again and receiving the Spirit.
- 2 Timothy 2:19   To receive the seal, we must give up our sins. This verse also teaches we must give up believing that we can never achieve a fullness of faith, which is perfection.
- John 6:26–29   The seal was given to Christ, and the summary of its meaning is contained here. Life is not about getting things in this world. We must come to the higher knowledge of eternal things by believing in Jesus. Notice though that a labor to receive the "meat" is implied in verse 27. It is about growing in faith and not just receiving faith.
- Deuteronomy 6:5–9   Here is a figurative description of the depth of importance the Ten Commandments has for us. We must choose to live right.
- Hebrews 10:15, 16   God wants to help us live a right life in Him.
- Isaiah 8:16   "Seal" is used as a verb, an action He does for us. To be sealed also implies permanence. A true born-again experience is one where a person wants to be good. To be a true follower of God, you must live His law continually.
- John 16:7, 8, 13   The Holy Spirit gives us what we need to live this way, by guiding us into

all truth and convicting us when needed (see also Phil. 3:15).
- Genesis 2:1–4   The Sabbath was founded at Creation.

> ## Words of Advice
>
> John's record of the conversation between himself, the Lord, and Peter in John 21:20–22 teaches us the lesson of professionalism in all our outreach efforts. If you have more than one study going on, do not talk to IAIN A about IAIN B. Keep what happens in each study separate from the other.

- Ezekiel 20:12, 20   The Sabbath is a sign of our commitment to God. The Sabbath being His day, He gives special blessings on it. When we participate, we receive the blessings and are changed little by little into better people. Thus Sabbathkeeping is an extremely practical method of achieving the spiritual growth that God wants for us.
- Exodus 20:8–11   The elements of a legal seal are in the fourth commandment. A seal has to have the name, title, and territory of a governing official. "The Lord" is His name. His title as Creator shows that He made the "heaven, earth, the sea, and all that in them is" and all is within his territory.

Extra Thoughts:

The seal of God is a three-step process on the Lord's part to make us perfect. He gives us His sacrifice, His law, and His Sabbath. We accept Him, obey Him, and make it complete by keeping His holy day. The seal is complete when the process is permanent as Paul said, "I have fought the good fight, I have finished the course, I have kept the faith" (2 Tim. 4:7). Do you want this seal? Give up your sins, accept His forgiveness, and give up the false gospel that says you can never be perfect. Believe that God will help you and He will, and keep the Sabbath as part of your complete commitment to Him.

Study #16 – The Mark of the Beast
- Revelation 14:9, 10   This is one of the sternest warnings in the entire Bible. The mark will be forced on the world, and all who accept it will be punished by the Lord.
- 2 Thessalonians 2:3, 4, 7, 8   The issue is worship. When the falling away happened, the man of sin changed the day of worship.
- Daniel 8:11, 12   The earthly temple was destroyed in AD 70, and Jesus entered the heavenly temple when He ascended. The casting down of the sanctuary refers to a humanized version of the truth. In AD 321 the passing of the Sunday law made the church more acceptable and gave it a measure of control in the then-known world. However, instead of converting the

pagans, paganism changed the church into what we see today in Roman Catholicism, i.e. the worship of the saints came about by taking local demigods and giving them Christian labels.

- 2 Peter 3:16–18   Most popular religious teachers today misquote Paul. The most common thought of those who do is that the Ten Commandments are done away with or changed.
- James 2:10–12   If one takes a stand for only nine commandments, it's worthless, which is what mainstream churches today are doing.
- Acts 17:30   It is when the conviction comes and is resisted that the mark is a sin. While God is merciful to those who do not know better, He also works to enlighten people as well. Then they are responsible.
- 2 Thessalonians 2:10–12   It is not enough to have truth, you must love truth. There has to be a desire for more. To have "pleasure in unrighteousness" is to be satisfied with a gospel that does not go far enough in its commitment to obedience.
- 1 John 2:3–5   Anyone who tries to downgrade the Ten Commandments is not a true follower of God.
- Matthew 15:3–9   Here is an example from Jesus' time regarding keeping the commandments.
- Matthew 24:45–51   There are two kinds of "servants," which represent two kinds of Christians. The difference is "meat in due season," which is deep truth at the appropriate time after someone has been brought to the point of conviction and renewal.
- Ezekiel 9:4–6   This imagery is similar to Revelation except the mark here is for those who are saved. Whereas, in Revelation, the mark is for those who are doomed. The place to begin is at the sanctuary. This means the issue of the mark starts first within God's people, the church.
- Daniel 6:5   Daniel was trapped by his enemies on a point about the law. The rest of the story features the decree they got their king to enforce, which dealt with worship. Human governments in our time will be used to enforce false worship in violation of God's law.
- Hebrews 6:1–3   People need spiritual growth. Once people find the Savior, they need to learn more about how to experience Him. Learning the truth on any issue (including the Sabbath question) helps people experience God.
- Exodus 31:13   The Sabbath is God's special sign.

Words of Advice

As soon as there is interest from someone who wants to study with you, take advantage of the opportunity. Make an appointment immediately. Do not wait to check your schedule, or the devil will bring something up to get that person to put it off. Once you get the first study finished and you have the plan in place for more, it is imperative that you do nothing to change the schedule you have committed to for at least three to six sessions. Once the study is off the ground and running, if you need to make the occasional exception it's okay.

- Isaiah 30:9, 10, 13 The desire to compromise the law always leads to false religion, which is based on "smooth things," or good feelings. This is symbolized as a breach in a wall.
- Isaiah 58:12–14 The symbolism of "repairing the breach" speaks to repairing the breach made in the law with the introduction of a false day of worship—Sunday.
- Ezekiel 22:26–28, 31 Those who caused the breach did it by instituting a false worship day.

Here are some quotes from the beast, the Roman Catholic Church, to show what she considers her mark of loyalty: "Perhaps the boldest thing ... the Church ever did, happened in the first century. The holy day, the Sabbath, was changed from Saturday to Sunday.... not from any directions noted in the Scriptures ... People who think that the Scriptures should be the sole authority, should logically become Seventh-day Adventists and keep Saturday Holy" (Saint Catherine Catholic Church Sentinel, Algonac, Michigan, May 21, 1995).

"The observance of Sunday by the Protestants is an homage they pay, in spite of themselves, to the authority of the [Catholic] Church" (Monsignor Louis Segur, *Plain Talk About the Protestantism of Today*, p. 213).

"Of course the Catholic Church claims that the change was her act.... and the act is a mark of her ecclesiastical authority in religious matters" (Letter from H. F. Thomas, Chancellor of Cardinal Gibbons).

The Bible does not word-for-word say what the mark of the beast is. By knowing who the beast is and understanding the description given by Bible principles and prophecies, it can be understood to be Sunday. This statement is further elaborated on by the following texts:

- Daniel 7:7, 19 Depending on the translation you are using, you will see uses of the word "stamped" or "trampled" with its feet here. Compare this to the statue in Daniel that had feet of iron mixed with clay.

    These feet were the nations of what became "Christendom" in Europe in the Middle Ages. Those same nations were used by the Catholic Church in their persecuting of the true believers in God. We had a union of church and state where the church would hold the trial, then hand the victim over to the state for punishment just as Jesus was tried by the Jews, the church of His day, and handed over to the Romans, the government at the time, for punishment.

- Revelation 13:11–17 American Protestants will act the same way the Catholics of the Dark Ages did by trying to control the government in the name of religion. The beast from the earth is the United States of America, which grew from nothing in a wilderness and has two lamblike horns, which are civil and religious freedom. For the prophecy to be complete, America has to speak to the people by passing national laws regarding worship. It will happen, and when it does, it is the signal for the end of the world.
- Revelation 7:2, 3 This prophecy will not be fulfilled until all who will accept the seal of God have done so.

Extra Thoughts:

Just as the seal of God is a three-step process of change the Lord makes in your life with the true Sabbath being an integral part, so the mark of the beast is a three-step counterfeit that is purely of human origin and, therefore, not of God. There is a false born-again experience with a false concept of the place for the law (both brought about by misquoting Paul) and a false Sabbath. Sunday will not be the mark of the beast until government enforces it. Since Sunday is not the true Sabbath that is found in the definition of righteousness (the law), it is therefore a self-righteous Sabbath. As such, it cannot be shared through the power of the Holy Spirit. It must be forced on people instead. Now is the time to take a full stand for the Lord.

Study #17 – Christian Standards
(This is a summarized version of all three Christian Standards studies in the Long Program.)

- John 15:5   Jesus will guide your whole life. In Him you can exist in this world of sin.
- Jeremiah 9:23, 24   The place in this world for you is nowhere near as important as your knowledge of God.
- 1 John 2:16   All sin can fit into these three categories.
- Psalm 101:3–7   Seek perfection in all areas of life so you can serve God. Let this principle apply to all you set before your mind's eye. This includes art, TV, music, etc. Also take stock of the activities of your life and ask prayerfully, "Is it really Christian?" Some things are just wrong like gangster rap or heavy metal music. Playing violent video games or watching Ultimate Fighting Champion would be other examples. Some things like card playing are so associated with gambling that they cannot be justified. Some activities don't seem to be wrong in and of themselves, yet they attract a wrong crowd, i.e., skateboarding, billiards. We must be careful how we indulge in them. Some activities may have nothing inherently wrong with them, such as stamp collecting, scuba diving, having a model train set in your basement, or playing or watching sports. However, so often people end up living for their hobbies. God has to be first.
- Philippians 4:8   This is not to say that everything in your life has to be directly religious. If there is something truly good in the world of art, science, literature, etc., God is there even if He isn't there by name.
- 2 Corinthians 6:14, 15   As a Christian, you are pledging brotherhood with all who believe the same. To do so with those who don't is not right. This bars you from secret societies such as lodges, college fraternities, and criminal organizations. It also bars you from political parties, labor unions, and activist groups.
- Colossians 3:16, 17   Spiritual music is better than worldly music.
- 1 Samuel 16:23   "Spiritual music" is not only music with Christian words but a style of music that is uplifting, ennobling, and inspiring with a calm rhythm and melody. Worldly music normally inspires a spirit of rebellion and self-exaltation.

> ## Words of Advice
>
> To know the studies does not necessarily mean memorizing them. That will come with practice. But memorizing scripture is a wonderful thing to do. Here is a suggested way to commit texts to memory for outreach. First, take each Bible chain and work on memorizing it as a whole. Start with only the book and chapter of each reference. You will be able to quickly look them up in any Bible then. For example, there are some great Sabbath verses in Genesis 2, Exodus 20, Nehemiah 9, Ezekiel 20, Mark 2, Acts 13, Revelation 1, and Isaiah 66. As you continue to give studies, focus next on the general gist of each verse. That way you can freely move from one translation to another and still remember the main point you need to share with each IAIN you meet. Then and only then, try book, chapter, and verse. Finally move on to exact wording in your favorite version of the Word. This will take years. Practice this by sharing and you will grow.

- 2 Samuel 6:14   This religious dancing is lost to history. It is not the same as the dancing of today, which is associated with bars and loose morals.
- Isaiah 3:16–26   Wearing jewelry is shown to be a thing of pride. Every possible kind is mentioned from head to foot. Also, being a slave of fashion is condemned. It is the responsibility of women not to present themselves to men as sex objects.
- Job 31:1   It is the equal responsibility of men not to treat women as sex objects.
- 1 Peter 3:3–6   Inner beauty is what our Father in heaven really wants us to have.
- Leviticus 19:28   Tattoos are banned completely. If you already have tattoos, this does not ban you from becoming a Christian; you just can't get any other tattoos.
- Job 40:6–14   The Lord invites Job to try to glorify himself. Part of this invitation is to do it by trying to make himself more beautiful than he is.
- 1 Timothy 6:16   Only God dwells in light. Jewels always consist of metal and rock that reflect light. Humans wearing these things are trying to create light of their own to dwell in.
- Exodus 33:1–6   When the Lord was about to lead His people into the earthly Promised Land, the call for revival included a "putting off of ornaments." As we are now so near the time when the Lord will open for us the true heavenly Promised Land, is it not logical we need to be ready in the same way?
- Deuteronomy 8:17, 18   The Lord controls your opportunities in life. What you have is part of His plan. The point to giving you wealth is so you can use it to further His cause in the world.
- Leviticus 27:30, 32   God claims ten percent of all we have as His own.

- 2 Samuel 24:24   The point to a sacrifice was not to kill something but to give something precious to God. True spirituality is in giving.
- Malachi 3:8–12   The only way we are allowed to test God is on the issue of money. Put Him first and He promises more than we can handle.
- Romans 12:1, 2, 21   By seeking the truth and separating ourselves from evil, we will be doing our part.
- John 17:15–17   Jesus wants to strengthen us from within, not shelter us. While it is important to guard ourselves, we must not make the mistake of being so focused on avoiding sin that we become fanatical or try to hide ourselves so much from the world that God can't use us to witness for Him.

Study #18 – The Importance of Health
Please see the identical study in the Long Program.

Study #19 – The Ten Tests of a True Prophet
Please see the identical study in the Long Program.

Study #20 – The Identifying Marks of the Remnant Church
Please see the identical study in the Long Program.

Study #21 – Baptism
Please see the identical study in the Long Program.

Special Thoughts on Public Evangelism

While working with Pastor Kelly Schultz planting the Canmore Church he once said to me that a sermon at an evangelistic meeting is basically a glorified Bible study. With that thought in mind, I'd like to share some ideas on public evangelism in case you are ever are in the position of leading out in a Revelation seminar. The following information will assist you in turning the Bible studies in this chapter into Revelation seminar sermons.

There is a basic structure that one needs to adhere to no matter how the exact details of the nightly plan go. You must interlock chains of thought on the following themes. (I don't take credit for this information. I read this in a textbook. I don't remember who said it first, but I have found it to be true in all my years attending and volunteering at Revelation seminars.)

Christ — Christ's Law — Christ's Sabbath — The Mark of the Beast

Usually the extras, such as the truths about the first and second deaths and Christian standards, go in between the Sabbath and the mark of the beast. The final topics of the Spirit of Prophecy, the remnant church, and the unpardonable sin wind up the meetings. The series runs in two cycles that come full circle. The first cycle explains what the truth is and builds the audience up until the Sabbath sermon. The second cycle then calls for a decision to take a stand for those truths, rising to a crescendo that ends with the mark of the beast. As the first cycle is in progress, just as in the study formats we've already discussed, there needs to be a description of the fact that there is such a thing as false and true Christianity. This idea needs to grow in the minds of the audience members until the Sabbath sermon where the difference is then made plain.

As Morris Venden said in the summary of his book *Uncommon Ground*, "The three angels of Revelation bear primarily a message *for* the everlasting gospel of Jesus Christ *not* against the beast" (p. 127). If you are going to use a study program like this as the basis for your sermons, keep Venden's thought in focus by always tying every topic to the cross and the born-again experience. Before you give any sermon calling Sunday the mark of the beast when it's enforced by law, present a sermon showing that the seventh day is the seal of God when received in true faith. Be sure to present these topics with the attitude that what mainstream Christianity is doing is not so much wrong as much as it's not right enough. You are calling your interest to a higher commitment than the commitment he or she has already made.

When you give the messages each night, don't just read from a script. Instead, talk to people—speak from the heart. If you've never written sermons before and want to use the contents of these studies as the basis for a Revelation seminar, an easy way to format a sermon is to simply start out with an anecdotal story that raises a question. The sermon itself is the answer to that question. As you share topics night after night, it is vital to not only talk about what the event is but also about how it applies to life. This is even more important in a public setting than in one-on-one outreach.

For a lot of people in today's online society the whole month-long process is seen as old fashioned, and they can't commit to that much time. Randy Barber has done seminars with as little as twelve meetings, and he's experiencing results. When I talked to retired evangelist Lester Carney, he told me he does one night on marriage and its importance, and he leaves out the sanctuary doctrine, which he chooses to cover in a follow-up Bible study class with the baptismal candidates.

Kelly Schultz also mentioned that the way a seminar develops has to follow a certain format. The first night sells the seminar and is designed to hook the interest of the audience. That night the speaker starts out in the mode of a teacher. Then he transitions into being a teacher/preacher over the next few nights. After that, he becomes more of a preacher than a teacher. And finally, he finishes the seminar as a preacher. Preaching

> **Words of Advice**
>
> Adrian, my friend and brother in Jesus, commented on the importance of learning the truth from someone who has already been through the salvation process. "You can't digest the book of Daniel by reading it yourself; you have to be shown."

is expounding on a topic in such a way as to convince people that it's true and ask the audience to take a stand for what they've heard. The only way you'll be successful is if you really believe in what you're saying with all your heart. That sincerity will be one of the biggest factors in convincing people to accept the truths presented.

Another important thing to consider in the order of presentation is when to share the truth about the beast and the antichrist. It really depends on who your audience is. If you are in a Protestant country where most of your audience will be filled with futurist believing evangelicals, then you need to bring the beast out early to shock your audience into understanding that the things they believe in are not true and to prepare them to accept what really is true. In a predominantly Catholic country this may simply be too much too soon, and you may want to discuss who the beast is closer to the time when you bring out what his mark is. Don't forget that in places that are not predominantly Christian, you have to spend more time on the first coming of Jesus and answering the first and second great questions of life than you would with those who have heard the stories of the Bible since childhood. Once you do invite the audience to come to church for their first Sabbath worship service, take Leo Schreven's advice into account. He said "give them a good old salvation sermon, give them a break."

The use of PowerPoint slides of charts, pictures, and/or Bible verses is very popular today. When you are speaking make sure the slides augment the speaker and not the other way around. It would be a good idea to have something written to hand out to the guests as they leave each meeting. This could include full transcripts of the sermon or simply the Bible verses you quoted for the night. I believe that Randy Barber gets results in twelve meetings, in part, because he uses a lot of handouts every night. Most of them further illustrate the points made in the presentation.

As important as the presentation is, so is what I call "seminar etiquette." Before the meetings, you must explain to the church members things like "don't get ahead of the speaker and give too much away to people who aren't ready for deeper truths"; "don't chase someone who walks out in a huff; he or she has made a choice"; and, of course, "don't talk about Ellen White until the speaker does." These and other topics about how to relate to potential interests should be covered. As mentioned in the "Psychology" chapter, you don't want to belittle a study with jokes or sidetrack it with conspiracy theories. This advice applies even more to a public setting.

As John the Baptist said, "He must increase, but I must decrease" (John 3:30). Jesus and the Bible are the stars of the show, not the speaker. Remember, most of all, David couldn't fight wearing Saul's armor. You have to do what works for you and follow as God leads you.

Chapter 7

Topics to Cover as the Need Arises

Here are some studies that can be inserted at any time into a study format and are meant to answer questions that may arise on side issues. If you are just beginning with IAIN, you may want to share only a verse or two from something here rather than going through a whole study on a topic. It may be all IAIN needs at the time.

I included one study that was especially meaningful to me. At the time I searched it out, Adrian and I had just got in touch again five months after the first study tapered off. He was then clearly being weighed down with a personal need of Christ, and the questions on his heart were more directly about his own relationship with Jesus. To help him, I prayerfully gleaned elements from a few studies such as "Michael the Archangel" and "Prophecies of Jesus," and then I put together "Jesus Is Because" just for him.

When the Lord brings someone into your life who is searching, He helps you to present what is right for that person. When the Lord gives you a perfect answer, keep a record of that answer. You will see many studies of your own come to fruition from that record.

The first three studies here are for helping to get the decision from IAIN when necessary. Louis and Carol Torres compiled them. The rest cover a wide variety of topics.

- Texts to Use in Getting the Decision
- Excuses Met With Scripture
- Difficult Texts
- The Search for Truth
- On Interpreting the Bible
- General Bible Helps
- Prayer
- Present Truth
- The 70-Weeks Prophecy in Detail
- How to Keep the Sabbath
- Baptized Into Christ, What About Doctrine?

Topics to Cover as the Need Arises

- Marriage and a Happy Home
- The Value of Work
- Michael the Archangel
- Bible Proof There's Life on Other Planets
- Prophecies of Jesus
- Jesus Is Because
- The Bible and Hot Topics (Abortion, Homosexuality, Remarriage, Euthanasia)
- The Manner of Christ's Return (No Secret Rapture)
- Events Surrounding the Millennium
- Speaking in Tongues
- The Role of Women/Women's Ordination
- Love Is the Fulfilling of the Law (The Ten Commandments and the Fruits of the Spirit)
- Gambling
- The Civil Laws
- Christians and Government
- The Case for Religious Freedom
- Once Saved Always Saved
- Challenges to the Truth About Death
- Stop Smoking Advice
- Bible Passages of Hope and Encouragement for Expectant Mothers

Texts to Use in Getting the Decision

- Immediate need—Psalm 18:44; 119:10; Hebrews 4:7; Acts 22:16
- Danger of putting off—2 Corinthians 6:2; Matthew 13:45, 46; 19:16–22; Luke 14:33
- To receive Christ—Revelation 3:20; Galatians 2:20; John 1:12, 13
- Pardon—Isaiah 1:18; 55:7; 1 John 1:9; Proverbs 28:13; Psalm 32:5
- Christ's keeping power—Jude 24; Hebrews 7:25; Philippians 1:6
- Victory—1 Corinthians 15:57
- Acceptance—John 5:24; 6:37; Isaiah 1:19, 20
- Last days light—Daniel 12:4; Proverbs 4:18
- Sabbath encouragement—Isaiah 56:1–6; 58:13, 14; Revelation 22:14

Excuses Met With Scripture

- Not good enough—2 Corinthians 8:12
- Gossip—John 17:14
- Can't leave old church—John 12:27, 42; Revelation 18:14 (This verse applies symbolically to IAIN's old church. The fruits of the Spirit that he once desired will be gone after now hearing

present truth.)
- Sabbath economic threat—Matthew 6:33; Psalm 37:3; Isaiah 65:13, 14; Deuteronomy 8:18
- Jobless—Matthew 16:25, 26; 2 Timothy 4:18
- Inconvenient—Matthew 16:24
- Sinned too much—1 Timothy 1:15
- Can't live it—1 Corinthians 10:13; 2 Corinthians 12:9; John 1:12

> ## Words of Advice
>
> This is from a pastor who chose to remain nameless for obvious reasons. On the subject of those who come into the church, get offended by someone or something, and later leave, he said, "It is a lot easier to give birth than to raise the dead." Too many people are worried about those who leave and are only planting doubt in the hearts of the rest of us when they repeat stories about our failure to keep everyone happy. Remember, the first test from the parable of the sower comes quite quickly.
>
> Another pastor observed that the real reason people leave is that they have some sort of control issue and are unwilling to die to themselves. Therefore, if you personally offended someone who is now no longer attending church, of course go and apologize, but if you did not offend them, do not feel one bit of guilt! There's a great book out by Mike Jones called *Sometimes I Don't Feel Like Praying*, which is designed for former Adventists. In it he doesn't say one word about how they can get justice for whatever wrong drove them away. His entire focus is on helping the wounded get back into a relationship with Jesus.

Difficult Texts

(The difficult text is listed first and then the "go to" text is listed second which helps to clarify the first text.)

- Romans 10:4   1 Peter 1:9 (The word "end" means "goal.")
- 1 Timothy 4:1–5   Genesis 1:29; Leviticus 11 (Does this justify eating pork? No. The verse means, "If you say grace before your meal, and the Bible says what you are eating is OK, then you can eat it." Paul's Bible was the Old Testament.)
- Colossians 2:14–17   Leviticus 23 (The fourth commandment is *the* Sabbath—Leviticus 23:3. The rest of the chapter lists each day as *a* Sabbath. They are the Sabbath *days*.)
- Matthew 24:40, 41   Jeremiah 6:11 (The word "taken" means "killed.")
- Deuteronomy 12:15   Deuteronomy 15:21, 22 (These verses are not referring to clean and unclean foods, but clean and unclean people.)
- Romans 14:1-3   1 Corinthians 8 (This is not talking about vegetarians; the whole issue was about eating meat offered to idols.)

Topics to Cover as the Need Arises

The Search for Truth

- There are three definitions of truth: Jesus, John 14:6; the Bible, John 17:17; and the Ten Commandments, Psalm 119:142.
- They are related: the Bible leads us to Jesus, John 5:39; Jesus showed us what the law is all about, Matthew 5:17; the Bible and the Ten Commandments show us what is right, Isaiah 8:20.
- Salvation and truth are spoken of separately but are equal, 1 Timothy 2:3, 4. Compared to this, Titus 2:13, 14 mentions Jesus' redemption and that He makes us into truly good people.
- There is an overall definition of sin in Romans 3:23. It can be further broken down to match point-for-point the three definitions of truth: not having faith, Romans 14:23; not living up to all that is revealed to you (thus Bible study is to be a personal experience), James 4:17; and violating the Ten Commandments, 1 John 3:4.
- The enemy of souls has developed three layers of counterfeits designed to hide the truth from us. They are false Christs, Matthew 24:24; scoffers, who either put the Bible down completely or misinterpret it, 2 Peter 1:3; 3:16, 17 and 2 Timothy 4:3; or false concepts regarding the law, Mark 7:9.
- What about the Holy Spirit who guides us into all truth? He glorifies the Son, John 16:13   15; He inspired the Bible writers, 2 Peter 1:20, 21; and you must obey in order to receive Him, Acts 5:32.
- Remember, love rejoices in the truth, 1 Corinthians 13:6. To really understand God and His great love, you need all the truth.

Words of Advice

As an example of adaptability, you could use the "Search For Truth" study in three different ways by changing how you conclude it. It could be used as a "hook" study with an invitation like this: "IAIN, would you like to know more of what the truth is? Why don't we make an appointment to study together again. There are some wonderful things from God's Word that I'd love to share with you."

You could also use it in the middle of a study program as a means to bridge into your commitment studies. In particular, running this study just after a Ten Commandments topic and just before covering the Sabbath would require an ending like this: "You see, IAIN, for a church to have all the truth, it must have Jesus, the Bible, and all ten of the commandments. If it only has nine of them, it is still falling short of God's glory."

Finally, you could use it if IAIN has been convicted but loves his sins and is now arguing some aspect of truth to the point that he will likely stop studying with you soon. You would then say, "I must clearly warn you that Proverbs 8:36 applies to any aspect of the truth. All who hate Jesus, the Bible, or any of the ten commandments love death. Therefore, those people will not be in heaven."

On Interpreting the Bible
- John 7:18; 5:41–44; Proverbs 3:5; 4:18; Matthew 7:29; and Acts 17:11 speak to the authority of the Bible and will answer someone who says, "That's just your interpretation."

General Bible Helps
- When tempted—Psalm 91
- Facing a crisis—Psalm 46
- Discouraged—Psalm 23
- God's power—Psalm 103, 104
- Poor finances—Psalm 37
- Lonely or fearful—Psalm 27
- Anxious for loved ones—Psalm 107
- Planning a budget—Luke 19
- How to live with others—Romans 12
- Sick or in pain—Psalm 91
- Weary—Matthew 11:28–30
- Things going wrong—2 Thessalonians 3
- Friends desert you—1 Corinthians 13
- Need inner peace—John 14
- Trust in God—Hebrews 11
- Severe losses—Romans 8
- Hard struggle—the book of Ephesians
- Sin and confession—1 John 1; John 3:1–21
- Fear of death—John 11; 17; 20; 2 Corinthians 4:5
- God cares for you—Luke 12:27–31

Prayer
- Matthew 6:6–9; 7:7–11   Prayer is an experience where you pour out your heart to the Father and ask for Him for help.
- John 14:13–15   Pray in Jesus' name.
- James 1:6   You need to believe He will answer.
- James 4:3   If we are asking for the wrong reason, He will hold back. Obedience is a condition of answered prayer.
- 2 Corinthians 12:7–9   Sometimes the answer is no.

> **Words of Advice**
>
> "When you do get the decision, seal that decision with prayer," said Louis Torres.

Topics to Cover as the Need Arises

- Mark 5:25–34 Sometimes we have to wait for the answer because the timing is not right. Sometimes His purpose cannot be discerned, but He always answers us.
- 1 Timothy 6:6–12 We should take this principle into account.
- Philippians 4:6, 7 We need to trust and be thankful.
- Matthew 6:33 With our will in tune with the Lord's will, everything we really need will be added to us. This is His promise.
- Philippians 3:15 If your prayers are not being answered in the way you think they should be, the Lord may be trying to get you to look at some aspect of your own life first.
- James 5:13–18 God will work more for those who ask more.
- Luke 18:1–8 Being persistent is the key to answered prayer.
- 1 Thessalonians 5:16–23 Some general advice about prayer.

Extra Thoughts:

Joseph's story of going from slavery to being prime minister of Egypt is an example of a prayer that may have seemed like the answer was "no" at first, but in fact was a gradually unfolding "yes."

We should also recognize that we do not need to assume certain positions in order to pray. Nehemiah offered a silent prayer before asking the emperor for something, and the disciples sat and prayed together as the Holy Spirit descended upon them. These are just two examples of times of prayer and answered prayers.

Present Truth

- Titus 2:11 All people throughout history have been given the opportunity to accept the gift of salvation. How can this be so?
- Romans 3:20, 21 The plan of salvation was first mentioned in the Old Testament. It was "witnessed" throughout history, not just from Jesus' day forward.
- Romans 9:4, 30–32 Just because the Lord raised up a set of people and gave them His plan did not make them superior. It was only those who complied with the plan in faith who were counted worthy.
- Acts 4:10–12 The whole point of the development of Israel was so that God could bring salvation into the world through Jesus. When He came, the majority of those who claimed to be looking for Him rejected Him. This will repeat itself today as the next text shows.
- Matthew 7:21–23 The many are the majority in the end time. These are people who felt completely safe inside the church but weren't really true in faith. They accepted Jesus by name, but used that name as a good luck charm.
- Matthew 25:31–46 This parable makes no mention of whether or not people accepted Jesus by name. It shows those who were kind and good will be saved and those who are not will be judged.
- Acts 17:30 Those who do not know that what they are doing is wrong will not be held

accountable for it. Each person is given enough truth in life so God can be fair in the judgment. The next three texts serve as examples of this.

> ## Words of Advice
> Something else you may find very helpful is to do your personal outreach work in tandem with a friend who has the spiritual gifts of encouragement and hospitality. My wife and I are like that. Whenever I've come on strong, speaking the truth a little too clearly and the person is offended, it's consistently been her loving, accepting words that have brought that person back.

- Genesis 12:3   Those who respected Abraham did so in part because of his commitment to God. Those who rejected him did so for the same reason. Thus one man could be used to test the sincerity of those around him.
- Matthew 8:5-12   This is an example of one man who came from outside God's people but showed true faith worthy of heaven. Notice what Jesus said about others like him.
- Matthew 10:42   This is another verse like God's promise to Abraham. Anyone who recognizes one of God's people as good recognizes God Himself.
- Romans 2:12-15   The definitive text on those outside God's people. Those who had a clear conscience will be saved. They did not know the religious aspects of serving Him, but they did know the practical ones.
- John 3:18-21   Jesus is the only way for humanity to be saved. But note that those who truly did good while not knowing Him by name, did it because He was working in their lives. They knew Him by His character, which is what the word "name" symbolizes. An example of this is Cornelius in Acts 10.
- 1 Peter 4:17, 18   Of those outside His people, there will not be many who are saved.
- Hebrews 6:1   Many Christian preachers today quote the verses in the Bible that say you need to accept Jesus by name and assume that means all those who have called Him by name will be saved and all those who don't will not. However, truth is a progressive thing.
- 2 Thessalonians 2:10-12   It is not those who have truth, it is those who LOVE truth who will be saved. It can be said that what direction you are heading in is more important than where you are on the scale of truth. Reread John 3:18-21. When God shines more truth into His people, if they are believers in name only, they will resist the new light. This explains how and why the "many" reject Him.
- 2 Thessalonians 1:8   Two kinds of people are shown among the lost here. Those with no knowledge of God (outside His realm) and those who do not obey the gospel (inside His realm).

Extra Thoughts:

This concept applies both on group and individual levels. A person in sin needs to know what Jesus did on the cross to save him. Then that person needs to know how to live properly, which is the rest of the truth. Someone in the church who is cherishing an error and refuses to give it up after having been enlightened, is as guilty as the vilest sinner.

The 70-Weeks Prophecy in Detail

Read Daniel 9:24–27 and cross-reference the following texts to clarify what the 70-weeks prophecy means.

- Seventy weeks—Ezekiel 4:6 clarifies that this represents 490 years.
- Thy people/city—Matthew 18:21, 22 states that this was the last chance for the Jews.
- Finish the transgression—Romans 5:18, 19 says that Jesus came to heal Adam's sin.
- Make an end of sins—Acts 3:26 records that Jesus' ministry was to show the whole truth to His people.
- Reconciliation/iniquity—Isaiah 53:5 indicates that the cross gives us forgiveness.
- Everlasting righteousness—Romans 8:2–5 says that the power of God gives us the ability to obey.
- Seal up vision/prophecy—Mark 1:14, 15 records Jesus's words that declare the prophecy to be now coming true .
- Anoint Most Holy—John 14:2, 3 shows us that Jesus is in the heavenly sanctuary.

Next, we have the specific prediction for the timing of the Lord's coming. On the command to restore Jerusalem unto the Messiah, three commands were given (Ezra 6:14; 7:7–10, 11–26). The last was the most complete with a command to restore the city. In effect it began in the fall of 457 BC. Adding the 69 weeks, or 483 years, on a calculator (negative 457 plus 483) gives you AD 26 for the start of Jesus' ministry. However, in the change from BC to AD there was no year zero, so the total is revised to AD 27. Luke 3:1 gives the year of Jesus' baptism. The fifteenth year of Tiberius was AD 27. A common error holds that "after" in verse 26 means the seventieth week is not part of the rest of the prophecy. This is incorrect. Verse 25 gives the timing of His arrival and the *beginning* of His ministry. This is at the end of, or "after," the sixty-nine weeks.

His ministry is a fulfillment of verse 27 in His "confirming the covenant with many for one week." Jesus preached, taught, and healed for three and a half years. It was the "middle of the week" when He was "cut off" on the cross. At this time the sacrificial system "ceased" because it lost its meaning, as shown in Matthew 27:50, 51; Ephesians 2:11–18; and Colossians 2:13, 14.

Then in Acts 1:8 Jesus gave the disciples the order to preach the gospel in Jerusalem, Judea, Samaria, and then the whole world. Acts 7:59, 60 gives the event that typified the Jews final rejection of their long hoped for Messiah, the stoning of Stephen. Obviously this was in AD 34. Acts 8:1 shows that the gospel was still only being proclaimed in Jerusalem when those rejecters drove the Christians around Judea and

Samaria. Jesus' appearance to Saul, at which time He called him to his mission (Acts 9:10, 11), combined with the Holy Spirit's outpouring on the Gentiles shows that the transition to preaching to all the world was now underway (Acts 11:18).

Now let's turn to Daniel 9:25 and 10:21. Who is the Prince to come? The answer is Jesus. Who then are the people who destroy the city? Here are two possibilities. See Psalm 17:13 and Jeremiah 29:17–19. When God's people fail Him, He brings judgment upon them in the form of handing them over to their enemies. The Roman soldiers who destroyed the temple in AD 70 can, therefore, be referred to here as the "people of the Prince to come" (Daniel 9:26). An alternate interpretation is to hold that the Jews are the people mentioned here, and by their rejection of Christ, they brought upon themselves the temple's destruction in the same event. His blood was literally on their children in fulfillment of their own words in Matthew 27:25. Either way this prophecy was fulfilled in AD 70 and has nothing to do with one single antichrist setting up a new literal temple in Jerusalem in the last seven years of earth's history.

What about the references to the destruction of the sanctuary and the desolations being poured out? The sacrifices now meaningless, the earthly sanctuary was no longer needed, hence He made it "desolate" (Matt. 23:38). In AD 70 Titus came and destroyed Jerusalem and the temple. Jesus knew of its impending doom as shown in Luke 13:34, 35; 21:5, 6, 20 and Matthew 24:1, 2. Matthew 24:20 shows that He expected some of His hearers to be alive at the time of Jerusalem's destruction.

In many places the New Testament refers to issues over old covenant practices and the high regard the disciples held for the temple. Therefore, they obviously didn't understand the significance of the change from the old to the new covenant right away and needed time to fully adjust to the new truth they were living under. Such is the greatness of God's mercy! He delayed destroying the temple until enough people understood that it was not needed. As Daniel 9:27 puts it "even until the consummation, and that determined shall be poured upon the desolate." The consummation was a fulfillment of Matthew 24:14 where the gospel was preached in all the known world. What was determined was destruction. It was poured out on a temple that was spiritually desolate and had been since the veil was ripped in two.

There is no evidence here to support any sort of "gap theory" leaving the seventieth week for today's Jews. Christ preached to them during His ministry for three and a half years and then through His disciples in Jerusalem for another three and a half years. This also explains why the prophecy gives an exact date for the Messiah and not for the destruction. That the prophecy ends in such an open-ended fashion should be enough to defeat any anti-Semitism that might be thought to exist in New Testament Christianity. Modern political Israel is meaningless from a prophetic standpoint as the Christian church replaced the Jews as God's chosen people in AD 34. But although the Jews rejected Him, there is no prophecy in the Bible that says they were permanently cast off either. Any Jew today who accepts Christ can be saved.

How to Keep the Sabbath

- Leviticus 19:30   Holy things must be treated holy.

Topics to Cover as the Need Arises

- Leviticus 23:32   Sundown to sundown is Bible time.
- Luke 4:16   Reading the Word is important.
- Hebrews 4:11   It takes an effort to be ready for the experience. This means physical and mental preparation.
- Mark 15:42   Friday is preparation day. This is the time to get affairs settled and extra work done so you can relax on the Sabbath.
- Exodus 20:8–11   The fourth commandment says do no work, which means paid labor and most of the regular duties of life. It is also inappropriate to get others to do your work for you.
- Exodus 16:23   An example of this is cooking.
- Mark 2:23–28   The disciples were not cooking. The principle here is that when you focus on Jesus, He will guide you through the dos and don'ts of Sabbathkeeping.
- Nehemiah 13:15–22   Make your heart and your home a fortress.
- Joshua 6:15, 16   It's possible the battle of Jericho was fought on a Sabbath. Spiritual warfare of today equals missionary outreach work.
- Luke 6:8–10   Acts of goodness and mercy are in keeping with the essence of His holy day.
- Matthew 12:9–13   Dealing with emergency situations that are beyond your control does not violate the Sabbath's holiness. As Jesus said here, it is lawful to do good on the Sabbath.
- Isaiah 58:13   Make the Sabbath a delight, a happy occasion. Not doing your own pleasure includes things that might not be work but aren't really spiritual, such as working on hobbies.
- 1 John 5:3   Don't let yourself be burdened by keeping His law.

Baptized Into Christ, What About Doctrine?

- 1 Thessalonians 2:4, 5, 9–13   Not everything comes straight from God. He will often give a message to one of his followers to then give it to the larger body of believers.
- 1 Timothy 2:3, 4   To be saved and to know truth are equal.
- John 14:23   Jesus' words here apply to all His teachings.
- 2 Timothy 3:15–17   The whole Bible is the word of God.
- Hebrews 6:1–3   The basics of faith are only a start.
- Acts 10:34, 35   There are two conditions to salvation.
- James 1:22–25; 2:17   Take what you learn and let it change your life. Prove your faith.
- Acts 5:32   To receive the Holy Spirit, you must be obedient.
- 2 John 9   Take any subject and ask, "Is this a doctrine of Christ?"
- Acts 20:24–27   A minister's duty is to declare the whole truth.
- Matthew 28:19, 20   The command to reach the world includes a command to teach "them to observe all things," therefore all true doctrine.
- 1 Thessalonians 5:21   Test all, but keep what's true.
- 2 Timothy 4:2–4   Many Christians are against the pluralism, rationalism, and relativism in

the outside world. However, when it comes to differing doctrinal points in various churches, the same person says, "It doesn't matter; you only need Jesus." That amounts to a form of pluralism inside the church.

Extra Thoughts:

Don't use Jesus to say doctrine doesn't count.

> ## Words of Advice
> To those who say "I'm baptized into Christ, not doctrine," you can respond with 1 John 3:7–10, 24 and inform the person that baptism into false doctrine is not true baptism into Christ.

Marriage and a Happy Home

- Genesis 1:26–28   Both male and female were made by the Lord to reflect His image.
- Genesis 2:18–24   The Lord knew Adam's need for a companion, but He waited to create her until Adam felt that need himself. Eve was a part of Adam. From "his side," shows she is equal to him.
- Matthew 19:3–6   Marriage is for life. For a man to be grown up, he must assume responsibility for his own home. That they are joined by God means there is to be harmony and unity in the home.
- Ephesians 5:25–31   As Jesus fully committed Himself to our salvation no matter what, so a husband is to love his wife the same way.
- Ephesians 5:24, 33   The wife is to submit to her husband as the church obeys the Lord. ("Reverence" is a very strong word; submitting means obedience.)
- 1 Peter 3:6, 7   The same point is made here.
- Colossians 3:18, 19   A wife must choose to submit. The man is not the boss; he is the leader. There is a difference.
- 1 Peter 3:1, 2   The wife here in this verse is married to an unbeliever, and submission is required as a witness to her husband even though his morals are not up to the higher standards of the Bible. How much more, therefore, should believing women submit who have believing husbands. In other words, it is not up to the wife to say, "My husband has to earn my submission." She needs to submit whether she feels he deserves to be submitted to or not.
- Genesis 21:12   The Lord's words to Abraham show that just because women are in submission to men does not mean the man is always right. A righteous man will accept good advice.
- Proverbs 18:22   A righteous man is given a wife as a gift.
- 1 Corinthians 13:4–7   These are descriptions of love. This is how a man is to love his wife.

- 1 Corinthians 7:3–5   Sexual privileges are part of the relationship and to be respected. Each is to meet the needs of the other.

Extra Thoughts:

The issue of submission on the part of the wife may be better understood with the Bible record of God telling Adam not to eat of the tree. We are left to assume then that God made it Adam's duty to tell Eve. The Lord will work within the system He ordained, won't He? Therefore, when the husband has seen God's will for the family, his job is not to command or demand her submission but to win it diplomatically as the leader. The wife's call to obedience through God working in her husband's life is, therefore, an act of faith in God. Yes, according to the prophecy in Genesis 3:16 many men have gone too far with the authority God gave them and women have suffered over the ages for it. This, however, does not negate the original plan.

Psalm 127 and 128 show that when the Lord is the center of the marriage it will work. With God's love at the center, husband and wife will be in harmony in their respective roles.

There is also no place in the Bible that says you have to be married to serve God. In fact, Paul says single people can serve Him because they are focused totally on Him (1 Cor. 7:32).

The Value of Work

- Genesis 3:17–19   Work was made hard because of sin. We need to occupy our minds to avoid temptation. Notice it is for our benefit.
- Ecclesiastes 9:10   Try your best at whatever you do.
- Romans 12:11   The Lord gives us work to do; we are working for Him.
- 2 Corinthians 4:17, 18   All suffering, including hard work, is covered here. It teaches us the lessons we need to learn in order to prepare for heaven.
- 1 Timothy 5:8   It is part of the practical aspect of religion. Being spiritual does not just mean sitting around and reading all day.
- 1 Timothy 6:10   Greed is a sin. Don't live for money.
- Ecclesiastes 4:6   Learn to be satisfied with what you have.
- Colossians 3:1, 2   We are to live for Jesus, not our jobs.
- Philippians 4:11–13   Through all our ups and downs, including in our careers, we are to look to Him. If we do, we'll have all we need.
- Exodus 20:8–11   The fourth commandment says that we are to rest on the seventh day and work the other six. This is the true Christian lifestyle. In our modern day most people only work five days a week. The verse says "all your work." Therefore the sixth day can be used for household chores or errands.
- Hebrews 4:4, 5, 10, 11   Again, this is to be our life pattern. We are to make an effort to be part of it.
- Matthew 6:19–34   Put God first and you'll have what you need.

Michael the Archangel

- Revelation 12:7   Michael is another name for Jesus.
- Exodus 3:2, 5, 6; Judges 2:1–4; 13:20–22; Zechariah 3:1, 2   It was an angel who spoke with Moses, yet He is clearly God. Samson's parents obviously met more than a regular angel. The rest of this final passage has the angel causing the high priest's iniquity to pass away. Only Jesus could do that.
- Joshua 5:15   Also, the same being is Commander of the Lord's host. Again, He is holy; therefore, He is no ordinary angel.
- Isaiah 59:1, 2; 1 Corinthians 15:25, 28   Since we in our sins cannot see God, it was the Son and not the Father who interacted with man in the Old Testament. John 3:16 was fulfilled the same day Adam and Eve sinned and Jesus was sent to the garden to deal with them after the fall.
- Daniel 10:13, 21   The word in verse 13 for "chief princes" actually refers to the Trinity. Michael is a member of the Trinity!
- Daniel 12:1   Again, this describes a position only the Son could have. Notice, He rules over the "children of thy people." Daniel's people were the Jews. The "children" therefore are Christians. Therefore, Jesus is Michael.
- 1 Thessalonians 4:16; John 5:28, 29   Take these texts together and you find that Jesus is the Archangel. The Lord descends, and it is His voice, which is the voice of the Archangel, that wakes the dead.

Extra Thoughts:

More than 300 names in Scripture are attributed to our Lord and Savior, some are titles, others are descriptions. None of them take away from His divinity. This includes the title of Michael.

Words of Advice

The "Michael the Archangel" study is best given with a New King James Bible. The translators of that Bible got something right that others have missed. Every time you see "Angel of the Lord" with that all-important capital "A" in the Old Testament of a NKJV Bible, that's Christ before He took on human form.

Bible Proof There's Life on Other Planets

The following is designed to challenge and encourage critical thinking. For many centuries Western civilization operated under the medieval worldview that there is a mysterious world above called heaven and another below called hell. As science developed, we now know we are a small part of a vast

Topics to Cover as the Need Arises

universe. Is this somehow incompatible with the Bible?

- Isaiah 40:22   The Bible teaches us that the earth is round. This verse also comments on what scientists know to be true today, that the universe is expanding. The Lord is responsible for this.
- Job 26:7   God's power is what keeps the earth in motion.
- Job 38:31, 32   Today we observe through telescopes that the Pleiades are a group of stars growing closer together, while the ones in Orion's belt are hurtling away from each other. Arcturus is said to be a bear with cubs. Could these cubs be planets?
- Isaiah 50:3   Astronomers have now discovered something they call "dark energy" in the universe. This verse shows that God was the One who created it along with everything else we see.
- Hebrews 1:1–3, 10; Isaiah 40:25, 26; Genesis 1:1, 2   The Father, Son, and Holy Spirit were involved in creating the physical realm. Notice the reference in Hebrews uses the word "worlds" in the King James Version. The New International Version uses the word "universe."
- Job 38:4–7   The creation story in Genesis 1 seems to suggest an earth-centered view. It is simply told from the point of reference of someone standing on this new planet. Whereas this text gives the point of view from an angel watching in heaven.
- Genesis 1:1, 17   The Lord set the stars in our sky. That does not necessarily mean He created the whole rest of the universe on day four. Verse one gives us an overview of the whole process, and mentions the heavens as being separately created from the earth, so they likely already existed. The creation story in Genesis 1 is the story of the creation of this solar system. It exists for the earth's benefit and, therefore, our benefit.
- Genesis 2:1, 2   Here is a declaration that Creation is finished. In other words, earth is the last planet He made. He made the seventh day holy as a memorial of Creation.
- Nehemiah 9:6   A host is a large group. The host of heaven worships God. These are beings, not inanimate objects. Elsewhere the Bible says, He is the Lord of "hosts."
- Isaiah 40:15   This is a comparison of the various cultures of earth to the rest of the universe.
- Job 1:6, 7   A sort of heavenly convention is discussed. Satan comes as earth's representative because he stole this planet from Adam and Eve (see Gen. 3:1–7).
- Luke 3:38   Adam is a son of God. The other sons of God at this convention are the Adam-type beings, the leaders, of the other planets.
- Isaiah 59:1, 2; Hebrews 10:12   We are isolated here because of sin. Jesus had to die here, so there is no other world in rebellion. Therefore, all the rest of creation is at peace with and in complete submission to God.
- 1 Corinthians 4:9; Ephesians 3:10   Good and evil are each active here, and the universe is watching to see who is really right.
- Luke 15:4–7   This parable applies to our whole earth and each person in it. Christ came to

save the world, and He wants to save you. The whole conflict between good and evil is played out in your own life (see Rom. 6:23; 5:6–12,17–19).
- Isaiah 66:22, 23   Here is a promise for all those who receive Jesus' victory on the cross.

Extra Thoughts:

Be careful how you present this study as it is very closely counterfeited within Mormonism. Be sure to bend over backward to depict Jesus as divine and not a space alien.

Prophecies Of Jesus

The Old Testament prophecy is given alongside its New Testament fulfillment.
- Birthplace—Micah 5:2; Matthew 2:1
- Virgin birth—Isaiah 7:14; Matthew 1:18–23
- Light bearer—Isaiah 9:1, 2; Matthew 4:12–16
- His work—Isaiah 61:1–3; Luke 4:16–21
- Healer—Isaiah 53:4; Matthew 8:16, 17
- Triumphant entry—Zechariah 9:9; Matthew 21:1–11
- Silence—Isaiah 53:7; Matthew 27:12–14
- Death—Zechariah 12:10; John 19:34
- Died beside criminals—Isaiah 53:12; Mark 15:27, 28
- His garments—Psalm 22:18; John 19:23, 24
- He rose again—Psalm 16:10 and Isaiah 53; Acts 2:30, 31 and Psalm 22

Words of Advice

The training seminars for high-pressure sales (say for instance, a door-to-door vacuum salesperson) teach that a good salesperson should try four times before accepting an answer of "no." For most people, this is too much, and they find salespeople to be rather annoying.

Notice how the Lord has only three messages of warning for the end-time. If you are in a situation where he has started to study with you and for no explainable reason has suddenly lost interest, I suggest you only try three times to get things going again with IAIN. After that let him go so you do not become annoying. Pray and wait for him to come back to you.

Jesus Is Because

As the Son of God, Jesus was the one who interacted with humanity before He took on human form. Man was cut off from the Father by sin (Isa. 59:1, 2); therefore, the stories in the Old Testament of God appearing to people are about Jesus. Here are some examples: Moses and the burning bush (Exod. 3:2–6, 13, 14) and Samson's parents (Judges 13:3, 8–10,15–22). In the book of Daniel, He is called "Michael, one of the chief princes"—the word for "chief princes" is the word for the Trinity (Dan. 10:12–14).

He spoke through His prophets ahead of time, telling when He would come and what He would do. If they weren't already convinced by His goodness and the miracles He performed, they could look to the prophecies He fulfilled, many of which were about what others would do to Him. A mere man could not control these. Here are a few: Numbered with the transgressors (Isa. 53:9, 12; Luke 23:39–42); thirty pieces of silver; not one bone from His body was broken and His side was pierced (Zech. 11:10-18;Ps. 34:20; Matt 26:14-16).

Those who did see Him assure us their testimony is true (John 1:1–4; 1 John 1:1–4; Luke 9:28–36; 2 Peter 1:16–19; Acts 26:12–23).

He changes the life of anyone who surrenders to Him. There is a joy and a lifting of your burden of guilt that you cannot fully describe. All you know is that you are new inside when you accept God's free gift of salvation (Ps. 51:10; John 3:3–8; Gal. 2:20; Rom. 5:6–11; John 1:12; Rom. 12:2).

The question Jesus asked His disciples, He asks each of us, "Who do you say that I am?" (Matt. 16:13–17). Remember, the Lord will reveal Himself to you. Just ask Him, and somehow you'll see and understand.

The Bible and Hot Topics

Proverbs 13:10 must be kept in mind in each of these studies. So many people on both sides of these issues are only proceeding from a human desire to be right. When this happens, there is no humble spirit of submission to God and His Word, and therefore, the person cannot be reasoned with. Even if that person is right, that rightness is tainted by human pride and, therefore, sin.

In any study on these topics, John 3:3 and 4:24 must be taken into account. Jesus was trying to reach out to two different unconverted people, one was inside the faith and another was without. They both showed their worldliness by trying to sidetrack the conversation. When a spiritual conversation gets sidetracked onto one of these hot topics, it's a diversionary tactic. Only when a heart is truly submitted to God can any truth be understood no matter how controversial. The first question to be settled then is "have you been born again?"

Abortion
- Job 31:15   God made us right in the womb. Life, therefore, begins there.
- Jeremiah 1:5   The Lord has a purpose for us from the womb.
- Exodus 20:13   The sixth commandment applies.
- Psalm 51:5   Often the reason given in support of abortion is to cover the guilt of the unborn child's parents for the circumstances the child is being born under, such as with teenage

pregnancy. All human beings are born out of the sin of Adam and Eve. Take all these verses along with verses that show God's love for sinners such as John 3:16, and you will see that though the baby may be born under the most terrible of circumstances, such as rape or incest, that's not the baby's fault.

Divorce and Remarriage
- Exodus 20:14   The seventh commandment forbids committing adultery.
- Matthew 5:27–32; 19:3–9   Jesus upholds marriage, and shows its depth. We must commit to our spouse with all our heart.
- Romans 7:2, 3   Marriage is for life. Obviously death ends the commitment.
- John 4:16–18; 8:3, 4, 10, 11   These are two examples of His compassion to those who failed to live up to this ideal. The one was "caught" in adultery, meaning if we have sinned and now realize it we can be restored from here on. However, we must not sin again.
- 1 Corinthians 7:10, 11   This answers the question "what if my spouse commits some horrible sin like abuse? Though it is not adultery, do I still have to stay married?" The answer is yes. However, there is an allowance for separation if necessary as Matthew 10:23 says to flee persecution. The ultimate goal must be reconciliation. If not, because there has been no adultery, there is no allowance for remarriage.
- 1 Corinthians 7:12–15   These are the instructions for mixed faith marriages. Remarriage would be possible here for a believer who has been left, but again reconciliation is preferable.

Capital Punishment
- Genesis 9:6   It was instituted right after the flood that a murderer should also die.
- Romans 13:1–5   Human government is God's appointed agency for carrying out justice in the world.
- Luke 23:42   The thief on the cross recognized the justice of his penalty. This was part of his true repentance, and because of this, Jesus could forgive him. If a condemned criminal is truly repentant, there can still be hope for heaven.
- 2 Samuel 18:33   King David shows his love for a son who rebelled against him and suffered loss of life in the process. The government must carry out justice with a spirit of benevolence.
- Proverbs 17:5   It is wrong to take pleasure at another's misfortune.

Euthanasia
- Exodus 20:13   The sixth commandment applies here also. It is still murder.
- Philippians 2:5–8; 1:23, 24   In the case of euthanasia, however, the victim may be the one desiring death to avoid living life handicapped. To want to die is suicide, which is wrong. This does not mean that every single thing modern medicine can do is okay either. The phrase "do

not resuscitate" has become popular and is acceptable as resuscitation would be carrying the life process beyond that which is natural. We are not to seek death, but we are to submit to it when it does come.

- 1 Thessalonians 4:13–18   With Jesus we have hope that goes beyond the grave.

Homosexuality

- Romans 1:18–22, 26–28   This statement is often misunderstood. The author is talking on a society-wide basis. The presence of homosexuality in a society indicates an extreme moral decline.
- Leviticus 18:22; Genesis 19:1, 2, 4–7, 11–13, 24   It is a serious sin that calls down judgment.
- Romans 3:23; 5:8   Jesus died for all sinners.
- Galatians 2:20   New life is available from Him.
- Philippians 4:13   Even this sin can be overcome.
- 1 Corinthians 5:9–12   For so long in society there was a stigma associated with immoral behavior. That has now been removed under the banner of tolerance, diversity, and acceptance. This verse guides us in how to treat the subject. Certain actions are not acceptable for Christians. However, in attempting to reach out to others, we need to manifest the same kind of patience Jesus did with tax collectors and prostitutes. We need to avoid the mistaken attempt at purity the religious leaders of the day exercised when they wanted to isolate themselves.
- John 3:17   Jesus came not to judge the world but to save it. The story of Lot shows the attitude we need to take toward open sins like those discussed here. When the men of Sodom wanted to rape the angels in Genesis 19:5–7, he implored them not to bring judgment on themselves. His highest concern was for their welfare, but this was expressed in a caring way that did not compromise the truth that their behavior was evil.

Words of Advice

The one hot topic not being dealt with here is suicide. Saul and Samson provide Bible examples. While the narratives suggest Saul is lost but Samson will be saved, they don't actually state these as facts. Therefore if IAIN lost a friend or relative to suicide, simply tell her we can't say for sure what will happen. We have to let God be the judge.

The Manner of Christ's Return (No Secret Rapture)

The devil's lies will be subtle and especially aimed at Christians as Christ's return approaches. The importance of the manner of Christ's coming is focused on here because of a falsehood running rampant today. It is called the secret rapture.

Matthew 24:26 refutes this theory. The lightning of verse 27 shows that His coming will be very visible and is not something that can be kept secret. Many people use Mathew 24:40, 41 to support their claim of a secret rapture, but the one "taken" is the one killed (see Luke 17:27).

A text that is often misquoted is the "thief in the night" reference in 2 Peter 3:10. People are reading only half the verse to get this teaching. The rest of the verse is quite noisy (see also 1 Thess. 5:4–6)! The point of the thief analogy is to illustrate the surprise of His coming and not the manner. The thief only comes for those who are not ready.

The second coming will also be audible and visual (see Rev. 1:7; 1 Thess. 4:16, 17). This text also proves that the righteous living do not go to heaven ahead of the righteous dead, as they are raised first.

Events Surrounding the Millennium
- Daniel 12:1; Amos 5:18–20   Just before, there will be a great time of trouble.
- Psalm 50:16; Isaiah 65:12; Hosea 8:7; Galatians 6:7–9   Those who think they are God's people but are not really living the truth will be lost.
- Isaiah 65:13, 14; 25:8, 9; Matthew 5:11, 12; Revelation 3:21   Those who have been true to Him must wait until He comes again.
- Amos 8:9; Zechariah 14:7   The day of Jesus' coming, which no one knows (Mark 13:32), is marked by a supernatural phenomenon. These two texts describe the supernatural movement of the sun from each side of our planet.
- 1 Corinthians 15:23, 24; 2 Timothy 4:1   These are two key texts that line up what happens before and after the millennium. His appearing is the second coming, which starts this time period. His kingdom comes at the millennium's end.

The following Bible references speak to each side of the millennium.

His Appearing
- "Jesus Christ … shall judge the quick" (2 Tim. 4:1).
- "They that are Christ's at his coming" (1 Cor. 15:23).
- "They that have done good, unto the resurrection of life" (John 5:29).
- "Some to everlasting life" (Dan. 12:2).
- "I will come again, and receive you unto myself; that where I am, *there* ye may be also" (John 14:3).
- "The Lord himself shall descend from heaven with a shout … the dead in Christ shall rise first: Then we which are alive *and* remain shall be caught up together with them in the clouds, to meet the Lord in the air: and so shall we ever be with the Lord" (1 Thess. 4:16, 17).
- "The great day of his wrath is come" (Rev. 6:17).

- "He hath ... avenged the blood of his servants" (Rev. 19:2).
- "The beast ... and ... the false prophet ... both were cast alive into a lake of fire" (Rev. 19:20).
- "The earth ... shall fall ... the LORD shall punish ... the kings of the earth" (Isa. 24:20–22).
- "He that hath part in the first resurrection ... the second death hath no power" (Rev. 20:6).
- "The Devil ... bound ... a thousand years" (Rev. 20:2).

His Kingdom

- "Jesus Christ ... shall judge ... the dead" (2 Tim. 4:1)
- "But the rest of the dead lived not again until the thousand years were finished" (Rev. 20:5).
- "We shall judge angels" (1 Cor. 6:3).
- "Thrones ... they sat upon them, and judgment was given unto them ... and they lived and reigned with Christ a thousand years" (Rev. 20:4).
- "The dead, small and great, stand before God; and the books were opened ... and the dead were judged" (Rev. 20:12).
- "Some to shame *and* everlasting contempt" (Dan. 12:2).
- "They that have done evil, unto the resurrection of damnation" (John 5:29).
- "Whosoever was not found written in the book of life was cast into the lake of fire" (Rev. 20:15).
- "This is the second death" (Rev. 20:14).
- "The holy city, new Jerusalem, coming down from God out of heaven" (Rev. 21:2).
- "And they went up on the breadth of the earth, and compassed the camp of the saints about, and the beloved city: and fire came down from God out of heaven, and devoured them" (Rev. 20:9).
- "Then *cometh* the end, when he shall have delivered up the kingdom to God" (1 Cor. 15:24).
- "Behold, the tabernacle of God *is* with men ... the former things are passed away" (Rev. 21:3, 4).
- "Blessed *are* the meek: for they shall inherit the earth" (Matt. 5:5).
- "For the first heaven and the first earth were passed away" (Rev. 21:1).

Extra Thoughts:

When Jesus returns He will destroy the living wicked. The living saints will watch as He raises the dead saints. Both are changed and fly off to heaven for a period of 1,000 years. Exceptions to this include a special resurrection for those who "pierced Him" (Rev. 1:7) and a special mini version of the lake of fire called "a lake of fire."

This millennium time has God's people with Him judging the fallen angels and the wicked. The "bottomless pit" of Revelation 20:1–3 is obviously symbolic of the earth as a wasteland as the rest of the chapter clearly describes events that happen on the surface of the earth. Satan will be "bound" by a chain of circumstance, as he will have no one to tempt into sin.

Since Jesus went to heaven and clearly warned us in Matthew 24:23 not to expect Him to touch the earth when He comes again, the prophecy of Zechariah 14:4 will be fulfilled at the end of the millennium. The city comes down to the earth; God raises all the wicked together; and this is the one point in history where every knee does bow before Jesus Christ in recognition of His justice. Satan makes his final effort to deceive the wicked, and one last time they show their contempt for God's mercy by trying to attack the city as described in Revelation 20:7–10. The second death punishment is the same as Malachi 4:1, which is also called His "strange act" in Isaiah 28:21. See Ezekiel 18:32 to learn how God feels about destroying the wicked.

After all sin and sinners are completely wiped out of existence by fire, God will make the earth anew, and it will be the home of the saved forever (see Isaiah 66:22, 23).

Speaking in Tongues

- Revelation 13:13, 14   The final deception includes a false fire from heaven.
- Acts 2:1–11   The true fire from heaven was an outpouring of the Holy Spirit, which gave them the ability to speak real languages.
- 1 Corinthians 13:1   Angels are said here to speak a different language. This language is not what is being spoken in Pentecostal churches today. Instead they babble and talk gibberish.
- Zephaniah 3:8, 9   This one language will be restored. Five texts ban repetition and babbling, they are 1 Timothy 6:20, 21; 2 Timothy 2:16; Matthew 6:7; Ecclesiastes 10:11; and Isaiah 8:19, 20.
- Acts 5:32   To receive the Holy Spirit, you must be obedient.
- John 16:13   The Holy Spirit guides us into all truth. If Pentecostals really have the Holy Spirit, why don't their churches keep the Sabbath?

> **Words of Advice**
>
> Normand Cote, a former Pentecostal who is now an Adventist Pastor said, "Don't attack speaking in tongues right away when you deal with a Pentecostal; you're almost attacking their salvation."

The Role of Women/Women's Ordination

- Genesis 2:18   Woman was created to be man's helper. Though equal in value, even in the perfect world this was an assistant's role. What made things perfect was that she was satisfied with this role.
- Genesis 3:6   Eve's sin was first coveting that which had been withheld from her. This weakness is passed on to all women.
- Genesis 3:15–19   As punishment for sin, the

> **Words of Advice**
>
> Kelly Schultz on home outreach: "When visiting a member of the opposite sex, converse with the spouse as well to avoid crossing social boundaries. That way he or she will not think something is going on."

Topics to Cover as the Need Arises

Lord took leisure away from men and power away from women. Implanted in a woman's heart was a desire for emotional fulfillment from the man in her life. She was now in service to him. His sin is specified as giving in to her. This affected the relationship by making him weak-willed. His weakness is that he can be manipulated with guilt. Now he has to work hard. His work was given to teach him life lessons to prepare for heaven.

- Job 31:9, 10   The wife's role is a role of service, including sexual service. The mention of housework shows that this is a biblical part of human nature and not just cultural that a wife's service is mainly in the home.
- 1 Peter 3:7   God defends women. Men and women are not equal in this world; they are instead balanced. A woman has no power, but she is a daughter of the King and deserves special treatment. This study really has a dual message. For men, they need to be reminded to take care of women and not abuse their authority. For women, they need to be reminded to respect male authority and not take advantage of their special treatment.
- Proverbs 31:10–31   Nowhere in the Bible does it say that a woman is to deny her gifts, strengths, and abilities. She is only to direct them in an unselfish way to support her husband and family.
- Luke 8:1–3   Jesus traveled with His disciples, who later became leaders of the new church, and a company of women who served the group. The Greek word for "ministered" or "provided" in verse 3 describes the service role of a deacon(ess).
- Luke 10:38–42   An example of male/female relations under sin. One woman is attempting to manipulate a man (Jesus) into doing what she wants through guilt. This is one of the reasons men were to be leaders in this world. It is withheld from women for their own good.
- Galatians 3:28   This verse is quoted by some to say that New Testament Christianity abolishes the roles of men and women and restores equality, especially regarding women as leaders.
- 1 Corinthians 7:20–22   This text balances out the previous one by showing that the order of society does not change as we are still in a world of sin. (The New Testament does validate women in the service role as they've been given.)
- Ephesians 5:22–25, 32   Submission is required for wives. "As unto the Lord" covers any case where there is conflict between the man's will and God's will. Please refer to the "Marriage and a Happy Home" study for more texts regarding this topic.
- 1 Timothy 2:11–15   Just as the first born was given authority so Adam had an authority Eve did not because he was made first. 'Learn in silence' here shows women are not to have spiritual authority. The reference to motherhood shows even in societies where women were discriminated against, the spiritual experience of mothering children parallels the life lessons of bearing responsibility men have in the world.
- 1 Timothy 3:2   It does not say one spouse generically here. An elder as a man must have only one wife.

Extra Thoughts:

Some point to the fact that Mary Magdalene was the first to bring the good news of Christ's resurrection as evidence that women are now approved for ministerial roles. Yes, the doctrine of the priesthood of every believer applies to women, and women can do many things for God. But Mary was not a disciple, and there is no record of any woman publicly preaching, performing a wedding, or baptizing people in the New Testament.

The household relationship is a symbolic representation of Christ and the church. This means that women moving into spiritual leadership roles such as pastors or elders breaks that symbolism. Having women elders and pastors is similar to having yeast raised bread and fermented wine at the Communion service when fermentation is a symbol of sin. The literal ceremony has to be matched by the symbolism for the lesson it teaches to be of value. Such actions are therefore unbiblical.

Words of Advice

A few years after the Lord gave me success winning Adrian, Melissa and I studied with a family who later took a stand for God and joined the church. At one point a red flag went up in their minds that almost derailed the study when the pastor's wife was chosen as an elder in the church. They knew from the Sundaykeeping church they previously went to that only men are biblically called to this leadership role. God gave me the right words for the situation when I said, "The Seventh-day Adventist Church is not perfect and does make mistakes. But everything I have shown you from the Bible is true."

This is a sensitive issue, and at first I thought about avoiding it so as not to stir up controversy and ruin the purpose of this book. I decided to include it in here but would like to advise you to keep this as a side issue. Although important, it should not be brought to the front in your witnessing efforts. Though I do not agree with women pastors or elders, since various churches and conferences within the North American Division and elsewhere are appointing them, I also do not think it is right to take it out on the individual women in these positions. As long as they bear these titles and roles, give them complete respect.

Biblical support for this respect comes from the two uses of the illustration of the watchman in Ezekiel, where a watchman is told his own salvation depends on his willingness to warn the wicked of the errors of their way. The first use in Ezekiel 3:17 has the Lord raising up the watchman. However, in Ezekiel 33:2 it's the people who appoint the watchman, who is then given the same responsibility.

Louis Torres said, "Four quarters and a dollar bill are equal; they just have different roles, different functions." And since the priesthood of every believer is a doctrine we hold to, he also made reference to it when he said, "Ladies, you are already ordained."

Topics to Cover as the Need Arises

Love Is the Fulfilling of the Law (The Ten Commandments and the Fruits of the Spirit)

Jesus' life on earth was one of love. He came to love us by sacrificing Himself for our sakes. Everything He did was love in action. Philip wanted to know the Father, and Jesus said, "He that hath seen me hath seen the Father" (John 14:9). In John 15:12–14 Jesus introduces a new commandment that we should love one another. Does this mean that the Ten Commandments are null and void and replaced with this one commandment? In verse 14 Jesus said that we are His friends if we do *whatever* He commands.

The following chart can be derived from Matthew 22:37–40. It is simply an expansion of the concept of love:

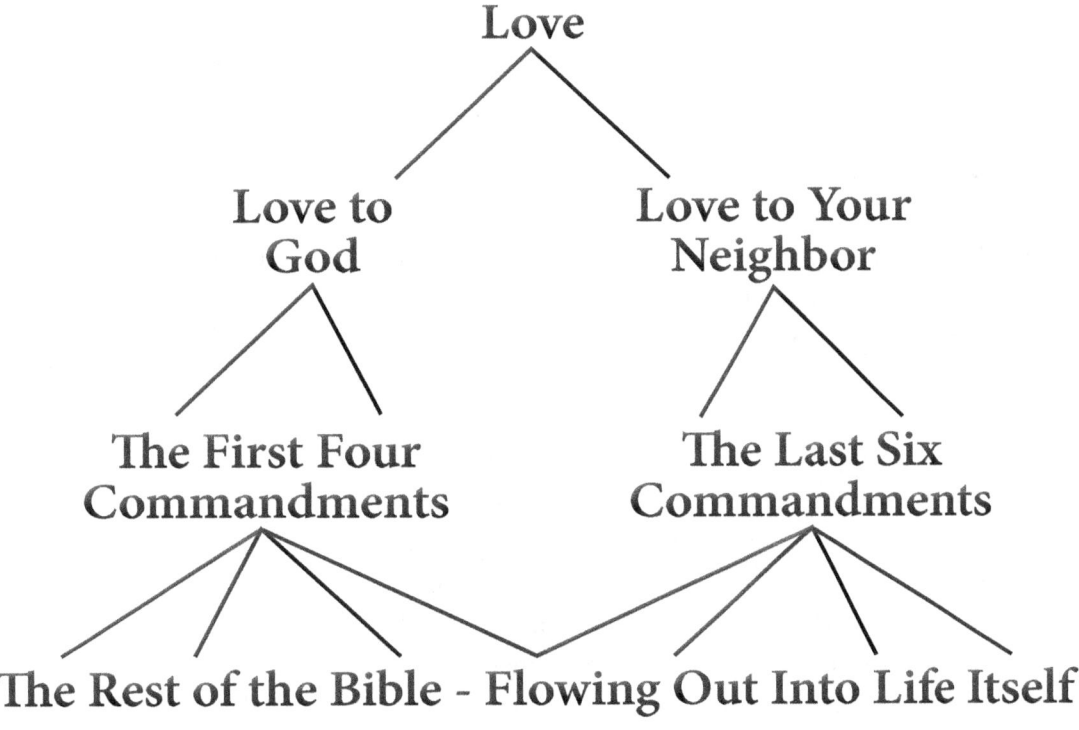

The law is simply a more detailed way of telling us how to love God and each other. The five books of Moses and the rest of the Bible provide stories and examples in further explanation of this love found in the Ten Commandments.

Jesus' first quote in Matthew 22 comes from Deuteronomy 6:5. Moses gave this admonition to love God at the conclusion of his speech in which he reiterated the law to the people. The second quote is from Leviticus 19:18.

Paul also mentions this point in Galatians 5:14 before going on to contrast the "works of the flesh" with the "fruits of the Spirit." The whole passage starts in verse 13 where we are told not to use our freedom as an excuse to sin. Notice that all the sins listed as works of the flesh are things forbidden by God's law—these include adultery, idolatry, and murder. Paul then goes on to list the fruits of the Spirit, or the results you get from a Spirit-filled life of faith and submission to the Lord. The most fascinating thing here is that when you look at the positive side of each individual law you see the corresponding fruit as the natural result of having your heart in harmony with it.

Following are each of the Ten Commandments reworded into positive concepts along with the parallel *fruit of the spirit as found in Galatians 5:22–24*:

- God is more important than anything else. *God is love, and knowing God is knowing real love.*
- We are to cherish only a true concept of Him and approach Him in a true way. *True joy comes from knowing Him truly.*
- Even His name is holy. This covers more than swearing. It is living right to give Him a good name. *The essence of this commandment is self-control, which results in peace.*
- We have our work in this world to do, and then He gives us His special day. The seventh day is His day. Keeping His day His way is following Him with all our hearts. *Longsuffering comes from regular, consistent, habitual faith-building experiences.*
- The first commandment with a promise covers all human authority. The Lord wisely starts in the home, the building block of society. *Gentleness is the benefit of a stable home.*
- Complete physical security starts in the heart by being free from anger, *which leads to goodness.*
- Sexual purity and marital security. *The New King James version translates faith to faithfulness. You are to be faithful to your vows, your spouse, family, and the Lord.*
- Home and property security starts with acceptance of one's situation in life. *Meekness is the essence of this commandment. Meek people are satisfied with what they have in life.*
- Total and complete honesty. By not calling good things bad or bad things good, we gain self-control. *Another word for this is temperance.*
- All sin starts in the heart. This commandment must be kept to keep all others. *To completely keep this, we need to crucify our flesh. The fruits of the Spirit are really the results you get from having the law in your heart.*

Gambling

- Luke 12:15; Exodus 20:17   Gambling is wrong because it is a form of greed.
- Genesis 3:17–19; Proverbs 13:11   Because of its emphasis on getting rich quick, gambling violates God's plan for earning a living. (See "The Value of Work" study for more information.)
- Philippians 4:11   The biblical principle is to be satisfied with what you've been given in life.
- Deuteronomy 8:18; Proverbs 13:22   Money is a gift from the Lord and is to be used for

His purposes. Gambling throws money away and is an irresponsible use of money. (See the "Christian Standards, Tithe" study for more information.)

Extra Thoughts:

Casino games of chance are the most often thought of form of gambling, but there are others. Lotteries, bingo games, and risky investments such as mutual funds and playing the stock market are also forms of gambling. Responsible retirement planning is one thing. However, how many people plan for the end of this life and make no provision for eternity? (see Matt. 6:33).

The Civil Laws

There are four kinds of laws in the Old Testament: the Ten Commandments; the ceremonial laws; miscellaneous laws such as the health and sexual purity laws; and the civil laws, which were not ceremonial but dealt with public and nonreligious affairs in the nation of Israel.

In 1 Corinthians 9:8–11 we find an old law quoted that is used to make a point about another issue. What we can deduce from this is that although these laws are not in affect now there are lessons contained in them that we can apply to our time. So how should we treat slaves when there is no slavery today? The principles contained within the fair treatment of slaves' laws can be applied to the employer/employee relationship. Are we still to take one "Sabbath" year off every seven? After seven sets of seven they were to celebrate the jubilee year and return property to its original owners. We see this concept reflected in laws preventing any one corporation from becoming a monopoly.

The civil laws were done away with when the Israelites were taken into exile. Since they lost their sovereignty, there was no longer a nation to enforce these laws (see Neh. 9:33–37; Lam. 5:16). Ezekiel speaks of the crown of Israel being overturned three times until the Messiah comes, who then keeps it forever (Ezek. 21:25–27). This happened as predicted as the crown was in Babylon's hand when the prophecy was given and then overturned to Persia, Greece, and finally Rome. This helps us make sense of Jesus' answer on the question of paying taxes to Caesar in Mark 12:17. Furthermore, 1 Peter 1:18 and Romans 13:1–7 confirm this. Because God has people in all nations now, we are to be good citizens of whatever nation we live in. Solomon's writings support this (Eccl. 8:2). The only exception to this rule comes in Peter's words to the council in Acts 5:29.

There is also New Testament evidence for the removal of the civil law in the Jerusalem Council in Acts 15. Verses 1–6 set the tone as the issue came up in the early church about circumcision and the law of Moses. The discussion of the topic is listed in verses 7–20 with verse 21 mentioning the Sabbath (therefore, it is still in force) and verses 22–29 are the result of the discussion.

Christians and Government

- Deuteronomy 5:16 The fifth commandment. This statement on respecting human authority starts in the home but can be extended to the rest of society as this study will show.

- 1 Peter 2:13–18; Proverbs 21:1; 20:28   All human authority is under the Lord.
- Psalm 105:7   He uses all government and human authority of any kind, even in ungodly nations.
- 2 Peter 2:10–13   Those who are rebels here would also be rebels in heaven.
- John 19:11   Jesus set the example of submission.
- Romans 13:1–7   If your heart is right with God and you are doing good, you have nothing to be afraid of.
- Matthew 22:16–21   Jesus shows that government has a different purpose than the church.
- Genesis 11:4   Nationalism is a form of selfishness.
- John 19:15   To place national pride above God is to show that one's heart is in this world.
- Jeremiah 29:4–7   By seeking peace in whatever government system we are under, we shall have peace.
- Jeremiah 50:28–30   The ones used to punish the Jews went too far (see Ps. 137), and they were later punished.
- Ecclesiastes 5:8   The Lord is aware when human government goes too far and there is injustice.
- Acts 4:18–20; 5:29   Where there is no conflict, obey human authority as if it is the Lord Himself.

The Case for Religious Freedom
- Genesis 15:5, 6   This was the covenant that God made between Himself and Abraham to establish Israel. It included a physical/political promise of a nation here and a spiritual promise for heaven through Jesus. (See Gal. 3:16.)
- Exodus 3:12   Moses was raised up to bring the promise for a nation into effect. Israel as a nation was to be a theocracy, directly ruled by the Lord as He spoke through His prophets and judges.
- Deuteronomy 18:9–13   God does not tolerate false religion.
- Joshua 1:8   As Israel followed God, they were blessed. They were used to punish evil nations.
- Judges 2:11–23   The storyline continues with Israel failing to completely follow God. They, therefore, could not be completely blessed.
- 1 Samuel 8:5–8   Israel sinned when they asked for a king. The theocracy was over.
- 1 Samuel 12:13–15   However, God's appointed rulers were still to rule according to His laws. Cross-reference this with Proverbs 20:28. Any system of government, if it upholds true justice, can have God's blessing.
- Jeremiah 5:6–9   The laws of the theocracy were removed by the removal of the nation itself in captivity. This prophecy parallels Daniel 2 with the great world empires to come. They were given control over God's people.

Topics to Cover as the Need Arises

- Ezekiel 21:25–27   The crown of Israel was overturned with each successive empire that came and went. The one with the right to it is Jesus. This prophecy, along with Galatians 3:29 and Romans 2:28, 29, shows that once the political promise was taken away it was no longer needed.
- Hosea 1:7   Jesus came to fulfill the spiritual promise, and only the spiritual promise.
- John 4:21, 23, 24   Jesus explains that there is to be a change. God was no longer going to have only one nation to serve Him.
- Luke 17:20, 21   Born-again Christianity replaces theocracy.
- 1 Kings 18:40   Here is an example of a prophet putting to death false prophets at a time when Deuteronomy 18:9–13 was still in effect in Israel.
- Daniel 2:24   Here is an example of a prophet who, while in captivity and not in Israel, saved the lives of many false prophets. Why? Because it was not his kingdom and he was not under theocracy.
- Matthew 22:21   In the Christian era, with no one nation belonging to God, there is to be a separation of church and state.
- 2 Thessalonians 2:3, 4   The issues of prophecy predicted that a false theocracy would rise up in the name of God during the Dark Ages.
- Revelation 13:11, 12   There is also to be a repeat in our time. A beast is a country. To be lamblike is to seem Christian yet to speak as the devil. The beast takes away freedom.
- Matthew 24:12–14   This passage describes the trap society is under today. Evil is abounding, thus causing Christians to hate their enemies. They must remember that God said, "Vengeance is mine" (Rom. 12:19). At the same time, the true gospel, which includes freedom, will go out to the entire world.
- Daniel 12:3   The promise to those who will stand for God.

Once Saved Always Saved

- Romans 8:29, 30; Ephesians 1:5, 11   These two passages are highly misunderstood by most Christians today, resulting in the assumption called "once saved always saved." This doctrine states that the Lord chose only a very few for salvation right from the start of history. They have always been chosen, and the rejected ones have always been rejected. To believe this you have to deny free choice and say that Jesus only died for a few.
- Romans 10:13   Anyone who calls on Jesus will be saved.
- 2 Corinthians 13:5   The Bible clearly shows that we need to challenge and examine ourselves.
- 2 Peter 1:3–10   Growth in grace is important. To say "all we need is Jesus and nothing else" is wrong in one sense because a relationship with Jesus helps us to grow in so many ways. The idea of once saved always saved leads one to feel no need to grow, and then the former purging of sins is forgotten. We need diligence.

- Ezekiel 18:21–32   It is best to read the whole chapter, but these verses point out that anyone who chooses to do right will be saved. There is no exclusive club with God. Notice the born-again reference at the end of the chapter. Doing right is only possible with His power working in your life.
- Hebrews 10:23, 26–32   The gift of God to change our lives takes effort on our part to keep. It is not automatic, nor is it a guarantee since it is possible to turn away. There are many references to God's power and consistency in the Bible. They are often quoted by once-saved-always-saved believers to say they can never lose salvation. Verse 32 is an encouragement to help us through the tough times. God will never give up on us. We must simply not give up on Him either.
- John 8:31   "If" says it all. God gives us free choice throughout the Bible when He uses this word.
- 1 Corinthians 9:27   Paul said he made efforts against his sinful nature. He recognized even he could fall away.
- Titus 2:11   Somehow, someway every human being has a chance to be saved.
- Esther 4:13, 14   Here is an example of someone "predestined" to do a great thing for the Lord. She is warned if she chooses not to do it He will find some other way to accomplish His purpose, but she will not be saved. The best way to understand predestination is that it is for the group. God has predestined a people who will do His will. Any one individual has the free choice to be part of that group or not.
- Romans 11:2   Chapters 9 to 11 explain the failure of literal Israel and the transition to spiritual Israel with the calling of the Gentiles. The "foreknowing" or predestination continued even though the definition of what was foreknown changed according to human choice.
- Romans 12:3   Believing in the idea of once saved always saved leads a person into pride and self-exaltation. The tendency is to say, "I'm saved" rather than "Jesus has saved me."
- Ecclesiastes 9:11   This verse clearly contradicts the conclusion of once saved always saved, which is that we have no free will, when it says time and chance happen to all.
- Exodus 9:12   Did God make Pharaoh reject Him?
- Exodus 8:32   Pharaoh hardened his own heart. The Lord simply knew what would happen and put him through the plagues until he drove the Israelites out.
- Revelation 3:5   When we are born again, we are promised our name is written in the book of life. It can be blotted out if we do not continue in our born-again state.
- Jude 5   Here are some examples of the Lord rejecting people who sinned after the Lord Himself gave them an initial form of salvation.
- Joshua 24:15   Choose to serve God.

Topics to Cover as the Need Arises

Extra Thoughts:

Here are some other points to consider. In Matthew 19:17–22 and Mark 10:17–22 the rich young ruler was loved by Christ. How could he be predestined to turn away? See also Proverbs 28:9; Isaiah 8:18–20; Romans 11:18; Jeremiah 5:1, 2, 6–9; 7:6–11; 8:20; 1 Timothy 4:16; 2 Peter 3:15, 17; and 1 John 2:4–6.

Challenges to the Truth About Death

(Note: use this study after you have shared studies on the first and second deaths and only if IAIN responds with these challenging verses to question what you have just taught him. Don't use any more of it than you need to. If IAIN only asks about one of these challenge texts, don't plant doubt in his mind by talking about the others.)

Saul and the Witch of Endor

Read 1 Samuel 28:3–20. If you want to believe this really was the ghost of Samuel, then you have to believe that God Himself had to obey this witch and let Samuel out of heaven, which is in violation of His own law in Deuteronomy 18:10–14. The Lord was not speaking to Saul by the means He normally used as it says in verse 6. In verse 9 we see the witch's fear, for Saul had previously obeyed the law.

The key reference in this story is in verse 14 where it says, "And Saul *perceived* that it *was* Samuel." In other words, the Bible doesn't actually say it was Samuel; it says Saul thought it was Samuel. There's a big difference there.

Following are more reasons why it could not have been Samuel:
- the spirit came up from the ground and not down from heaven (verses 11, 13, 15).
- the spirit was in the form of an old man yet we are promised in heaven we'll all be young.
- the spirit said Saul would be with him tomorrow (in other words dead). The implication of being with Samuel would be to go to heaven, yet the tone of the remark was as if to say Saul would be punished, therefore, in hell. Why would Samuel, a good man, be in hell? The words of the spirit lead Saul to commit suicide the next day. Would God lead someone to commit suicide? In the Lord's prayer, we are told to pray for the deliverance from evil and in Ezekiel 18:32 we are clearly shown God doesn't want to lose anybody.

Taking the truth about death and the story of Satan's lie to Eve in Genesis 3:4, 5 into account, it must have been an evil angel who appeared to look like Samuel and was, therefore, trying to lead Saul astray.

The Thief on the Cross

Where did Jesus go after He died? Why did He tell the thief on the cross they'd be together in paradise *that day* in Luke 23:43, since He supposedly went to hell as 1 Peter 3:18, 19 appears to say and then He told Mary on Sunday morning that He *hadn't yet ascended to the Father* (John 20:17)?

There were no commas in the Greek text. The comma was misplaced by the King James Version translators. (There's another misplaced comma in the KJV rendition of Acts 19:12.) Move the comma to follow the word 'today' and you'll see the promise to the thief was given that day; paradise itself was to be later. Jesus spent that weekend resting in the grave; He didn't go anywhere.

The Spirits in Prison

People think 1 Peter 3:19, 20 refers to ghosts burning in hell right now that Jesus went down to save. However, in Revelation 20 we read that the events of the second death happen on the surface of the earth and at the end of the millennium. Is it not well understood that those who receive the second death have already been judged? What would be the point of Jesus offering a second chance to anyone He chose to punish in the first place? There is no such thing as a second chance for the wicked (see Heb. 9:27).

Look at verse 20 in 1 Peter 3. The word 'soul' does not mean 'ghost' because there were eight living people on the ark! We find the key in 1 Peter 4:6. The gospel "was" preached to them that "are" dead. Look again at 1 Peter 3:19, 20 which starts with "by which" or "by whom." What is this referring to? It is referring to the Holy Spirit as mentioned in verse 18. The Spirit inspired the holy men of old and lives to glorify Christ (2 Peter 1:21; John 16:14). The Old Testament heroes of the faith were godly men who were inspired by God Himself. Therefore, Christ was preached unto the people of Noah's time through the Holy Spirit using Noah's example as a means of convicting these people of their sins.

God patiently offered them salvation while Noah built the ark. If they had boarded the boat, they would have been saved. Why then are they called "spirits in prison"? These spirits are living people. They are in prison in the sense that they were enslaved to their sins (see John 8:34). The proper understanding of 1 Peter 3:19,20 and 4:6 is that Christ was preached to them while they were still alive!

The Rich Man and Lazarus

We find the parable of the rich man and Lazarus in Luke 16:20–31. Lazarus didn't go to heaven but to "Abraham's bosom." If there is a great chasm between heaven and hell, why are they able to talk freely back and forth? The key is verse 31. The parable ends with the rich man asking Abraham (not God) to allow people to come back from the grave and warn the living.

But the message of the parable is that people who want to believe Satan's lies about death won't believe the Lord's truth no matter how much God tries to teach them through the Bible. Jesus is using the popular misconceptions about death, heaven, and hell to show how absurd they really are.

Absent From the Body

This verse, 2 Corinthians 5:8, above all others seems to be quoted to support the idea of a believer going to heaven immediately after death. Does this one verse outweigh the following twenty-five texts: 2 Samuel 7:12; 1 Kings 1:21; 2 Chronicles 16:13; Job 7:21; 17:13; 19:25–27; 27:3; Psalm 17:13–15; 104:29; 115:17; Ecclesiastes 9:10; Ecclesiastes 12:7 cross-referenced with Psalm 146:3, 4; Ezekiel 18:20; Matthew 27:52; John 11:11–14; 1 Kings 2:10 cross-referenced with Acts 2:29, 34; 1 Corinthians 15:51; 1

Thessalonians 4:14; 1 Timothy 6:16 cross-referenced with Job 4:17; James 2:26; 4:14?

There is simply no way that this one verse can contradict all the others and teach that we become ghosts and go to heaven as soon as we die—it simply can't mean that. What does it mean then? In 2 Corinthians 5:1–10 Paul is talking about being clothed, which leaves us with three possibilities. We are clothed in our earthly house of this tabernacle, that is to say our body. There is also our house from heaven, which we do not yet have, which is our glorified body. And then there is the state of being naked, meaning asleep in death.

Paul is saying that we groan in this tabernacle (our present body) but not that we would be unclothed (that is dead) but that we would be clothed in immortality. He then sums it up by saying that we would *rather* be absent from this body and be present with the Lord. But that is not possible for anyone yet, since in verse 10 we must all first appear for judgment. Remember, Paul said he would not have us be ignorant; therefore, believe his words to you.

(Special thanks to my brother in Christ, Al Graca of British Columbia, Canada, for his insights on this verse.)

Words of Advice

Since the belief systems of the world are the darkness we are to call people out of, when reaching those not raised in the Judeo-Christian thought structure of Western society, you have to take culture into account to some degree. People who accept Jesus do not have to accept all that Western society thinks is Christian. Since the devil's lies are always attached to some truth, that which agrees with the Bible from IAIN's individual heritage can be kept, and that which does not should be discarded.

However, there are also gray areas. When you think about it, there is a lot of paganism still around us. Why are the constellations named for Greek gods? Why do we have sixty minutes in an hour and sixty seconds in a minute, or why do we shake hands as a greeting in the West? These things and many others come from superstitious and pagan origins.

Louis Torres put it this way, "What the Bible calls 'the vain traditions handed to you by your fathers,' the world calls culture. Where Bible truth does not conflict with local custom, honor local custom. Where it does conflict, Bible truth supersedes."

Stop Smoking Help

- Make the decision ahead of time when to quit. Smoke your last cigarette by choice.
- To clean out your body, fast the first day. Also, drink plenty of water and shower often the first few days. Take walks to get fresh air.
- Caffeine and alcohol only increase the cravings. Give yourself a break from them too.
- The physical craving goes away quickly. The rest is on the mental level. You will be a

non-smoker when you believe you are.
- Observe non-smokers. What do they do with their hands? Is there any other way they conduct themselves differently?
- The subconscious mind cannot process negative expressions. Let this be an experience of freedom rather than some great thing you have to do. Smoking is the burden. Enjoy your liberty.
- Help yourself through distractions. Carry a pen or stick to give your fingers something to hold onto in the transition. Chew on it if you need to.
- When a person feels overwhelmed with temptation, remember that it usually lasts only a few minutes. Take a short walk or shower. You will get through it. Prayer helps.
- Purge your home of all smoking materials such as ashtrays. Let no one else smoke around you.
- Don't hang out with smokers anymore. This does not mean cutting off your friends, but don't go out to the smoking areas when they smoke. Talk with them when they are not smoking.
- Some people get bothered when they see you achieve success over a weakness they have. They will try to trip you up. You must be aware and ready to handle the situations as they arise.
- You will get into areas where you know you will be tempted, such as Christmas parties. Decide ahead of time to say no, and the temptation will not be as strong.
- Reward yourself at anniversaries. When one week, month, and year pass by, spend some of the money you would have spent for cigarettes on a treat for yourself.
- Be willing to give yourself to God and let Him give you victory. Believe in Him (1 Cor. 15:57).
- Smoking is now dead in you, you're free (Rom. 6:11).
- Don't give yourself a chance to go back (Rom. 13:14).
- Don't forget! He who maded this world in six days can make you a non-smoker (Ps. 51:10).

Bible Words of Hope and Encouragement for Expectant Mothers

- Psalm 100:3; Job 31:15; Jeremiah 1:4, 5   These verses show God's involvement in our existence.
- 1 Timothy 2:15   This verse provides encouragement for mothers.
- Proverbs 22:6   Advice on childrearing. Teach your child Bible principles early.
- Judges 13:3, 4, 13, 14   The Lord takes the influence of prenatal care very seriously. Take responsibility for the health of your baby. Do not indulge in wrong pleasures such as drinking and smoking. Also eat only healthy foods. What the Bible calls unclean is listed in Leviticus 11.
- The following are miracle baby stories: Genesis 21:1-3   Isaac was born to Abraham and Sarah; Luke 1:57, 58   John the Baptist was born to Zechariah and Elizabeth; Isaiah 7:14; 9:6   Jesus Himself was a miracle baby.
- Isaiah 49:15, 16   This illustration compares a mother's love to God's even greater love.
- Luke 18:15–17; Psalm 127; 128   Jesus loves children.

Chapter 8

Mentoring New Converts

During the mentoring phase of your relationship with IAIN, you will experience some of the greatest joys you've ever had in life. All the sacrifices have been worth it, and a new convert is alive in the church and on-fire for God. Now he is looking to Jesus on his own for faith, but he still has a special place in his heart for you. He will look to you as more experienced and need you to show him how things are done. The Lord can still use you in many ways to influence him for good.

This chapter provides a wide variety of suggestions on how to engage IAIN in the life of the church after he has been baptized. Of course, there will also be challenges that IAIN will experience in this phase of his spiritual journey. Here is some advice on many of these issues and how best to deal with them as you nurture each new IAIN in their faith as a newborn Christian..

Very soon after IAIN gets baptized, let her know that although God has worked many changes in her life, her basic personality has not changed. If IAIN is more of an introverted person, she may not be teaching Sabbath School in years to come. If she is a social butterfly gifted in hospitality, maybe she'll end up having people over to her house for Sabbath afternoon fellowships. Leo Schreven's advice for new believers in the church is to "find their ministry." They've been fed through the efforts made to win them. Now it's time for them to seek ways to give back. It may take time for the Lord's leading to be obvious, but new people need to be encouraged to get involved.

Unfortunately, the devil is trying to sidetrack us on our journey home. One way he does this is by getting us to pay attention to things other than the gospel. Little debates happen within our ranks that could easily be solved with simple study and prayer. While studying with IAIN, don't mention anything that may currently be a raging issue in these inner debates. Your job is to make him an Adventist only, not a conservative or a liberal one. If after joining the church, he finds out about some hot topic and comes to you for advice, share your thoughts from your own study,

> **Words of Advice**
>
> Marlene Littman, wife of retired Pastor Elmer Littman, has some good words for new converts who get too involved too quick, "Warn them not to church themselves out." One way I've seen this happen is in new people's self-imposed guilt for getting behind on their Sabbath school lessons. I always tell them "get what you can out of it, and then move on".

but leave him to study it out for himself. Encourage him to make his own decisions, relying on the Holy Spirit's revelation.

Staying away from side issues when trying to reach new people is important for two reasons. The first is that when you talk about controversial subjects, people often get riled up and passionate one way or the other. When people divide into camps and argue about something, even if they're right, they're reasoning from their own ideas and not from a point of view of dependence on God. The second is that we are trying to get people to learn of and imitate Christ, not us. IAIN needs to see the difference between moral issues, which you are called to take a firm stand on when you study with him, and personal growth issues, which you are not. For instance, it is a sin to eat pork or any other unclean food. This needs to be clearly communicated before baptism. It is not a sin to eat clean meat though being vegetarian is preferable. If IAIN is simply not ready, he's not ready.

The short list of taboo topics includes any political questions, including moral issues that are being debated in the political realm, such as abortion. There is a study on these hot topics in the previous chapter. But try to avoid covering these topics until after IAIN has been broken and made new. Women's ordination is another hot topic, and the same advice applies. Some others include the question of whether the festival days are still to be kept and extreme forms of vegetarianism such as the raw food movement (eating only raw foods because there is life in that food which is lost when cooked). Another side issue is whether or not to have sex with one's spouse on the Sabbath. Still another side issue is whether or not to celebrate Christmas and Easter.

Another side issue often surrounds whether the church likes the pastor or not. Here's some advice from Louis Torres: "Support your pastors and other leaders, and do not speak out against them if there are things happening in your local church or conference that do not violate biblical principle, but are only matters of policy. Cooperate even if you don't fully agree."

> **Words of Advice**
>
> On the issue of sharing the health message with IAIN, Carol Torres said, "Teach only what you know." You won't be able to guide her any further than you have gone yourself.

For example, maybe you like singing old-fashioned hymns right out of the hymnal and now your church has decided to modernize things with a projector and screen. This issue is not enough of a controversy to attempt to sway IAIN's opinion on. Feel free to state your case to the pastor and/or the church board, but accept their decision. In archery the first goal is to get a good grouping of all your shots on the target, rather than a few of them hitting the bulls-eye. The pastor is the one the Lord uses to hold the group together. If he is not quite on target with something, it will be worse to speak out against him. This will only plant seeds of rebellion. The Lord can bring in a new pastor to help get even closer to the target when the time is right.

Mentoring New Converts

For new converts the Sabbath is a new experience. When IAIN comes to the faith she will need help. You need to show her how to keep the Sabbath. This is a great time to exercise the gift of hospitality. Have her over for lunch. Take a nature walk in the afternoon. Introduce her to church members you know. Invite her to different activities such as fellowship meals, prayer meetings, or church socials and look for other ways you can help her make friends.

One thing new Adventists can find hard to do is to strike the balance between isolating themselves from the world enough to avoid temptation and not so much as to become monastic and therefore have no ability to witness. A rule of thumb that helps is we should only associate with "them," i.e. our non-Adventist friends, as much as we can do them good. This is especially true on the Sabbath. This will provide a safe environment on Sabbath to serve others or to fellowship with like believers.

If IAIN comes to church dressed inappropriately before baptism, let it slide. However, once IAIN is baptized he or she needs to be made aware that a church service is as formal an event as a wedding or a funeral. The verses that use garments as an illustration of righteousness in the "True Grace Is Power to Live Right" Bible study have the practical application that coming before God in anything less than your best clothing is symbolic of wanting to be saved in your sins. This may be an issue if IAIN is extremely poor. He or she should be free to decide what constitutes "their best."

When the tithe issue has been covered and he shows willingness to give the Lord control in this area of his life, show him an offering envelope. Explain how to fill it out and what the various kinds of offerings are for and how our system works.

Communion is another service that may be new to IAIN. And as far as I know, we are the only denomination that practices foot washing as a regular part of the communion service. Go through this with him for his first time if you can. If possible, wash his feet. Obviously, if IAIN is a member of the opposite sex, you can't do this. But if you can, this will provide a very special bonding experience for the two of you and help him get through something that may seem strange at first.

Another issue may come up in regards to ethnic diversity. One time I was at a church in the Calgary area that was ethnically diverse, and I was so happy to see such a spirit of camaraderie in the worship service. They were a great example of what the love of Jesus can do. Then at the fellowship meal I noticed something interesting. All the white people sat at one table, all the black people sat at another, and all the Asians sat at a third table. At first I thought, *What's going on?* Then I realized the issue was not one of racism; it was simply what I now call "cultural comfort." If IAIN is the only black or Asian person at a white church or vice versa; if IAIN is a young, single person who joined a church filled with older, married people; or if there is any way IAIN does not feel he fits in and he wants to transfer his membership to

> **Words of Advice**
>
> Pastor Warman had a story of a man who became an Adventist and a year and a half later was only taking twelve oranges to work every day for lunch. "That really does shame the church," he said.

a nearby Adventist church that will meet his needs better, tell him to go ahead. This situation may be of the Lord. He used you to draw IAIN to Himself, and now it's time for you to drop out of the picture. Even if you and IAIN do stay at the same church for years and years, remember, you are not joined at the hip. Let him make his own friends. Just be there if he needs support and guidance.

If IAIN's initial contact with the church came through one of our health seminars, she already knows much of what we believe. If not, get whatever health information you can to her. Encourage her to be open to vegetarianism, but don't make it a test of faith. The best advice to give her is to seek for slow, permanent changes. It is enough for many to give up tea, coffee, alcohol, and pork so quickly.

> ## Words of Advice
> How can you tell when a new Adventist is falling into the trap of fanaticism? Side issues are brought to the front and become an all-consuming passion, leading to in-house only evangelism. Suddenly IAIN is no longer concerned with winning new people to Jesus but with winning the existing membership to his or her point of view.

Seventh-day Adventists who are fanatical about health can be very annoying. Unfortunately, this is an experience too many of us go through. When I go to health seminars put on by the church, I see speakers who are reasonable, well-balanced Christians. They are capable of being vegan because it is important enough to them to make the effort to do it. But they prove their sincerity by their willingness to accept those who don't go that far on the issue of health. What is unfortunate is that many church members come out of these seminars and tell their friends what they should and should not eat. Do whatever you can to help IAIN avoid going down that road. Otherwise the center of IAIN's faith can easily become skewed to whether or not to eat fruits and vegetables in the same meal rather than focusing on the Savior who gave His life for her on the cross.

Here's a great quote from *Counsels on Diet and Foods* that every new Adventist needs to see: "I have had great light from the Lord upon the subject of health reform. I did not seek this light; I did not study to obtain it; it was given to me by the Lord to give to others. I present these matters before the people, dwelling upon general principles, and sometimes, if questions are asked me at the table to which I have been invited, I answer according to the truth. But I have never made a raid upon any one in regard to the table or its contents. I would not consider such a course at all courteous or proper" (p. 493). For more on this topic, I suggest you read the chapter titled "Extremes In Diet" in *Counsels On Health*.

Many today are unsatisfied with the mainstream healthcare system and think they are doing a good thing by turning from western medicine to the alternative health movement. Whether you go to a doctor and he says, "Take two aspirin and call me in the morning," or you go to a naturopath and she says, "Take two ginseng and call me in the morning," it really is the same thing. I like to call it "magic pill thinking". Most people want a quick fix without making any real changes in their lifestyle. Naturopathy, homeopathy, therapeutic touch, reiki, ear candling, iridology, reflexology, acupuncture, acupressure, and a host of others may have some treatments that work for specific diseases. However, in all the years I've interacted with the alternative health community, I've always seen great animosity toward Christ and Christianity. Church members need to beware of health practices that do not believe the healing power comes from God and be warned to avoid the trap of thinking that all modern medicine is bad.

> ## Words of Advice
>
> One of the reasons reason why the many self-supporting health ministries (such as Uchee Pines and Weimar Institute) are nowhere near as popular today as the Battle Creek Sanitarium was in the early 1900s is not because of any fault on our part as Adventists. It's because the world has rejected the approach to health God called us to share in favor of "magic pill thinking". For more on this see *Adventism in America*, pages 193–205.
>
> The health message in Ellen White's writings puts the onus on personal responsibility. You do your best (through nutrition, exercise, water, sunlight, temperance, air, rest, and trust in Him), and when you do have a problem, go to a doctor. That's what we taught then and still do now.

Now we turn to the issue of music. The original Hebrew word translated *timbrel* in the King James Bible denotes a small hand drum. In some places in modern English Bibles, it is translated tambourine. This type of drum music would likely not have been the same as the hypnotic constant beat of the ancient pagan religions that is mimicked so much throughout modern secular music.

In evangelical churches where the worship service is essentially nothing more than a rock concert, we are seeing a false attempt to fulfill the call to reform worship in the first angel's message. The old worship format seemed to be an expression of a theology that was dry and stale to them, so some people think that by livening up the service with a more exciting worship style on-fire Christians will be the result. According to the first angel's message, however, the real reason worship needed reforming was because of the Sabbath question. You can't have a special experience with God on a normal day of the week no matter which type of music you play. If IAIN came out of a church that emphasizes this emotional worship style, tell him plainly and clearly that our faith puts enlightenment above entertainment. If he loves the truth, he'll adjust.

"The things you have described … the Lord has shown me would take place just before the close of probation. Every uncouth thing will be demonstrated. There will be shouting, with drums, music, and dancing. The senses of rational beings will become so confused that they cannot be trusted to make right decisions. And this is called the moving of the Holy Spirit" (*Maranatha*, p. 234).

Now let's look at the issue of relationships. If you find out while studying with IAIN that he's actually in a common law relationship and not a marriage, he will need to repent of this sin against God and be properly married before baptism and church membership can occur. Assess the situation. If you find this out before you see conviction and conversion, you will have to let it slide off you until then.

During study and possibly after, you may get drawn into IAIN's marital problems. This is especially the case if IAIN is a woman who is unfulfilled in her relationship. She may be looking for more than her husband can give her, which is why she is looking to the Lord. In having won her trust, you may be trusted with helping here in her marriage. If in your opinion the couple's problems are beyond your ability to deal with, go ahead and encourage them to seek the help of a professional *Christian* counselor.

However, you can do quite a lot more than you think for the couple because you have the truth at your disposal. Show them the Sermon on the Mount, and tell them that in the middle of their most heated arguments to "turn the other cheek" and "love your enemies." Take them to verses on the subject of respecting authority. Tell them about God's authority in the marriage and their need to commit to their spouse no matter what. Their vow was to the Lord, and to each other. Their vow was a vow to give, not get, and it was not dependent on the reaction they got later on from the one they vowed to love.

Most likely you are studying with only one member of the family. Transitioning for a while to discuss their problems may be a way to draw the other partner into the study as well. Don't let their problems take over the study though. Two studies are included in "Topics to Cover as the Need Arises," which should be helpful. One is on marriage and another is on the role of women. There is only one way to make a marriage work, and that is to follow the biblical model with the man as leader of the house and the woman in a support role.

When one tries to take the other's role, it results in nothing but heartache. Lay out the various roles and clearly get across to each one the need for individual responsibility. As with so much else in life, we can only do our part. *Manuscript Releases*, volume 7, page 268, says, "You have not been appointed to talk about others' faults." The marriage cannot grow until each person forgives the other and focuses on improving him or herself.

> **Words of Advice**
>
> Richard Warman's thoughts on marital counseling: "If I can bring them both to Christ, they can be brought to each other."

The New Testament references to family structure quoted in the two studies clearly show that the woman has to be the one to choose to accept her role. The man has to love her with the same self-sacrificing love Jesus had for the church. This means he cannot pull rank. Men and women both have the same lesson to learn in different ways. That lesson is: can you love someone even when that person lets you down? They both ultimately have the same calling, which is to affect the world for good. The difference comes in their definition of what constitutes affecting the world. For him it is in his work. For her it is in her home. Her work is to be his wife and mother of their children.

"It is no evidence of manliness in the husband for him to dwell constantly upon his position as head of the family.... The Lord has constituted the husband the head of the wife to be her protector; ... even as Christ is the head of the church and the Saviour of the mystical body" (*The Adventist Home*, p. 215).

"Could the veil be withdrawn and father and mother see as God sees the work of the day, and see how His infinite eye compares the work of the one with that of the other, they would be astonished at the heavenly revelation. The father would view his labors in a more modest light, while the mother would have new courage and energy to pursue her labor with wisdom, perseverance, and patience. Now she knows its value. While the father has been dealing with the things which must perish and pass away, the mother has been dealing with developing minds and character, working not only for time but for eternity" (*Ibid.*, p. 233).

In a truly Christian relationship, neither one will feel they have any power. The woman won't because biblically she doesn't. The man won't because his power is really God's, and he is to use it accordingly. His quest is to discover God's will for the family and then win his wife to it.

On another note, to help IAIN overcome the challenges of the sleeping church mentality, be sure to implant in his heart a desire to share what he has learned as soon as you see signs he really believes it. The great commission in Matthew 28:18–20 now applies to IAIN after he gets baptized. Take him through a study of the parable of the sower from Mark 4 as outlined in this book, and warn him of the pitfalls to come. Encourage him to seek the good ground by sharing his faith, but be realistic. He will go through those pitfalls in his spiritual walk.

After IAIN gets baptized, one of the best ways to expand your outreach efforts and help her share her faith is to run a small group where IAIN brings friends to you for study. She will of course be so full of love for Jesus that she will be witnessing everywhere she goes. Much of this will be without you around, but maybe she'll want to give studies to others like you have done with her. Does she have any friends she can bring to you for study? If so, have her there as an apprentice study giver. Her knowledge of them and her presence will help break the ice if you don't know them.

> **Words of Advice**
>
> Retired Pastor Gordon Miller once said, "Counseling will help you to find out what your problems are if you don't know them, but Christ is the answer."

The information in the chapter "The Psychology of Giving Bible Studies" was designed for use in one-on-one situations. When studying with more than one person, things are a little different. You have to take all of that chapter's advice completely into account, plus account for a few extras in the dynamics of a small group setting. There will be two people in the group who will need your attention more than the rest: one is whoever comprehends the most of what you share week by week and the other is whoever comprehends the least. It is a very tricky thing to do, but you must balance the pace of the study to meet the needs of both. If the pace is too fast, your slowest learner may drop out. Remembering Daniel best candidate to call 8:27, that may be okay so long as you keep in contact with this person and try to schedule a separate study or host another group later that will more closely fit the studying needs of this individual.

As the group study continues and transitions to the point where a call for decision is made, it will be the person who is the quickest learner who will be the best candidate to call for a decision from first. When this person does make the choice to get baptized, the rest will be strongly encouraged to do so as well, and getting decisions from them should be easier.

We can compare this to the sport of bowling where the object is to get a strike by knocking all the pins down with a bowling ball. The pins are arranged in a V-shaped pattern with the headpin in the center. One place just slightly off from this pin is where to aim the ball as you roll it down the bowling lane. When you hit it just right, the ball moves one way, knocking down pins, and the headpin moves the other way, doing the ball's job of knocking the rest over.

Carol Torres commented on the fact that 120 were filled with the Holy Spirit but only Peter rose up among them to speak to the crowd in Acts 2. She said, "People bond with the speaker, so in order to preserve this bond, you need to have only one speaker." This applies to small group study. Definitely seek to include a few helpers with you who are established in the faith as you try to reach new IAINs. They can certainly converse and interact with these people, but have only one person as the teacher/leader of the study.

The previous advice from the Psychology chapter to to keep all socializing to the start of a study bears repeating for a small group setting, but this is made more difficult with the extra people involved. Try to stick to this plan without giving the impression you are policing the study. Sometimes when one of these helping church members blurts out too much too soon, it is the Lord, in His wisdom, making use of them to quicken the pace of the study. Sometimes a problem will arise in a small group where your helpers become too chatty and distract from the lesson. Take a cue from a successful evangelist who would start out a visitation session with everyone talking, but when he knew it was time to get the decision from the interest, he would lean forward and continue speaking in that position. That was the cue to his helpers to do nothing else but pray silently.

> **Words of Advice**
>
> Dr. Robert Logan, a church growth consultant and the Seeds '96 church planting seminar keynote speaker, said this about growing through small or 'cell' groups: "Always have one study leader and an apprentice. When the group divides, the apprentice becomes leader of the new group."

Once he does take a stand, IAIN is a newborn babe in the faith. He is inexperienced yes, but he has made a decision. What is needed most of all now is encouragement and friendship. It is up to you to change how you deal with him. As this person is now a member of the church, treat him as you would someone who has been a member for quite sometime. Do absolutely nothing to in any way send the message to your new friend that he or she is some sort of junior church member!

We don't police each other; we pray for each other. This is especially true if IAIN is a new friend who just came in through an evangelistic series. In one month he has absorbed what others take years

Mentoring New Converts

to consider. Let the pastor's Sabbath School class for new people take care of his doctrinal education. He has had enough for now. Just be his friend.

Manuscript Releases, volume 7, pages 267 and 268, contain some help for new converts. These words would be good for all people to read as soon as they take a stand for God. To continue in growth, those of us who have been in the church a while also need to read them ourselves: "Here is where the work of the Holy Ghost comes in, after your baptism.... You are born unto God, and you stand under the sanction and the power of the three holiest beings in heaven, who are able to keep you from falling. You are to reveal that you are dead to sin; your life is hid with Christ in God.... When I feel oppressed, and hardly know how to relate myself toward the work that God has given me to do, I just call upon the three great Worthies, and say; You know I cannot do this work in my own strength. You must work in me, and by me and through me, sanctifying my tongue, sanctifying my spirit, sanctifying my words, and bringing me into a position where my spirit shall be susceptible to the movings of the Holy Spirit of God upon my mind and c h a r a c t e r ."

> **Words of Advice**
>
> At the Seeds '96 church planting seminar held at Andrew's University, North American Division Evangelism Institute Director Russell Burrill pointed out that at the beginning of the book of Acts they counted people. By the end, they were counting churches.

The Lord's format for accomplishing growth in His people is as follows. First, there is an initial enlightening. Then comes a dark period or wilderness experience to test sincerity and faith. Finally, a second refreshing comes if the person is willing to wait for it. IAIN's experience is the end of one journey toward the light and the beginning of another. Whatever previous truth he held has now grown into the message for the last days. But this is a coming full circle to the start of a new journey. The new second light ahead is the hope of seeing Jesus face to face.

The hardest test will come as his fire dies down, and he goes through the crisis of faith that every Adventist has to go through. He will get to the point where he realizes the calling God has laid out for him is higher than he can attain to. Reminding him of the following promises will help him get there. "Looking unto Jesus the author and finisher of our faith; who for the joy that was set before him endured the cross, despising the shame, and is set down at the right hand of the throne of God" (Heb. 12:2). "Now unto him that is able to keep you from falling, and to present you faultless before the presence of his glory with exceeding joy" (Jude 24).

As we close this chapter, it is important to remind you, as the leader, of the process for reaching souls and the potential to burn out. The "sowing" is when you look for people to study with; the "cultivating" is when you give those studies; the "reaping" is when you obtain a decision; and the "conserving the gains" is when you shepherd the new souls. This entire process is what is needed to bring someone fully to the Lord.

Don't overextend yourself with too much of any one portion of this process while it is in motion. In other words, once you start to see results from sowing, cultivate what you have, reap it, and get it into the barn. Then go back out and sow some more. It is better to win one or two completely than to partially win a hundred.

Finally, remember not to let a continual outreach effort burn you out and cause your own faith to suffer. We read in Mark 6:7–12 about the Lord sending His disciples out on their first missionary journey. They return full of stories, both of successes and failures, and He says to them, "Come ye yourselves apart into a desert place, and rest a while … And they departed into a desert place by ship privately" (Mark 6:31, 32).

Chapter 9

Understanding Evangelicals

Being raised in what I call a nominal Christian environment, the Lord used evangelical Christians to prepare me to receive Him into my life. I value what I was given before becoming an Adventist, as I needed to hear that Jesus would be my Savior if I asked Him. After being shown the Savior anew along with doctrinal truth through studying with my wife and Pastor Warman, the Lord kept bringing evangelicals into my life. As I interacted with them, I was driven to study the word even harder to find answers to the challenges they brought me on issues of difference between our faiths.

This chapter is meant to help you understand the practical ramifications of what evangelicals teach in comparison to what Seventh-day Adventists teach. Knowing where others agree with you in concept, but maybe not in wording, should help you to relate to them better. There are many sincere people in every church who have truly been born-again. They simply haven't been led to the point in life where they have questioned the Sabbath yet. Ellen White wrote the following comment on Malachi 3:17: "God has jewels in all the churches, and it is not for us to make sweeping denunciation of the professed religious world, but in humility and love, present to all the truth as it is in Jesus" (*S.D.A. Bible Commentary*, vol. 4, p. 1184).

Philippians 1:18 says, "What then? notwithstanding, every way, whether in pretence, or in truth, Christ is preached; and I therein do rejoice, yea, and will rejoice." In *Evangelism* we read, "We are not to pass judgment on those who have not had the opportunities and privileges we have had. Some of these will go into heaven before those who have had great light but have not lived up to the light" (p. 173).

Therefore, let us as Adventists not think we're better than they are in any way. There are many Adventists who do not understand the church's message and are legalistic. It is easy to be lured into a false sense of security that they are in the "right" church and that the end-time issue only revolves around the Sabbath/Sunday question. The real issue for all humanity is whether or not we are going to make a full commitment to Christ, which includes keeping His holy day the way He wants us to.

So why are there so many churches? When the Lord raised up a leader during the Reformation and a new church was started, why didn't He find a way to do away with the previous churches? Let's consider the story of "Phil." This is a fictional account of something that likely happens in some form every day.

I Was Saved in a Living Room

Phil goes to Las Vegas for a weekend and scores big at the roulette table. To celebrate his winnings, he finds a drug dealer on the street, buys a gram of cocaine, gets himself a prostitute, and considers this a great weekend. Monday morning he's back home and on his way to work. When he arrives at his office building, there is a little old lady standing near the entrance holding up a pamphlet. From Phil's perspective he sees all religions as equal, and he has no interest in any of them. Does it matter then which church this lady is from or whether or not the doctrines in that pamphlet are truly biblical or not? In that immediate moment, God can use this lady's example to convict Phil of a better way.

This story illustrates a principle that is confirmed by Exodus 3:18. When you really look at this text, all God told Moses to ask Pharaoh for was a weekend off. The principle then is if they would reject some of the truth, they would reject all of the truth. Though I am completely willing to stake my eternal life on the fact that the Adventist understanding of the Bible is the real truth, I do rejoice that Christ is being preached in some form by all Christian denominations, including the Catholic Church. Those among the wicked who reject whatever form of truth given to them, be it complete or not, will have no excuse on judgment day.

Though they vary greatly in many peripheral beliefs, evangelicals define themselves as having three common core characteristics. First, they believe that Jesus is the Son of God, the Savior. Second, the Bible is the Word of God. And third, people must be born-again. So an evangelical is anyone who is preaching that people are flawed and need renewal from God above in order to get to heaven. This theology emphasizes the cross and that a person must first repent of sin in order to be saved.

The word "evangelical," meaning an emphasis on evangelistic methods, thus implies that their main tool for growth is the sharing of the gospel. Personally, I would class fundamentalists, Pentecostals, charismatics, and non-denominational Bible churches as evangelicals. I would even say that Adventists can be thought of as evangelicals in that we agree with the three main points of their faith.

Nominal Christianity, in name only, may talk of the same, but there is not much practical application of these ideas in everyday life. The central focus of this Christianity would, therefore, be church attendance and not a born-again understanding with a whole life commitment. Personally I would class most churches that don't accept the

> **Words of Advice**
>
> One of the reasons for the variety of denominations today is that many churches deduced from the Reformation that a highly centralized leadership structure will eventually cause corruption. They go with a congregational method instead. This means the tithe stays with the local body and pays that particular minister's salary. As Nancy Eirich pointed out, "There is then no motivation for a pastor to preach a strong message such as give up your jewelry for Jesus. The sermon is essentially just a sales pitch."

Bible as historically accurate in its entirety and teach infant baptism and use it as their main method for growth as nominal. They don't really promote their understanding of Jesus; they just expect those born into their ranks to stay with them.

> ## Words of Advice
>
> Another item of misunderstanding between evangelicals and Adventists is on Christ's human nature. When you really think about it, what we both believe in is very similar. They just aren't wording their view in as great a detail, and this throws them off. We both believe that Jesus had to really experience life here as one of us in order for the cross to have value.
>
> Confusion comes because of a difference in understanding the doctrine of original sin. Both believe a brokenness from God was created by Adam and Eve's choice. Both believe weakness of character has been passed down to all. However we only believe in individual responsibility for sin and don't believe in a guilt that has been passed down with that weakness like they do.
>
> Therefore we can see Christ as having a post-fall human nature and not thinking of it as a sinful one. (He felt the pull of sin but never surrendered to it. That pull did not defile Him.) To evangelicals this is blasphemy because they equate anything post-fall as being defiled already. To solve this dilemma, word your position on the subject this way, "He had a perfect, godly mind in a weak human body."
>
> That's all that needs to be said. Anymore and you're over-thinking the issue.

You may have friends from other churches who seem interested in the truth. They come to you with some amount of Bible knowledge and are at least willing to talk to you about spiritual things. Are they really interested though? If in trying to share with these people you find them continually turning the discussion into a doctrinal debate and trying to get you to come around to their point of view that should tell you something. By meeting them point for point, you may think you are advancing the truth, but you are only validating them, essentially telling them their points are worthy of being refuted. *Mind, Character, and Personality* says, "Love will gain the victory when argument and authority are powerless" (vol. 1, p. 210). When they see that their doctrinal arguments have no effect on you, that's when they can be convicted by the Spirit.

They believe in Christ, and their basic understanding of the gospel is essentially the same as ours. However, although evangelicals may use the same words and quote the same Bible verses you do, they put a spin on what they say that distorts those teachings into something different. I would liken evangelical theology to looking at the stars at night from a telescope in one's backyard, whereas Adventist theology can be likened to seeing pictures of the universe taken from the Hubble Space Telescope. It is much richer and clearer. Their theology focuses on salvation from humanity's point of view while ours focuses on God's point of view. Certainly the Lord has led in their lives so far. That needs to be respected in any dealings you have with them. However, He wants to use you to lead them into a deeper experience with Him and a clearer understanding of His Word.

There is a concept I like to call "human-centered thinking" drawn from the second commandment, which is the basis of all pluralism and false religion. Its emphasis is not on God revealing truth but on human opinion of truth. Christians of all faiths understand that when a Muslim, atheist, or Buddhist asks, "How can you tell who is right?" they are using human-centered thinking. What most Christians don't realize is that when they say to Adventists "that's just your interpretation" or "that's only the doctrine of your church" *they are doing the exact same thing.*

One reason more evangelicals don't want to take a stand with us is simply a prideful unwillingness to give up their own human-centered thinking. In some ways it's not surprising. To find out their sins put the Savior on the cross and to be shown beyond all doubt that no other way but accepting Jesus has any power to get them off this planet is incredible. They can't believe that anybody else could have even more truth. Think how it must feel for an evangelical, especially one with a very dramatic conversion story to tell, to be brought into contact with an Adventist who, by emphasizing doctrine, is essentially telling them "there's more to the experience than that." Some woman may stand up in her home church and say, "I was a prostitute for twenty-five years, and God rescued me in one weekend," but she's telling this story wearing huge, gaudy jewelry with thick makeup on her face while holding a cup of coffee in her hand. Does God want to do more in her life? I would say, "Yes!"

The question that is facing today's Christians is do people study the Bible for themselves or do they take a minister's word for it because he is a minister? Is their faith really in Jesus and in God's Word, or is their faith in the church? *Testimonies for the Church*, volume 9, has an answer. "The testing message for this time is to be borne so plainly and decidedly as to startle the hearers, and lead them to desire to study the Scriptures" (p. 109).

The Bible is one book with one message. If there's any hope of winning people with this mindset, you have to convince them what you're showing them is from the Bible and the Bible alone. You will hear a lot of taunts accusing you of blindly following Ellen White, whom they'll say made up or stole all this information you're sharing. Of course this is not true and you know it. Say to them plainly, "It's not my church against your church; it's what does the Bible really say?"

Every true revival from Martin Luther to present day had two things in common. One was a re-discovery of the plan of salvation. The other was some lost truth had been recovered and become an issue of contention, thus dividing the people of God into camps. They are either for the new truth or for the status quo—the true followers being the ones to advance with the new light. Luther is known as the re-discoverer of justification, which is the plan of salvation itself. Wesley is known for bringing us sanctification. Today, the sanctuary, state of the dead, and the Sabbath fill the place alongside forgiveness by Jesus' shed blood and build on top of baptism by immersion, sanctification, and tithe, which all had their place at one time or another during the Reformation.

The modern popular gospel comes from the trend toward church unity by ignoring doctrinal differences. It is very important to remember the exact wording of Matthew 24:14. Jesus said, "*this* gospel," not "*the* gospel," would be preached in all the world. Paul in Galatians 1:6–9 speaks of "another gospel" that all who believe would be cursed.

Paul also said, "I speak as a man" (Rom. 3:5).

I will speak in human terms here referring to evangelical theology as "their gospel" and Adventism as "our gospel." Adventists and evangelicals do have a lot in common. They are both Christians. They hold to the same basic doctrines such as the Trinity, Creation, the nature of humanity, and the need of the Savior. That's pretty much where their gospel ends.

Whether evangelicals would be willing to admit it to themselves or not, their gospel is still in the sixteenth century with its traditional beliefs about a soul going to heaven above or hell below as soon as someone dies. Their gospel understands the events of the first four books of the New Testament only in terms of contemplating Jesus' time on earth as a man and not thinking in terms of the great controversy theme and the plan of salvation being worked out through every generation of human history. This is why the "Michael the Archangel" study is important. It was God the Son who interacted with man in Old Testament times. When you combine the Bible study on life on other planets with the ones teaching the truth about death, the sanctuary, and Michael the Archangel, you end up with our gospel that shows heaven is as real as our world is. For every other belief system in the world, both in and outside Christianity, heaven is a wispy fairyland or in some other dimension of time and space. These are both simply saying the same things.

Words of Advice

Embracing the Adventist worldview also affects your understanding of the creation/evolution debate. The "creation science" movement coming out of the evangelical camp is based on the traditional Christian worldview of a person going to heaven or hell immediately after death as a ghost. Therefore, they bend over backward to try to show this earth as the only possible place in the universe where intelligent life could exist, and they say the entire universe is 6,000 years old. So was Lucifer created on day four, and then he rebelled on day eight? In the mind of an evolutionist, we might as well try to prove the earth is flat.

As you read Ellen White's descriptions of Satan's fall and the war in heaven, its obvious these things happened before the earth was created. It's entirely possible the universe is 14 billion years old as the astronomers theorize. Genesis 1 and 2 describes the creation of this planet and the solar system that serves it. This does not invalidate creation in favor of evolution though. Every other solar system in the universe must have been created one at a time using the same literal seven-day process God used for this one.

When their gospel says, "Christ died for you," what they mean is that He suffered a gruesome, horrible physical death, which is true. However, that's the most minimal way to understand the cross. Our gospel talks of the value of Christ's suffering and death in that it was primarily on the mental and legal level. With the proper understanding of the first and second deaths, we know He did not feel the fire of the second death, but He did feel the anguish of it, that separation from God that all sinners will face on judgment day.

The question of righteousness by faith becomes a very tricky thing. Evangelicals are quick to declare that works have no place in salvation and faith is what it's all about. However, when they quote, "Love is the fulfillment of the law," or say, "The law is now in our hearts," what they mean is, "Because I have a warm fuzzy feeling inside about Jesus, now I don't have to make any changes in my life." The two most important Bible studies in this book are "True Grace is Power to Live Right" and "The Differences in False and True Christianity." They describe the truth about righteousness by faith. It's at this point that the two gospels diverge from each other before the Sabbath question is discussed.

Because of this, their idea of what constitutes justification is different from ours. Their gospel teaches that when a sinner finds Jesus that person is declared righteous. It is thought of as a legal transaction done only in heaven. Our gospel teaches that when a sinner finds Jesus he or she is *made* righteous. When we talk of God giving us His goodness, we don't just mean we wear it like a covering label. We mean it is a living experience and we are actually changed by it, so long as we continue to accept it.

The greatest difference in these two gospels is on this subject of righteousness by faith. Their gospel says, "God's love gives me an excuse for my sins." While ours says, "God's love gives me power to rise above my sins." The reason for the difference here is because of the influence of what's known as once saved always saved. This is also called the doctrine of eternal security or predestination.

Not all evangelicals claim to be adherents to the ideas put forth originally by John Calvin, which states that only a select few are predestined by the Lord for salvation and the rest are doomed with no real choice for either side. However, the influence of these ideas has colored the question of what exactly it means to say we are saved by grace. This is commented on in *The Great Controversy*, "The sanctification now gaining prominence in the religious world carries with it a spirit of self-exaltation and a disregard for the law of God that mark it as foreign to the religion of the Bible. Its advocates teach that sanctification is an instantaneous work, by which, through faith alone, they attain to perfect holiness" (p. 471).

> **Words of Advice**
>
> Louis Torres has a story of a major university that did a study and concluded people's characters are set within them by the age of five. Only three things can later affect anyone—personal trauma, the death of a loved one, and a genuine born-again Christian conversion.

One parable helps us understand the development of church history and our place in it. Jesus compares Himself to the sower of wheat and the devil to the sower of tares in Matthew 13:24–30, 37–43. It begins with Jesus sowing and ends with the harvest. Since He sowed the Word with His first coming and the harvest is the end of the age, it is, therefore, a description of the entire Christian era.

As you read the entire parable and the Lord's explanation, you will notice something very interesting. How many parties are involved in the parable? Three: the wheat, who are His; the tares, who are Satan's; and finally the field, which is the world. You may have heard someone interpret this to mean that the tares are the Buddhists, Muslims, New Age Movement followers, etc. However, this is not true. Imagine all the belief systems of the world as a circle and Christianity as another circle inside it. Then imagine a pure dot of absolute truth inside the circle of the church. All that is outside the circle of the church is the field. It is the stage on which the conflict takes place. This point is illustrated in Figure A. As far as issues go in the conflict, all that is outside does not count.

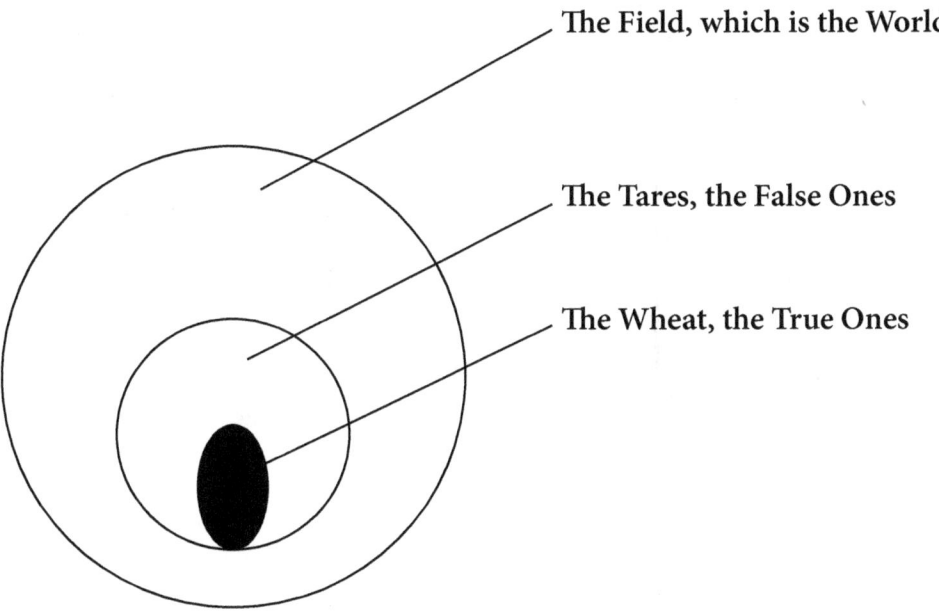

Figure A

Christ died for all people, of course, but the conflict described in this parable goes on *inside the church*. This is where true and false interacts in the Bible narrative. In the entire storyline of the Bible and church history, the ones who have turned from God and need to be called back have always ended up as the majority within the faith, while the true followers of God are the minority. Revivals come when it is necessary to call God's people back to the Bible. If the people will accept the preacher of truth and his or her message, they will be saved from whatever calamities have threatened to befall them.

Now consider the thought structure of most evangelical pamphlets. They have illustrations with a human being on one side and God on the other with the cross as the only way to bring the person across the great chasm to God (see Figure B). Sounds correct, doesn't it? This is why we have the dynamic described in Phil's story (at the start of this chapter). There is a certain amount of value to this theology, especially with all the quoted verses that focus on our inability to achieve heaven through our own good works.

However, read an evangelical pamphlet through, and you will see its emphasis is almost exclusively directed to the non-Christian who needs to hear this message of general conviction of all sin, along with an invitation to accept the Lord. Unfortunately, there is little, if any, direction in how to live life as a Christian afterward or what doctrines to accept or reject from the different denominations out there. By only emphasizing the core elements of Christianity and making no difference in doctrines, their gospel changes the third of the three great questions of life from "What does He want me to do for Him in return?" into "What do I want to do for Him in return?" The love of God then becomes the vehicle for bringing false doctrines into the church because of a lack of scrutiny.

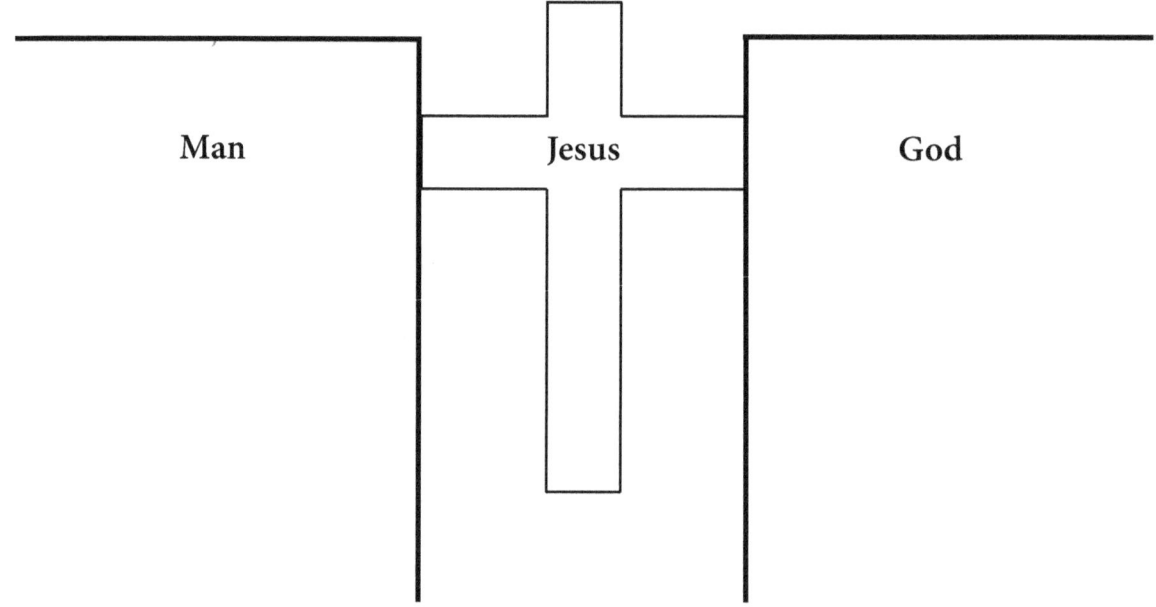

Figure B: "Evangelical Bridging The Gap Theology"

True faith includes good works. They come after conversion and are evidence that conversion is genuine. The thought structure implied in their gospel is of two groups instead of three. There are those who accept the Lord and those who do not. The field in the parable would not fit into this system—the wheat would be all Christians with the tares being all else. This is simply inadequate theology; thus making the standard of righteousness a lot higher than the evangelicals believe. This is also what makes things so tricky because it is not wrong, it's just not right enough. Their gospel is telling the world, "You need to become a Christian." But their gospel is not making any difference within Christian faith, while our gospel is telling the world, "Yes, you do need to become a Christian, but here's what kind of Christian you need to become."

Once again, we cannot judge. We showed we weren't ready for Jesus to come back with the way

Jones and Waggoner, who were speaking on true righteousness by faith, were treated at the Minneapolis General Conference in 1888. Though the message of Adventism is Bible truth, we as church members have the same struggles living up to the truth as everyone else. Every Christian of every denomination must realize that the call to holiness the Bible sets before us is higher than a human is capable of attaining to. We can either play games with words, trying to avoid our responsibility in life, or we can throw ourselves at Jesus' feet and believe He will help us.

The differences in the two gospels also affects how one views Christian unity. To say doctrinal differences don't matter and the love of Jesus is all we need creates a unity in the church based on church politics. All organizations that teach the three basic core elements can keep their existing structures without worry or fear of anyone losing their job. The concept within Adventism of the remnant church is one actual church. This is not only a unity of belief but of the actual church organization.

Words of Advice

One of the most encouraging books to read when considering the differences between their gospel and ours is *Seventh-day Adventists Answer Questions on Doctrine*. (Yes, I know there are those who call themselves "Historic Adventists" who want nothing to do with *Questions on Doctrine* and say 5 percent of the book is wrong. I am talking about the other 95 percent that is right.) The overall tone behind each and every question Martin and Barnhouse asked our leaders was, "You're not one of us; therefore, you must be wrong, justify yourselves," which is the same attitude the Jewish leaders took toward Jesus.

What's fascinating is that's exactly what the authors of the book did! They knew these men couldn't be reached using Bible texts as the differences in the two gospels would affect their view of what any one verse meant. So *Questions on Doctrine* is full of references to the exact same Protestant scholars Martin and Barnhouse themselves would have had confidence in. *Questions on Doctrine* shows that it's not Adventism that has departed from the spirit and power of the Reformation, it's evangelical Christianity.

There are of course other differences that need to be understood when discussing prophecy issues and end-time events. The mainstream evangelical churches have almost completely given themselves over to the false system of prophetic interpretation known as futurism or dispensationalism. Seventh-day Adventists are believers in the historicist view.

Futurism is entirely based on what's known as "the gap theory." It says that the last week of prophetic time in the 70-weeks prophecy of Daniel 9:24–27 is meant for the Jews and will be a seven year time period just before the second coming. There is much confusion within the futurist camp because the second coming is presented as a two-stage event where the true believers suddenly disappear in the rapture one day and all that is left are the wicked who get one more chance to be saved before the absolute end. Some are pre-tribulation and others believe in a mid- or post-tribulation rapture. The focus of this system is entirely on the literal, political nation of Israel in the Middle East today with an understanding of the mark of the beast as some literal hand stamp or credit card issue like an RFID chip or UPC code.

Almost everything we take as symbolic, they take as literal and vice versa. The place a rebuilt temple in Jerusalem has within futurism is the same place the sanctuary has within Adventism. Whereas evangelicals are looking for the antichrist to be a political leader who will try to create a one-world government, we are looking for a spiritual leader who will try to create a one-world religion.

Their view of Armageddon is one where a literal war will be fought between the so-called Christian west on one side and some foreign, ungodly enemy on the other in the actual valley of Megiddo in Israel. Who they think that enemy will be happens to be whomever is the current enemy in the headlines. When Hal Lindsay wrote *Late Great Planet Earth* in the 1960s, the enemy of the day was the communists in either the USSR or China. These same ideas have been repackaged by Tim Lahaye in his *Left Behind* series, and now Muslims are the enemy.

Though it may be hard for your friends to handle, when you understand the 70-weeks prophecy correctly, modern Israel has absolutely no place in Bible prophecy! The battle of Armageddon will be and now is a spiritual battle. It's the last time anyone on the planet will have a chance to make their decision for or against Jesus and His truth. It's interesting to note that they use the day for a year principle with this prophecy because it cannot come true any other way, but then they ignore the day for a year principle in interpreting every other time prophecy. The 70 weeks work out perfectly to AD 34 just as is shown by the Bible study included earlier. Trying to make futurism work is like trying to build a pyramid from the top brick down. On paper everything seems to fit, but when it comes down to an actual application of these ideas, they just don't work.

> ### Words of Advice
>
> This is why you need to examine the situation with IAIN as you begin studying together. If you are studying with someone who has little to no knowledge of God and spiritual things, use bridging the gap theology at first. Then go beyond it when IAIN is ready. More importantly, with so much emphasis on love and so much animosity toward doctrine, odds are IAIN may not be practicing in real life what his church teaches on paper anyway!

Matthew 13:40–43 says, "As therefore the tares are gathered and burned in the fire; so shall it be in the end of this world. The Son of man shall send forth his angels, and they shall gather *out of his kingdom* [which is the church] all things that offend, and them which do iniquity; And shall cast them into a furnace of fire: there shall be wailing and gnashing of teeth. Then shall the righteous shine forth as the sun in the kingdom of their Father. Who hath ears to hear, let him hear."

One thing that puzzled me for years was the fact that the order of events at the end of the parable of the wheat and tares directly contradicts the order of end-time events as shown in the book of Revelation. Just a few years ago, I realized the reason. The sending forth of the angels here is not a reference to literal angels gathering the wicked a short time before the second coming. Jesus is speaking here about the preaching of the three angels' messages. Since 1840 these messages have caused a change in the Christian world, dividing them into two camps just as in the Reformation.

How is this gathering happening? The answer is in the chapter "Modern Revivals" in *The Great Controversy*. There Ellen White describes how William Miller preached in a logical fashion, providing Bible verses to prove his point, but by 1888 when *The Great Controversy* was first published, popular preachers used emotional appeals instead. She then goes on to describe how the Ten Commandments fit into true faith.

What other reason could there be for this change but for the preaching of the true Sabbath? The ministers of other churches likely said in their hearts, "If that's true, I'm out of a job," and they started teaching that the law wasn't so important after all. It is this attitude that has directly led to the great moral decline we have seen in our time. In each generation since then, mainstream Christianity has lost more and more of its hold on western society with its watered down gospel, and secularism has risen up to take its place.

When you think about it, the last time the Christian church had enough influence in the western world to get the government to do its bidding was in the prohibition era. Since losing that battle after prohibition was repealed, the church has lost on every other moral question: evolution, rock and roll music, feminism, divorce, abortion, and homosexual rights. Now we are seeing a meanness of spirit in what the U.S. media calls "the religious right" as they struggle to regain lost ground. This is actually a fulfillment of Matthew 24:12: "And because iniquity shall abound, the love of many shall wax cold." Verse 13 says, "But he that shall endure unto the end, the same shall be saved."

> **Words of Advice**
>
> One time some evangelicals from a local Bible college came to the Airdrie church to visit. Ken Eirich told them in conversation how in his twenty years as a Pentecostal pastor before becoming an Adventist he had been exposed to six different views on the rapture. Jesus is only going to come back one way. The confusion on the issue is proof it's not true.

The gathering together into bundles corresponds with Paul's words in 2 Timothy 4:3, 4: "For the time will come when they will not endure sound doctrine; but after their own lusts shall they heap to themselves teachers, having itching ears; And they shall turn away their ears from the truth, and shall be turned unto fables."

By believing things about end-time events that aren't true and getting angry as the evil ones gain more and more power, Christians will be tempted to the point where they say, "That's it, we're taking over." As the end-time finally does break upon us, the supposedly better world established by secularism will fall apart, so they will attempt to take over. However, since they hold to an inadequate theology that leads them to overlook the false doctrines not only of their own churches but also of the Catholic Church, millions of people will be led astray and will be on the wrong side. This is described in *The Great Controversy*: "When the leading churches of the United States, uniting upon such points of doctrine as are held by them in common, shall influence the state to enforce their decrees and to sustain their institutions, then Protestant America will have formed an image of the Roman hierarchy, and the infliction of civil penalties upon dissenters will inevitably result" (p. 445).

Now of course we want to reach out in friendship and present the three angels' messages to all concerned. There is nothing we can do to prevent the fact that many will disagree with us. The two gospels are not the same. The question has to be asked plainly and clearly and is proven by the Bible studies in this book, who is really preaching this gospel and who is really preaching the other gospel?

> ### Words of Advice
>
> For those who think we should try to be like other churches as much as possible consider this. Lester Carney, after years of successful evangelism, said, "You have to give them something they are not getting in their own church. Otherwise why should they change over? They won't come to get the same thing they get already. So you see, the differences [in our faith] make all the difference."

This is the reason why those from within the evangelical camp who are opposed to us call us a cult and try to downgrade Ellen White. She can't be a true prophet to them because she isn't telling them what they want to hear. John 1:22 documents the Pharisees asking John the Baptist, "What do you say about yourself?" (NKJV). This implies they approached issues of faith from a human-centered thinking point of view.

It is interesting to note that they also accused Jesus of doing the same thing in John 8:13. His words in Luke 7:29–35 indicate that Jesus knew He couldn't satisfy them. If this happens to you, do everything you can to show that what you believe comes from the Bible, and follow this advice when facing criticism: "Those who were in pursuit of the earthly [crown], mocked them, and threw black balls after them. These did them no injury while their eyes were fixed upon the heavenly crown, but those who turned their attention to the black balls were stained with them" (*Testimonies for the Church*, vol. 1, p. 349).

On page 353 we read "The black balls which were thrown after the saints were the reproachful falsehoods put in circulation concerning God's people by those who love and make a lie. We should take the greatest care to live a blameless life, and abstain from all appearance of evil, and then it is our duty to move boldly forward, and pay no regard to the reproachful falsehoods of the wicked. While the eyes of the righteous are fixed upon the heavenly priceless treasure, they will become more and more like Christ, and thus they will be transformed and fitted for translation" (*Ibid.*).

It's also interesting to note how on page 341 of Jud Lake's book *Ellen White Under Fire*, he remarks that the sum total of all of Ellen White's statements her critics take issue with "amounts to … 0.1% of her writings." He admits he is not addressing the plagiarism issue in this calculation. He's not talking about any question regarding the source of her statements but the statements themselves. Think about that. Just as in the Bible, the Lord has literally given 99.9 percent proof of Himself in Ellen White's writings, and yet that's still not good enough!

If only those who put out so many anti-Adventist materials could see they are fulfilling her prophecy in *The Great Controversy*: "As the controversy extends into new fields and the minds of the people are called to God's downtrodden law, Satan is astir. The power attending the message will only madden those who oppose it. The clergy will put forth almost superhuman efforts to shut away the light lest it should shine upon their flocks. By every means at their command they will endeavor to suppress the discussion of these vital questions" (p. 607).

When the character of Christ is reproduced in enough members of the Seventh-day Adventist Church that the Lord can see fit to pour out the latter rain upon them, the sincere-hearted evangelicals will finally see the Sabbath in its true light. However, what we face with the evangelicals who refuse to give up their human-centered thinking, Paul faced with the Jews. In his time they were the ones who thought they knew the truth, and in pride they resisted as the Lord called them to higher truth than they were willing to attain to. Paul did try to reach them, but he also gave up when he saw they just wouldn't listen.

If you have a friend who is constantly debating with you, maybe it is time to do the same. Maybe someone else around you will hear the truth, and you will win a soul instead of an argument. "Reject a divisive man after the first and second admonition, knowing that such a person is warped and sinning, being self-condemned" (Titus 3:10, 11, NKJV). "Then Paul and Barnabas grew bold and said, 'It was necessary that the word of God should be spoken to you first; but since you reject it, and judge yourselves unworthy of everlasting life, behold, we turn to the Gentiles. For so the Lord has commanded us'" (Acts 13:46, 47, NKJV).

But as you've probably noticed yourself, when we hold prophecy seminars, most of the attendees are evangelical Christians. In the end they may become our greatest enemies, but until that day, they are the best candidates to share the truths of the Bible with. Many will come to the full truth through a partial experience first, which prepares them to hear the rest. Our purpose as a church is to call out of Babylon those who are God's. Some will come in directly from the world, but we are primarily a reform movement within Christianity.

Make it your goal to show not only by your words but also by your character that what you believe in really is what the Bible says. We read in Daniel 12:3, "And they that be wise shall shine as the brightness of the firmament; and they that turn many to righteousness as the stars for ever and ever." The many are the majority of today's sincere believers in God. What are they to be turned to? Righteousness. This is the rest of the Christian experience.

Words of Advice

I've briefly surveyed a number of anti-Ellen White materials and have noticed two elements in common. The first is the bad example of some church member who caused the author of the book, video, or Web site to lose confidence in us as a people. This is of course sad, but not really a valid criticism of what we believe. The author is merely disgruntled and does not have the faith to discern between the perfect message and the imperfect people who struggle to live up to that message.

The other is quite a bit more serious—a rejection of the sanctuary doctrine. The sanctuary is the one doctrine that we alone hold to be true. It's as important as the Sabbath and the Spirit of Prophecy to understanding the significance of last-day events. Because evangelicals believe in a soul going to heaven or hell right after death, they can't embrace the sanctuary. Why have a judgment now to decide if all the ghosts up there in heaven can be allowed to stay or not?

It will help to reach your evangelical friend by tying the sanctuary to the truth about death and also by explaining we are forgiven in two ways, though evangelicals only emphasize the first. That emphasis is on the individual experiencing forgiveness. Jesus offered to erase the record of the wrongs done by human beings. He made this offer during their lifetimes as His voice spoke to their hearts through the Holy Spirit and the Word. Now Jesus is making that offer real for all who accepted it from every generation of history. Since 1844 He has been erasing those records with the clerical assistance of the angels mentioned in Daniel 7. He is essentially proving to the rest of the universe that the ones He will save can be trusted with eternal life, are sorry for all their sins, and will completely submit to His will.

Chapter 10

The Three Angels' Messages in One, Easy Five-Minute Lesson

Our calling is not only to tell the world the truth but also to prove it to be true by living it. We need an experience of Jesus and His forgiving love like never before. We need to understand what it means to say that He has saved us from all our sins. The evangelical understanding of justification makes it essentially a label or a rubber stamp applied in a one-time experience with no real change in us. It makes no room for sanctification. What about our understanding? How does doctrine and Christian growth fit in with accepting Jesus as our personal Savior? *Evangelism* says, "Several have written to me, inquiring if the message of justification by faith is the third angel's message, and I have answered, 'It is the third angel's message in verity'" (p. 190).

Marvin Moore concurs in his book *The Crisis of the End Time*: "It is crucial to understand that our standing with God after the close of probation—our assurance of salvation during the time of trouble—will be grounded on exactly the same foundation as it is today: justification, not sanctification.… here, unfortunately is where many Seventh-day Adventists have gotten themselves off track. They think that justification provides our standing with God before probation closes, but that sanctification—a perfect character—must provide our standing with God after probation closes. This is totally false! It is a deception that will cause you untold grief and unnecessary spiritual anguish during the time of trouble.… I urge you to read through the chapter 'The Time of Trouble' in The Great Controversy and notice that not once does Ellen White say that character perfection will be the basis of salvation during that time. The basis for assurance then will be exactly what it is now: repentance and confession of sin, and faith in the blood of Jesus to forgive those sins. When we stand before God during the time of Jacob's trouble, we must plead His righteousness to cover our confessed sins the same way we do now, and that will be our assurance of salvation then just as it is now" (pp. 220, 221).

We need a new understanding of how justification and sanctification relate to each other. With this we can avoid the traps of legalism, which says that we can get to heaven by our own good works or "sloppy agape," which is the faith only, works free, impractical gospel taught so much today. But if we are saved by faith, why when Jesus comes again will He reward people according to their works?

James 2:18, 20–24 gives us an answer, "Yea, a man may say, Thou hast faith, and I have works: shew me thy faith without thy works, and I will shew thee my faith by my works.... But wilt thou know, O vain man, that faith without works is dead? Was not Abraham our father justified by works, when he had offered Isaac his son upon the altar? Seest thou how faith wrought with his works, and by works was faith made perfect? And the scripture was fulfilled which saith, Abraham believed God, and it was imputed unto him for righteousness: and he was called the Friend of God. Ye see then how that by works a man is justified, and not by faith only."

We can't get to heaven on our own because we don't have the power to be good. Evangelical pamphlets are very adamant to stress that point. They also stress Jesus had to come and die for our sins to pay our debt to God, which is true. But what they don't stress is that with God uplifting us we can recover our noble dignity and become the people He wants us to be. This is the true solution to the crisis of faith we all have to go through. Romans 8:3 says, "For what the law could not do, in that it was weak through the flesh, God sending his own Son in the likeness of sinful flesh, and for sin, condemned sin in the flesh."

Look carefully at these words. The problem is not the law but our ability to keep it. Jesus had to die to satisfy the penalty of the law, but this verse does not discuss that. His condemning of sin is a condemning of the excuse that we can't obey. He came with a perfect godly mind in a weak human body and lived a sinless life by depending on the Father above. When our mind is renewed, we can do the same thing if we depend on Him! That is what righteousness by faith really is. It is being good by faith!

One of the most freeing experiences of a Christian's life is the realization that just because one may be tempted, that does not mean one is already defiled. If Jesus was tempted the same way we are and He did not sin, then it is not a sin to be tempted. When you first come to accept Jesus as your Savior, the Holy Spirit takes the merits of His sacrifice and applies them to your own life as you come to believe with all your heart and ask Him to do this in response to His wooing. You are justified, or purged, of all that you knew to be sin at the time when you repented of it. It is His work. But it is a work He works in you! The cause and effect relationship is that as you receive His justification you are born again and become a new person in Jesus.

Sanctification can be rightly understood as justification all over again. As your Christian life goes on, you are given new opportunities to learn about other aspects of your life that you did not then know to be sinful. The Lord winked at them then, but now He commands you to repent on a sin-by-sin basis with tailor-made experiences just for you. Any lesson you learn in life that makes you a better person, you ultimately learned from God. These lessons themselves constitute our sanctification when we accept them in faith.

The true understanding of how justification and sanctification relate to each other is best illustrated by the growth rings of a tree. When a sapling newly emerges from the ground and begins growing, it is surrounded by bark. As the tree grows, the bark gets thicker, and the tree changes. It is not the same as when it started. Examining a cross section shows a pattern of rings. Each ring is the place where the bark used to be. The inside of the tree filled the place as the bark expanded on the outside. When the tree is mature it bears fruit. A tree is perfect in the sense that at each stage of its growth, it is a perfect specimen for that stage. It's not perfect in the sense that it hasn't finished that growth process until there's fruit.

2 Peter 1:3–8 starts and ends with references to the true gospel of Jesus' covering mercy and righteousness by faith: "According as his divine power hath given unto us all things that pertain unto life and godliness, through the knowledge of him that hath called us to glory and virtue: Whereby are given unto us exceeding great and precious promises: that by these ye might be partakers of the divine nature, having escaped the corruption that is in the world through lust.… For if these things be in you, and abound, they make you that ye shall neither be barren nor unfruitful in the knowledge of our Lord Jesus Christ."

The middle section of the passage lists the growth process that happens as one acts on the promises given them of God. "And beside this, giving all diligence, add to your faith virtue; and to virtue knowledge; And to knowledge temperance; and to temperance patience; and to patience godliness; And to godliness brotherly kindness; and to brotherly kindness charity" (verses 5–7). So Peter's words describe a growth process that is continually in motion as long as you live. Yet it comes around full circle—from knowing Jesus initially, through all the phases of your faith development, to knowing Him anew.

Verses 9 and 10 include a useful rebuttal of the once saved always saved argument: "But he that lacketh these things is blind, and cannot see afar off, and hath forgotten that he was purged from his old sins. Wherefore the rather, brethren, give diligence to make your calling and election sure: for if ye do these things, ye shall never fall." If these things—in other words the growth we obtain from our relationship with Jesus—abound, we gain a greater knowledge of Him. Therefore when someone has truly experienced the Lord and grown for the better because of it, this experience leads to a greater sense of dependence on God than ever before.

One of the fatal flaws in evangelical theology is that with such an emphasis on faith and a corresponding downgrading of works in the salvation experience, they don't fully know what it means to repent. Repent of what? They will say repent of sin, but what sins? Without the Ten Commandments in their proper place there is no practical, clear definition of sin to work from. When you are sharing and the word comes to IAIN to accept the Lord's death on the cross for forgiveness and he or she does, that is following God, which the evangelicals agree with. When other words such as "keep the Sabbath" are brought out in the study, accepting those words are also acts of submission to His will.

When I was in the world, I needed to be saved from it. From the Baptists, Pentecostals, and even a few on-fire members of the United Church, a church I would not class as evangelical but as nominal, I learned that the life of the singles bar was unfulfilling. As an Adventist I still agree with that statement. When I found Jesus, He saved me from alcohol, drugs, and loose morals. However, He did not stop there. He gave me contact with Adventists to teach me pure doctrine. The reason I don't drink alcohol is the same reason I now don't drink coffee. It's also the same reason I don't wear jewelry, because these are additional things that can separate me from God. My iniquity was purged by mercy in the form of forgiveness, and also by truth in the form of teaching me a better way.

Jesus also saved me from false understandings of what it means to keep the fourth commandment. He did that by teaching me what the Sabbath is all about. And He saved me from the trap of spiritualism by teaching me the truth about death, heaven, hell, and the events surrounding the Millennium. I was excited to learn all these things and so much more from my wife's example and her pastors' Bible studies. It was the Spirit speaking through them that wooed and changed me as I submitted to what I was being shown. All the doctrine I learned only enhanced my knowledge and experience of what it meant to say that God loved me.

Previous to experiencing conversion, you were operating under a false understanding of what goodness was and how sinful sin was. After conversion, you are humbled by the knowledge of the sacrifice of Christ and want to go on to serve Him better than you ever have before. As life goes on, it is easy to think that you, as a new Christian, have to look to yourself for this change and think that you do the work with His help. This is not the case. Read 2 Peter 1:11: "For so an entrance shall be ministered unto you abundantly into the everlasting kingdom of our Lord and Saviour Jesus Christ."

Notice that Peter said that the entrance would be "ministered" unto you. To some degree you will feel that you must make changes in your life, but when you try on your own, you will feel only frustration and difficulty (and if you did succeed God would owe you salvation). As you are brought to points in life where you say to yourself (of sin habits you once cherished and struggled with), "never again will I do this, it has caused me to suffer too much," you will realize that all the changes for the better that have happened were from God working in your life.

No matter where you are on the path to heaven, you will always have a humanness that taints you and creates in you a need of Jesus to cover you with His goodness. If all of a sudden, prayers are not being answered and your conscience is being pricked about something, then He is giving you a chance to grow in some area of your walk with Him. By study, prayer, and reflecting on your circumstances, you will find the answer as to what change He wants you to make in your life. When you make that change, it's because He led you through this process. The proof of that is when the change becomes permanent. Therefore, instead of trying in your own strength to be good, you are trusting and following as you respond to what He reveals to you. He is the one really doing the work because He orchestrates the experiences and grants the empowerment once you make the decision to follow Him.

This practical understanding of how justification and sanctification relate to each other is so powerful. If people would accept it, I honestly believe it would heal the rift *Questions on Doctrine* created within the Adventist church between those who now call themselves "Progressive Adventists" (liberals) and those who call themselves "Historic Adventists" (conservatives). If people would accept it and be willing to be led further by the Holy Spirit, it could heal the rift between evangelicals and Adventists. It could even heal the rift created when the Catholic Church rejected the teachings of Martin Luther at the Council of Trent and make us all into one truly unified church under Christ.

The Three Angels' Messages in One, Easy Five-Minute Lesson

This process of sanctification is also highlighted in the Beatitudes of Matthew 5:3–12. The "poor in spirit" refers to those who come from the world and search for Jesus. Like the prodigal son, they decide to go home. They find Jesus when He comes as a seed of truth. If they are truly interested, the devil can't take them away and that seed will grow into a harvest of conversion. They "mourn" as they are sorry for their sins. Becoming "meek" by the knowledge of the sacrifice He made on their behalf. They "hunger and thirst after righteousness" when they are changed by the renewing of their minds. With a knowledge of what true goodness is, they see the world in a whole new light.

Immediately after conversion, people are on fire for God. Since they are newly acquainted with the truth, they don't know much yet so they spend more time sowing seeds than cultivating or reaping. Then comes a time of darkness in the wilderness. It is "dark" when there is cherished sin to deal with. They are in the "wilderness" when there is a right relationship with God but are in need of a greater understanding as to who He is. Here is where the sleeping mentality takes over for believers. Interest in outreach becomes secondary to their own problems. Whatever they share with others in the way of cultivating comes from what they themselves are learning.

It's easy to get caught off guard and lose sight of Jesus when people focus on their problems instead of His solution. The dark time is needed to help them deal with the root causes of the remaining sins they struggle with. They need to understand fully that it is not just the guilt of the individual wrongs that God wants to deal with; it is also the character flaws themselves that make people commit those wrongs. What brings people out is the second refreshing. This is the true understanding of righteousness by faith—that the Lord will give them the power to be good. He works with them to teach them the lessons they need to learn in a way that is right for them, preparing them for the more glorious future ahead. It is also a time to test their faith. Unfortunately, not everyone successfully comes out of this time. This is where the thorns may choke out the Word. The advice in *The Acts of the Apostles* page 105 is especially useful.

After being brought through this time and realizing the Lord's forgiveness anew, they understand His mercy even more. In seeking sanctification, they find justification again in a greater sense. This leads to purity of heart and a desire to help others find the same thing they have. This is also where they have removed the beam out of their own eyes and can see clearly to help their neighbors in love. They are now "peacemakers," ready for the good ground in which to grow in grace by leaps and bounds. Their growth is in faith and in numbers. Now they are on fire again, but it is more like hot coals instead of a raging bonfire—this fire is quiet, deep, and much more intense. Now they reap results from their previous efforts at sowing and cultivating. This explains why it's worth it for the Lord to wait for the sleeping church to awake. The sleeping mentality, being simply an immature state of faith, will awaken when it grows to maturity.

As each of us looks back on how in our young understanding of the truth we were sleeping Christians for so long, we will say, "That is what I needed to go through to get to where I am now," and we'll rejoice in God and His leading in those very experiences. We thought we knew the Lord, but now we have been shown more. We want to share Him more, and our sharing is now much more effective because of the humbling experiences we've gone through. This allows us to be more compassionate to sinners around us.

What is really fascinating about the Beatitudes is that in each step of the process Jesus says those who are there are "blessed." He is with us the whole way. In Isaiah 54:4 we read, "Fear not; for thou shalt not be ashamed: neither be thou confounded: for thou shalt not be put to shame: for thou shalt forget the shame of thy youth, and shalt not remember the reproach of thy widowhood any more." It is such a joy to be brought through the process and emerge on the other side. The joy is greatest when we realize we were brought through by a loving God.

The three-phase system of growth is mirrored in the lives of many Bible characters and the whole history of the world. The time up until the flood was a demonstration of how bad things can get under sin. Then a first refreshing in the form of the Exodus was given. The people tried to obey in their own strength and failed, so Jesus came to provide forgiveness, restoration, and righteousness by faith.

The life of Jacob, starting at the vision of the ladder, is another example. *Patriarchs and Prophets* puts it this way, "In the vision the plan of redemption was presented to Jacob, not fully, but in such parts as were essential to him at that time…. All this was revealed to Jacob in his dream. Although his mind at once grasped a part of the revelation, its great and mysterious truths were the study of his lifetime, and unfolded to his understanding more and more" (p. 184).

Consider how Joseph's life impacted Egypt, the known world of his day, and how that is a symbolic representation of Jesus. Joseph went to prison but then became the Egyptian's savior when he told pharaoh his dream and formulated a plan to make it through the drought. Similarily, Jesus saved us from the prison of sin by becoming sin for us. Moses then was a second refreshing for Israel as they were called into the Promised Land, which we can compare to heaven on earth. The first and second comings are symbolized also in the fact that the plagues that befell the Egyptians who had enslaved God's people came after they had been given an offer of salvation through them. How different would Egypt have been if they had all accepted the God of the Hebrews after Pharaoh's dreams. Their mistreatment of their friends, the Israelites, showed their contempt for God.

Our Lord went through this process of growth too. He never sinned, but mirrored our experience coming out of sin into conversion by coming out of Egypt. He then lived a normal life, the life of a sleeping Christian, which was not wrong, just not finished. After that His public ministry represents a more active service, a higher level of faith that we all need to attain to. Jesus did not go all the way to Rome or Spain, He stayed within His own circle, but just think how much that circle expanded beyond the people He personally knew!

Those who accepted Him caught the vision laid before them by His great commission, and they went to the rest of the then known world for Him. Church history also mirrors this process, both in the entire Christian era and in the history of our denomination. The "former rain" of Hosea 6:3 corresponds to Pentecost. The first century church went into the Dark Ages and came out during the Reformation.

The Three Angels' Messages in One, Easy Five-Minute Lesson

Each reformer's message was a second refreshing for the people. Each time the people only went as far as that reformer would lead them, they were going back into darkness. The final reform came in the form of the Advent movement. The first vision given to Ellen White showed how we received a great first light in the form of the Millerite movement and were on a journey to heaven with a second light ahead of us. Today we look to the same second refreshing promised to the whole church—the "latter rain" promise of the final outpouring of the Holy Spirit and Jesus' return to rescue His people.

Sanctification is also described in the parable of the growing seed in Mark 4:26–29: "And he said, So is the kingdom of God, as if a man should cast seed into the ground; And should sleep, and rise night and day, and the seed should spring and grow up, he knoweth not how. For the earth bringeth forth fruit of herself; first the blade, then the ear, after that the full corn in the ear. But when the fruit is brought forth, immediately he putteth in the sickle, because the harvest is come."

The stony ground, thorns, and good ground of the parable of the sower represent the three phases of evangelism—sowing, cultivating, and reaping. And the initial enlightening, dark or wilderness time, and final refreshing that many Bible heroes had to go through all parallel that of the blade, ear, and then full corn in the ear. They all tie in together; they are just different aspects of the same process of growth that each of us is put through by God to prepare us for heaven.

Christian Growth Chart

Sower	Blade	Evangelism	Personal Experience	Description	Prodigal/ Beatitudes
1st Test - Immediate growth, then scorching.	"First the blade ..."	Sowing - Small truth far and wide.	What God has done for me.	Birth of a dream.	"Give me my inheritance"/ "Poor in Spirit"
2nd Test - Thorns.	"Then the ear ..."	Cultivating - Feeding interests.	What I can do for Him (wilderness).	Death of a dream.	He wastes it and suffers/ Thirsts after righteousness
Good Ground - Results in the lives of others.	"Then the full corn."	Reaping - Getting decisions to accept.	Full trust and submission.	Supernatural fulfillment.	Comes back, is kissed and restored/ Peacemakers Ready for persecution

Since justification by faith is the heart of the third angel's message, and this message includes the other two (see *The Great Controversy*, p. 611 and *Early Writings*, p. 277), therefore the full understanding of justification with sanctification is what is implied by the second refreshing. For us to be ready to give the final message to the world, we need to fully go through this process and see doctrine return to a faith relationship with Jesus in our own lives and as a church.

Einstein's theory of relativity includes a mathematical formula that says an object's mass will increase as it approaches the speed of light. From one-tenth on to about 70 percent of light speed (*c*), the change is not too noticeable. Once the object gets to 90 percent and beyond, however, the increase is almost off the scale. It is the same with our Christian faith. The beginning of our faith journey when we are born again is like the starting point on the graph below. As we approach the second refreshing, we grow in faith by leaps and bounds. Our success in finding others will also proportionately increase.

It is the same for the church in general. We went from about 50 people after the Great Disappointment, to 3,500 in nineteen years, to around 100,000 by the turn of the century. Another century has passed and we are at around 17 million. Let's hope since the end has not yet come that this represents the slow gradual incline and we are just now rounding the curve to massive growth.

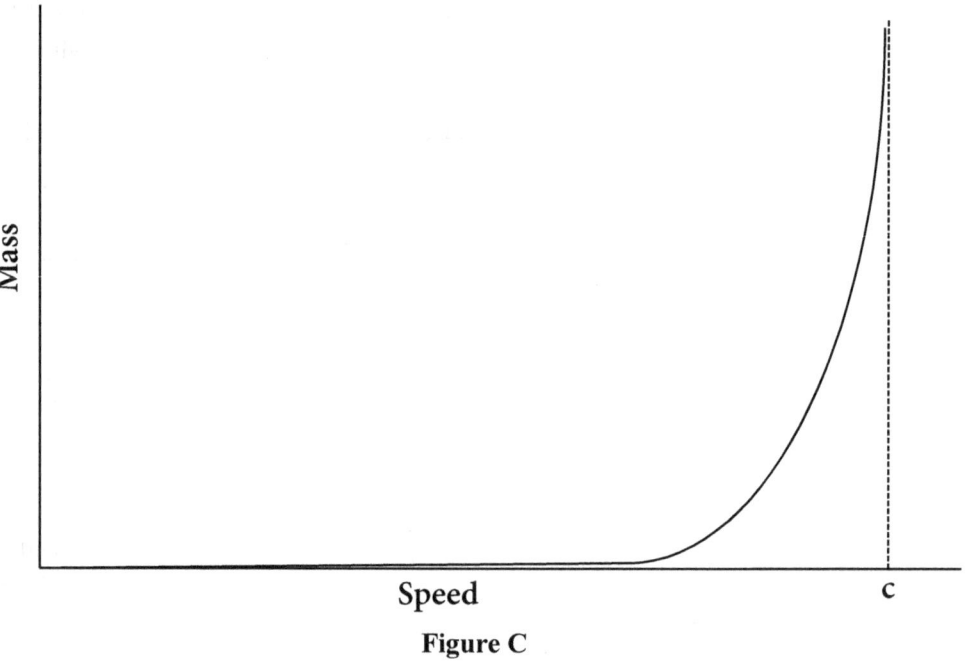

Figure C

As you seek for the Holy Spirit to refresh the church, ask for the refreshing in your own life. Ask for a new understanding of God's mercy to you. Ask Him to show you how much He has led in your life over time. As we come out of our wilderness experience and this understanding of justification is restored within our ranks, this second refreshing will also include a greater understanding of what our calling is, and we will be more prepared than ever to receive the special outpouring from on high that the Bible refers to as the latter rain. God will bless us with the latter rain when we get to the point of "primitive godliness as has not been witnessed since apostolic times" (*The Great Controversy*, p. 464). And we will do that when we give up all that is holding us back, including all the fears mentioned in chapter 2. Notice also from Mark 4:29 that the harvest is as soon as the fruit is developed. In other words, when we all understand our place as His people and are willing to do our work, we will see the final outpouring of the Spirit.

The message of the three angels found in Revelation 14:6–12 is the summation of all that we hold dear as a movement of prophecy. That is the gospel we have been called to give. We ourselves need the revival in our own hearts in order to be used of God to revive the world. Let's see how these messages fit into our Christian experience. First off, they begin and end the same way, with the truth. "And I saw another angel fly in the midst of heaven, having the everlasting gospel to preach unto them that dwell on the earth, and to every nation, and kindred, and tongue, and people, … Here is the patience of the saints: here are they that keep the commandments of God, and the faith of Jesus" (verses 6, 12).

The whole point of these messages is the whole point of the entire history of the world—the cross and the plan of salvation. The "everlasting gospel" is the gospel of born-again faith and all ten of the Ten Commandments. It is the gospel that says through God's working in me I can become good. God's purpose in giving the gospel is to give humankind a way to recover from sin and become perfect again.

When the Lord sends a message to people and it is rejected, it takes a larger display of His power to get their attention again. That is what hardening one's heart does. While the majority in the world rejects the gospel itself, the majority within the church also reject it by stopping at some point along the road to perfection. This is because some detailed application of the true gospel points out some cherished sin. There are three messages, each stronger than the previous, because there are also three levels of rejection people go through.

The first message given by the angel is "fear God, and give glory to him; for the hour of his judgment is come: and worship him that made heaven, and earth, and the sea, and the fountains of waters" (verse 7). As we are now living in this end-time judgment, it is time for a serious commitment to Christ, which includes worshipping Him. The Sabbath becomes an issue because with their unconverted hearts people are unable to see the core heart issue of righteousness by faith. Instead, they focus on the difference that has flowed from the heart into everyday life. They say to themselves, "What does it matter what day I keep?" The Lord is calling for a reform among those who call themselves His people by responding to this question with "keep the Sabbath."

"And there followed another angel, saying, Babylon is fallen, is fallen, that great city, because she made all nations drink of the wine of the wrath of her fornication" (verse 8). The second message now takes the differences in Christian faith quite a bit further in answer to the next level of rejection. If someone's heart is still not subdued, they will respond with "but I like my church." "My church," "my faith," "my philosophy," "my religion," "my belief system," all these phrases have one thing in common—they're all ways of saying that what I believe in is nothing more than an extension of myself. Since only truth comes from God, only a truly born-again person can understand it. Even if what people believe is 99.9 percent the same as the truth, all who hold to it will be folded into the great deception called Babylon in the end.

"And the third angel followed them"—this implies a time delay, which there has been since the first message went out in the 1840s. It is also spoken of as with a "loud voice," which the second message wasn't, confirming the time delay and thus implying a revival. "If any man worship the beast and his image, and receive his mark in his forehead, or in his hand" (verse 9). True Christian faith includes a true understanding of the place for the Ten Commandments, and with that, the true Sabbath shines in glory. In that sense it is the seal of God, the sign of complete submission to His will. The false, popular gospel includes a false understanding of the place for the law and along with it a false Sabbath. Since it is human based and, therefore, self-righteous, it follows that it will not come to the world in humility but in self-exaltation. It's not Sunday itself that is the mark of the beast, it is when Sunday is forced on the world that it will become the mark.

If time continued and every prophecy from the Bible and the writings of Ellen White came to pass except for the actual second coming, we would end up with an updated version of the Dark Ages. A new one-world religion would be formed with the pope at its head and "Saint Buddha," "Saint Mohammed," and "Saint Billy Graham" underneath him. Instead of an antiquated Swiss Guard, papal bulls and decrees would be enforced by the combined military, cultural, and financial power of the United States, courtesy of a unified evangelical church. The big difference is that this time there would be no wilderness to hide in. The significance of end-time events is that when the true gospel has finally gone out to "all the world" and the false gospel has come right behind it, there will be no more field. Everyone will essentially be either wheat or tares.

The third self-righteous rejection comes from anger at the sins of others and a lack of love for the enemies of God which says, "But I honestly believe if we make them obey us by strict Sunday laws, we will save them." It is a little more than that though. It may sound like a way for the church to take over the world, but it will be revealed to be a jealousy of the people who are free from the world through their true faith once the contrast is made plain. It will be an attempt to conquer them. The Lord's response to this full rejection is, "do it and you will die," which is what is meant by the warnings contained in verses 10 and 11. As there are three rejections of truth, there are also three threats of death through the seven last plagues, the second coming, and the final judgment. This is how strongly He feels about freedom to choose.

The remnant church is not the *one* true church—it is the *last* true church. When Luther, Wesley and all the other great reformers were preaching present truth, the movements raised up after them were remnants in their respective times. The church is the basket God wants to put His people in despite its flaws. "But we have this treasure in earthen vessels, that the excellency of the power may be of God, and not of us" (2 Cor. 4:7). Isaiah 54 has a promise to claim in verse 2: "Enlarge the place of thy tent, and let them stretch forth the curtains of thine habitations: spare not, lengthen thy cords, and strengthen thy stakes."

It is time for an expanded concept of what it means to be a Seventh-day Adventist. It is time for the laity to come to the maturity of faith that the good ground offers and rise up to fill the places that are too numerous for the pastors to fill. It is time to do outreach beyond our comfort zones. It is time for us, the church members, to reach the whole world instead of relying on our satellite evangelists.

The Three Angels' Messages in One, Easy Five-Minute Lesson

May the Lord bless you. By applying the concepts presented here, may you find all that you need to become an on-fire Christian standing for God in these last days. May you understand not only what the truth is, but also how to pass it on to others. May it all come from Jesus and flow back to Him in a living faith experience. And may He reward your efforts with changed lives all around you. Acts 4:13 says, "Now when they saw the boldness of Peter and John, and perceived that they were unlearned and ignorant men, they marvelled; and they took knowledge of them, that they had been with Jesus." Furthermore, 2 Timothy 4:5 says, "But … do the work of an evangelist, make full proof of thy ministry."

I wish you well.

Appendix A
Understanding Temptation

When the New York Police department finally caught the Son of Sam killer, he informed them that he did what he did because he heard voices in his head telling him to. This must be an awesome force upon someone. Even without voices, temptation is still overwhelming for us at times. Question? Just because I hear a voice or feel a pull on my heart to do anything wrong, where is it written that I have to give in to that voice? The Son of Sam killer could have said no, now couldn't he? Let's turn to 1 Corinthians 10:13 for an answer: "No temptation has overtaken you except such as is common to man; but God is faithful, who will not allow you to be tempted beyond what you are able, but with the temptation will also make the way of escape, that you may be able to bear it" (NKJV).

Here are some common causes for temptation and some ways to escape:

1. When you are tempted, you may already feel defiled just for having the desire in the first place. "Temptation is not sin, and is no indication that God is displeased with us" (*Signs of the Times*, December 18, 1893). "Cleanse the fountain, and the streams will be pure. If the heart is right, your words, your dress, your acts, will all be right" (*Evangelism*, p. 272). "You should control your thoughts. This will not be an easy task; you cannot accomplish it without close and even severe effort. Yet God requires this of you; it is a duty resting upon every accountable being" (*The Adventist Home*, p. 334).

    Put these quotes together and you will realize that if we are making the effort to control our thoughts and something does come into our minds, we have not sinned if we repel that thought immediately. The process of corruption has to be divided into two parts. There is temptation, the desire for something, and then there is sin, which is acting on that desire.

    How many times have you given in just to get the conflict in your mind over with? How many times have you done the same thing several more times just to punish yourself? If you choose to believe that God will help you and repel the thought right away, you will have victory.

    So fight back by remembering that you are not yet defiled.

2. Another reason is a lack of faith. Not a lack of faith in God, but a lack of faith in your ability to follow God. That is what the Israelites suffered from when they refused to go into the Promised Land and were punished with forty years of wandering. They were supposed to be

a model of heaven on earth, and they were afraid of the responsibility they would have to bear in living that holy of a lifestyle. John 3:19 says, "And this is the condemnation, that the light is come into the world, and men loved darkness rather than light, because their deeds were evil."

George Orwell said, "On the whole, human beings want to be good, but not too good, and not quite all the time." This lack of faith situation would be like Jesus offering to heal a crippled man and the man saying, "No, thank you. I prefer the crutches because if you heal me I will have to get a job. And begging is easier." The solution here is to remember that if God calls you to a certain level of holiness He will empower you to live at that state. This is part of not being tempted beyond your ability to bear the temptation.

3. Sometimes people give in to temptation because they are embarrassed. They say to themselves, "I should be strong enough to face this; I'm going to prove how strong I am by facing this head on." However when they do that, they are trying in their own strength. In 1 Corinthians 6:18, in the New King James Version, we read, "Flee sexual immorality." To flee is to run away. Run from the devil by running to God, and you will have victory. This is also why His faith is made perfect in weakness. When we do get success from our strength, we sometimes give ourselves a break, and then temptation comes in stronger. The only safe way to heaven is by continually recognizing our need of the Lord to work in us and for us.

These last three points are especially for someone who is in the faith and struggling with a pet sin. Time after time, in so many conversion stories, you'll hear people share how sins that caused great grief to them disappeared right away, while others didn't, and the person in question struggled with them for quite some time. Those initial victories were over sins that never really had a hold on the person or, because of the suffering they caused, were easy for the person to give up.

4. Admit to yourself that the real reason you're holding on to the sin in question is because deep down somewhere within you, you still like it. I knew of a lady who was an Adventist for thirteen years but still struggled with smoking. Finally, one day she was sitting in her house with a Bible in one hand and a cigarette in the other. She realized one of them had to go. There is nothing complicated about this; give up your sin for Christ, simple as that.

5. Next is another form of a lack of faith. This time the lack of faith is in God. When you are in the middle of a temptation and it is at its strongest, it is easy to forget that God is still more powerful than this pull to sin. You end up giving in because you feel you have no choice, but it is your own desire talking to you. You essentially forget that you are still in God's presence. James 1:13, 14 says, "Let no man say when he is tempted, I am tempted of God: for God cannot be tempted with evil, neither tempteth he any man: But every man is tempted, when he is drawn away of his own lust, and enticed." In 2 Peter 1:4 it says, "Whereby are given unto us exceeding great and precious promises: that by these ye might be partakers of the divine nature, having escaped the corruption that is in the world through lust."

A pastor once recommended studying the Bible for an hour each day trying to answer the question, "How much does God love me?" That was his solution to a sin problem someone was struggling with. What miraculous answers to prayer have you received? How did it feel the first time Jesus washed your sins away? What powerful promises from Scripture can you meditate on? The solution here is to make efforts to remember that you are always in God's presence. Remember the great things He has done, not only throughout human history but in your own life as well.

6. You may have truly wanted to give up your sins in your heart. You may believe in the greatness of God's power, but you may still be struggling because in your own mind you really can't see yourself existing any other way than how you are right now. The solution here is to look to something better. If you focus too much on giving up the sin, you are still thinking about the sin. Find a positive replacement instead.

Appendix B
Dimensions of the Cross

As mentioned in the chapter "Understanding Evangelicals," one difference between Adventists and those of other denominations is in the emphasis on Jesus' suffering and what it means. Though to human eyes He died a gruesome and horrible death, the significance was far more than the physical pain. However, we cannot deny there was pain, and lots of it. Morris Venden draws from archaeological discoveries and describes it well in *Common Ground*.

"Apparently, the soldiers placed a person against the cross sideways, so that his feet were side by side against the cross, and then they drove a huge spike through both heels … After the soldiers had secured the body tightly to the cross sideways at the feet, they swung the shoulders around, stretched the arms out tight, and nailed them to the cross through the wrists. I tried standing in that position after I heard about it, and it wasn't long before my muscles began to jerk. When you … realize that it was God's Son who became subject to such a death, it will move your heart.

"When I think of this, I am dumbfounded at the genius of the Lord in arranging such a death for His Son to die. God's truths are always put simply at first and then as you dig deeper you learn more, but then you realize eventually that what you learn is only an extension of that same simplicity. To the most simple minded of person, one who has no experience in things of eternity and spirituality, there is Christ dying for him. An example of this might be the Roman Centurion who declared 'this must be the Son of God'. Even without any understanding of the deeper mental level of the cross, there is the whole plan of salvation in a nutshell, Christ died for you!" (p. 58).

Venden puts it well, but let's look at other dimensions of the cross. Just what was happening on the mental level? Romans 5:6–8 says, "For when we were yet without strength, in due time Christ died for the ungodly. For scarcely for a righteous man will one die: yet peradventure for a good man some would even dare to die. But God commendeth his love toward us, in that, while we were yet sinners, Christ died for us."

If Jesus had been a normal man living a life of sin, His sin would have been enough to keep Him out of heaven even if He did grow to become perfect while on earth. He had to live a perfect life for the whole time He was here. If He had been a perfect man (but only a man) and died, He would have only been able to save one other person. He would not have been able to get out of the grave Himself, because someone had to pay for sin. It is because He was God (and therefore infinite) that He could make an infinite sacrifice and save as many as will come to Him. But it was humanity who sinned, and humanity must die for sin. As God alone, He could not save human beings. Therefore, for the infinite God to make this infinite sacrifice, the infinite God had to become a finite man.

Because death is the penalty for sin and Christ never sinned, He should have been able to walk into heaven without dying as Enoch and Elijah did. Instead, He chose to die so Enoch, Elijah, and every other person who comes to Him from one end of human history to the other can go to heaven and be with Him forever. So the first dimension (beyond the physical pain) of the cross is this trade off: "Christ was treated as we deserve, that we might be treated as He deserves. He was condemned for our sins, in which He had no share, that we might be justified by His righteousness, in which we had no share. He suffered the death which was ours, that we might receive the life which was His. 'With His stripes we are healed'" (*The Desire of Ages*, p. 25).

The biblical truth regarding the second death gives us the next dimension of this mental level to consider. Just what was this sacrifice? Matthew 7:23 answers this question. "And then will I profess unto them, I never knew you: depart from me, ye that work iniquity." Now how can someone go away from the presence of the all-seeing, all-knowing God who is everywhere? When the Lord punished Adam and Eve, He reminded them that they were dust (Gen. 3:19). Only God has power to give or take away life. This "depart from Me" statement is a statement that says He will remove life itself from the wicked. In other words, they will no longer exist. That is how complete the brokenness is between humanity and God that sin causes. No wonder Jesus said there would be "wailing and gnashing of teeth" on that day. And this is why Jesus felt forsaken. Because of His perfection, He had an unbroken connection with the Father, and upon the cross Jesus was treated as a sinner. The Father broke that connection with His Son to the very same depth that He will with all the wicked on judgment day.

Since sin is what causes this brokenness, think also how much more sharp Jesus' conscience would have been in His perfection. As you have grown as a Christian, there are things you used to think were no big deal—little sins that didn't bother you that now make you hurt inside when they happen around you. If Jesus had changed His mind and not gone to the cross, He would have been saying that sin is no big deal or that life is too hard. He would have been giving human beings permission to sin. He simply couldn't do that.

Now there are other dimensions to the cross as well. When someone hits you, you can hit back or you can follow Jesus. You can even hit back harder if you have some sort of weapon. But Jesus said, "Turn the other cheek." He kept his own word when He was beaten, spat on, whipped, and finally nailed to the tree. His weapon, if He wanted to use it, was his godly power. He could have wiped those guards right out of existence in a second. He could have wiped the whole universe itself right out, started over, and no one would have ever known. The whole process of trial from the Sanhedrin to Pilate to Herod and back to Pilate with no Bible record of food, water, or sleep (in addition to the physical abuse He had to undergo) had to have pushed His patience to the limit. And what did He say? "Father, forgive them; for they know not what they do" (Luke 23:34). The cross shows the greatness of God's love, but it also shows the greatness of God's character.

And the cross also shows the pain sin has caused the heart of God. With one member of the Trinity coming to earth with the approval of the other two, it was the Lord's way of acting out how much He hurts. Isaiah 49:15, 16 says, "Can a woman forget her sucking child, that she should not have compassion on the son of her womb? yea, they may forget, yet will I not forget thee. Behold, I have graven thee upon the palms of my hands."

We touched briefly on the fact that the cross would not be of value without that perfect life. The Bible speaks of Jesus as perfect, but it also says He was made perfect through suffering. He went through the same process of growth we all have to be put through. That's why He is a compassionate High Priest, because He knows what it's like. That's why He can also judge us fairly. And the cross wouldn't be of any value without His resurrection either. It was because He came up out of the grave that we can have hope we will too.

We invite you to view the complete
selection of titles we publish at:

www.TEACHServices.com

Scan with your mobile
device to go directly
to our website.

Please write or email us your praises, reactions,
or thoughts about this or any other book we publish at:

P.O. Box 954
Ringgold, GA 30736

info@TEACHServices.com

TEACH Services, Inc., titles may be purchased in bulk for
educational, business, fund-raising, or sales promotional use.
For information, please e-mail:

BulkSales@TEACHServices.com

Finally, if you are interested in seeing
your own book in print, please contact us at

publishing@TEACHServices.com

We would be happy to review your manuscript for free.

www.ingramcontent.com/pod-product-compliance
Lightning Source LLC
Chambersburg PA
CBHW081838170426
43199CB00017B/2775